PERSPECTIVES

ON THE WORLD CHRISTIAN MOVEMENT

Study Guide

2009 Edition

Steven C. Hawthorne
Curriculum Development
Institute of International Studies

1605 Elizabeth St
Pasadena, California 91104

2009 Edition

Rights and Permissions
William Carey Library
1605 E. Elizabeth St
Pasadena, California 91104
Phone (626) 798-0819

Published by
William Carey Library
1605 E. Elizabeth St
Pasadena, California 91104
Phone (626) 798-0819
ISBN 978-0-87808-391-6

Cover Design: Chad M. Upham, modified by Katie Koch
Cover photos courtesy of Caleb Resources, International Mission Board and Create International

Printed in the United States of America
3rd Printing - April 2009

2009REV4UGI10000

Library of Congress Cataloging-in-Publication Data

Hawthorne, Steven C., 1953-
Perspectives on the world Christian movement : study guide / by Steven C. Hawthorne.
p. cm.
ISBN 978-0-87808-391-6
1. Missions--Textbooks. 2. Evangelistic work--Textbooks. I. Title.

BV2061.3.H39 2009
266--dc22

2008046697

Contents

Introduction

Perspectives: A Course of Vision, Hope and Passion

As the name implies, the *Perspectives* course is about vision. It's the same vision which empowered Jesus to live His life with joy, hope, and single-hearted passion. This course explores that vision and will help you respond to Christ's invitation to live for the same purpose and significance that He did.

There's joy in this vision. Jesus told His first followers that the value of living fruitfully for His Father's glory was "that My joy may be in you, and that your joy may be made full" (John 15:11).

What was the vision? Jesus summed up the vision in one of His final prayers to His Father, "I glorified You on earth, having accomplished the work that You gave me to do" (John 17:4). Jesus' life purpose was to bring about God's glory on earth. Throughout His life, Jesus kept the vision of God's greater glory before Him. He believed His Bible as it told the story and described the prophetic certainty that God would be delighted by worship from every people. The vision of God's glory focused His life choices and filled His daily affairs with immense significance. Passion for God's glory energized and integrated His life. Life with purpose was so satisfying that He said, "My food is to do the will of Him who sent Me, and to accomplish His work" (John 4:34). As He set His life toward the hope of finishing God's work, His life became a daily feast of purpose. This course aims to help you live strategically toward that same hope.

"Missions" is a loaded word for most Christians. Many people are exposed to missions in the context of appeals for volunteers or funds. Missions has often been reduced to a limited question of whether you will be a missionary or not. Most Christians would admit that they don't really know enough about what missions is to know what they would do or be if they were to aspire to be a missionary. Even less clear is how someone can live for God's global purpose without being a missionary.

The point of this course is not to persuade you to become a missionary. Neither is it to train you in skills you need to serve as a missionary. The point of exposing you to many of the practicalities and challenges is to persuade you of the feasibility and to set you on a path of ongoing learning to play your part wisely and well.

The primary idea is that God will fulfill His purposes. The certainty that He will see it fulfilled makes His invitation to join Him in His mission a matter of heart-blazing hope. We are not called to perform dull religious duties. He is enlisting His followers to lead lives of huge significance.

We are convinced that God has a "world-sized" role for every Christian in His global purpose. Whether people go to distant countries or stay at home is a secondary issue. The primary issue is what most people are hungry to discover: vision to live a life of purpose. Discovering that vision makes this course valuable, and perhaps crucial, for any Christian.

What's In This Course?

The course is designed around four vantage points or "perspectives"—Biblical, Historical, Cultural and Strategic. Each one highlights different aspects of God's global purpose.

The Biblical and Historical sections reveal why our confidence is based on the historic fact of God's relentless work from the dawn of history until this day. That's why the essence of this course is the record of what God has been unfolding for thousands of years toward a certain, and perhaps soon-coming, culmination.

As we wind our way through history, we will meet the largest and longest-running movement ever in history—the World Christian Movement. You will find that virtually every innovative approach you can think of has been attempted by those who have gone before us. We are in league with the most substantial movement of creative and self-sacrificing people the world has ever seen.

The Cultural and Strategic sections underscore that we are in the midst of a costly, but very "do-able" task, confirming the Biblical and Historical hope.

The Biblical Perspective

1. **The Living God is a Missionary God**
   God's purpose is three-fold: against evil—kingdom victory; for the nations—redemption and blessing; and for God—global glory in worship. God's purpose revealed in promise to Abraham. Exploring God's purpose for the nations: Blessing to the nations described.

2. **The Story of His Glory**
   Exploring God's purpose for Himself: How God has been steadily unfolding a plan throughout all nations and generations to bring about His greater glory, ultimately drawing to Himself the worship of all the peoples. Passion and prayer for God's glory.

3. **Your Kingdom Come**
   Exploring God's purpose regarding evil: How God has accomplished a defeat of evil powers in order to open a season of history in which the nations can freely follow Christ. The kingdom of God as the destiny of all history. Christ's mission seeks a hindering of evil to bring about a sign of the coming peace of the kingdom of God. Our prayers contend with evil in order to bring about the transformation of society with Christ's kingdom in view.

4. **Mandate for the Nations**
   Jesus shows great strategic interest in Gentiles; wise strategic focus by initiating a global mission on a few disciples among the Hebrew people. The Great Commission and the ways of God's sending in relational power. Dealing with the ideas of pluralism (all religions the same) and universalism (all persons saved).

5. **Unleashing the Gospel**
   The first followers of Jesus: obedient in costly, foundational ways. The climactic act of the book of Acts is the freeing of the gospel to be followed by Gentiles without Jewish traditions as a requirement. A foundational act of God which speaks to the situations where the gospel is hindered today. Strategic suffering and apostolic passion.

The Historical Perspective

6. **The Expansion of the Christian Movement**
   The story of God's purpose continues relentlessly from Abraham's day until the present moment. An overview of the largest and the longest-running movement ever in history—the world Christian movement. How the gospel surged through the peoples and places of the world. Important insights for our own day.

7. **Eras of Mission History**
   The greatest explosion of growth ever has taken place in last 200 years in three "bursts" of activity. Why we could be in the final era of missions. The global harvest force comprised increasingly of non-Western missionaries.

8. **Pioneers of the World Christian Movement**
   Today we anchor the race by continuing what others have begun. It's a day of finishing. All the more reason to learn the wisdom and the heart of ordinary people who did extraordinary things in earlier generations. Reading the writings of William Carey and other leaders to discern what these people have left to us. Exploring the contribution of women in missions throughout the centuries.

9. **The Task Remaining**
   God's pressed His purpose forward until the present hour of amazing opportunity. Understanding the concept of "unreached peoples" to assess the remaining task. Recognizing the imbalance of mission resources shapes strategic priorities. The basic minimal missiological achievement in every people group opens the way for working with God against every kind of evil so that the gospel of the kingdom is declared and displayed with clarity and power. The need and opportunity of urban mission.

The Cultural Perspective

10. **How Shall They Hear?**
    Culture and intercultural communication of the gospel. Communicating the gospel with relevance

at the worldview level helps avoid syncretism (blending of cultural error with God's truth) and also enables powerful movements of the gospel. Sensitive missionaries will look for ways that God has preserved or prepared people to hear the gospel, often finding redemptive analogies for God's truth.

11. **Building Bridges of Love**
The incarnation as a model of missionary humility. How missionaries can enter appropriate roles in order to form relationships of trust and respect to develop a sense of belonging, and thus to communicate with credibility for understanding. Explore the intricacy of identification in another culture. Explore the even greater complexity of presenting identity with integrity in a globalized, terrorized, pluralized world. Recognizing the dynamics of social structure in order to initiate growing movements of ongoing communication throughout the society.

The Strategic Perspective

12. **Christian Community Development**
A survey of world need. Dynamic balance of evangelism and social action. Hope for significant transformation as a sign of Christ's Lordship by Christian community development. Exploring the charge that missionaries destroy instead of serve cultures. Healing the wounds of the world between the peoples.

13. **Spontaneous Multiplication of Churches**
Look beyond institutional features of churches to understand churches as dynamic movements of Christ Himself being followed. Such a view of churches as organic, living things opens up the practicality of seeing them multiply rapidly as movements and also flourish in society bearing the fruit of social transformation. Churches as counter-communities, acting as salt and light, bringing change to their cultures. How movements multiply by connecting with entire families and larger social structures.

14. **Pioneer Church Planting**
The hope of planting churches among unreached peoples. How the breakthrough of the gospel in an unreached people requires that the gospel be "de-Westernized." The difference of contextualizing the message, the messenger and the movement. Distinguish and appreciate people movements, church planting movements and insider movements.

15. **World Christian Discipleship**
What it means to integrate life for Christ's global purpose as a "World Christian." Into the great story for His glory: a Person-driven life as a way of pursuing a purpose-driven life. The basic practices of world Christians: going, sending, welcoming and mobilizing. The essential disciplines of World Christian discipleship: community, giving, praying and learning. Simplifying your lifestyle as if in "war-time." Exploring the practical ways of pursuing God's purpose. Business and mission. Short-term mission. Welcoming international visitors. Wisdom in working with local churches and in partnership with Christians in different parts of the world.

Improvements Over Earlier Versions

This is the fourth major edition of the curriculum called Perspectives on the World Christian Movement. The first edition of the curriculum appeared in 1982. A second edition was released 10 years later, in 1992. The third edition, which appeared in 1999, was a significant overhaul of the course.

Changes in the Fourth Edition

Since the basic themes and core ideas have not changed, the fourth edition will be familiar to the more than seventy thousand people who have worked through the *Perspectives* course. The lesson titles are almost identical. But watch for surprises! Many articles which have been part of the curriculum for years have been greatly revised. Some have been edited to make them accessible and more clearly organized. Others have been updated with current vocabulary and ideas. We have also sought to add more biblical substance throughout the course so that the paradigm shift of hope is a stronger, life-integrating vision.

In the biblical section you'll find new material clarifying the powerful idea of blessing, exploring how God endowed humanity with responsibility for creation care and showing how the kingdom of God gives hope in our world. In the history section we explore how the gospel moved eastward, how the Christian movement is shifting southward and some interesting research that dispels some of the anecdotal myths about missionaries harming societies. The culture section contains some new material about orality, story-telling, and the complexity of ethnicity and missionary identity in a globalized world. In the strategy section we have new material giving hope for churches to bring change in their culture and, working together, address the great problems of our day.

For many the highlight will be several new case studies describing the dramatic and costly work of God among the unreached. A new section about world Christian discipleship is designed to help every believer move beyond filling roles and integrate their lives with others to fulfill God's great global purpose.

How to Use This Study Guide

This *Study Guide* is designed as a companion to the book *Perspectives on the World Christian Movement: A Reader*. Even though the *Reader* is the larger book, don't be fooled. The articles in the *Reader* were selected and edited carefully to fit together as a course. In a very real sense, the *Study Guide* constitutes the course. You can compare the *Study Guide* to an interpretive guide in a museum who helps you to understand and thereby appreciate and remember what you see. The integrative outlines show you how to read different authors and articles in a way that helps you evaluate and integrate what they are saying. The outline summarizes and organizes the main points. In some cases, the *Study Guide* adds material and short paragraphs of reading to what you'll find in the *Reader*.

Three Parts to Every Lesson

We've organized each lesson in three roughly equal sections or modules: Key Readings, Certificate Readings, and Credit Readings. The Certificate Readings build on the essential material found in the Key Readings. There are about 15 pages of readings in each of these modules. The Credit Readings go further to explore the ramifications and add detail with fascinating case studies. The end of the key readings is marked by this bar:

Conclusion of Key Readings for this lesson.

You'll find a similar bar signalling the break point at the end of the Certificate readings. Don't let the markers stop you from going on to study every part. Many of the most fascinating highlights are in the material beyond the key readings. We encourage you to skim every article for highlights as you are able. Don't be surprised to find that the readings are engaging and meaningful. We've not only gathered material from some of the best authors and leaders, we've sifted and edited their writing. Every page contains valuable vision and practical insight.

Study the Readings

The *Study Guide* will cue you to read selections from the *Perspectives Reader*. You will often be asked to read portions of articles. You will find the range of pages with beginning and ending points described not only by the page number, but also by a letter. The letter indicates which quadrant on the page you will find the starting or the ending point. Most of the starting and ending points are at break points above subheadings. The diagram to the below left shows which letter corresponds to which quadrant. If there is no letter, assume you need to read the entire page.

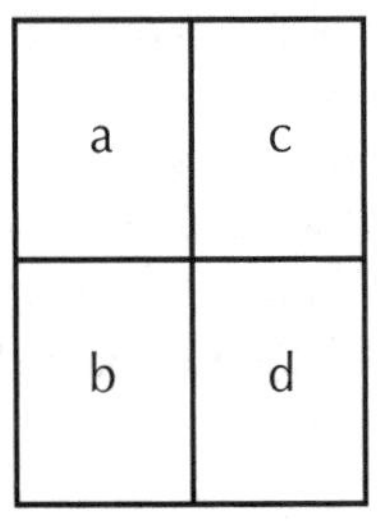

Focus on the Objectives

Each lesson opens with important introductory paragraphs and a list of objectives. This list should help focus your attention on the basic ideas.

Take in the Key Word

The "key word" at the beginning of each lesson is designed to stimulate interest and signal what may be of primary value to you. It is not intended to be a one-word summary of the content of the lesson.

Reflect on the Thought Blocks

Sometimes we invite you to stop and reflect on an idea, look elsewhere in the notebook for an illustrating story from another article, or examine some scripture that will deepen your grasp of the topic.

You'll find the reading assignments in a shaded, gray screened box like this.

You'll find these Thought Blocks in an outlined box like this.

Learn from the Reviews

The reviews are designed to be completed with an open book and open Bible, if you prefer. There is no time limit to completing the review. The left column is designed to help you prepare for class discussion with your written answers. The right "in-class review" column is designed for you to write down information gleaned from class or mentor discussion which corrects or extends your answers.

1 The Living God is a Missionary God

Studying this lesson will help you:

- Explain how the covenant with Abraham discloses God's purpose for every people.
- Explain how God's promises are an important part of our mandate for mission.
- Describe how God has fulfilled or will fulfill His promise to Abraham progressively through history: first, in lives of Abraham and his descendents, next, in Christ and those who have followed Him, and finally, at the coming of Christ at the close of the age.
- Explain why the hope and the responsibility of the covenant with Abraham have been inherited by all those who have joined themselves with Christ by faith.
- Explain how the promised blessing of the nations is fulfilled primarily by the provision and invitation to be part of God's family in Christ.
- Explain how the promised blessing can also mean God's people will be used to bring measures of tangible goodness and societal transformation among the nations.
- Describe God's mission purpose as it unfolds in three directions: toward God, on behalf of all nations and against satanic evil powers.
- Describe how the most compelling mandate for mission comes from the entire story of the Bible.

God is a God of global purpose. He has already put in our hearts the longing to be a friend to a great God, to somehow become a co-worker with Him, living in the dignity of a purpose larger than ourselves. We really want to serve God in the biggest way we know how. What prevents us? Although we know better than to treat God as if He were a personal problem-solver, it's still common to regard Him from our point of view, as if He were on call to help us whenever we face difficult circumstances.

Our problem may be a matter of shriveled vision. We cannot devote ourselves to that which we cannot envision. Our vision is limited by the horizon of our own concerns and culture. But, there is a better destiny—a larger purpose. We can lay hold of it by knowing and following God toward a vision which extends far beyond ourselves.

In this lesson we'll begin a journey to discover what God has revealed about His purpose through the story of the Bible. His purposes make best sense when they are stretched out end-to-end on the timeline of the Bible's story. Walking with God through the story of the Scriptures will catapult us into the center of the significance of the rest of history.

The later it gets in history, the better God looks, because it's all coming about as He promised. Because He is a God of grand purpose, and because there is a mission He has set Himself to fulfill, our God is a missionary God.

purpose We were made to live for purpose. God Himself lives for purpose. The way to live with significance is to devote yourself to a purpose that is larger than your life.

I. God's Promise Reveals His Purpose

God could have revealed His purpose in the form of direct commands about what He wanted to see done. Instead, God chose to reveal His purpose in the form of a promise, a promise that was both personal and immensely global: to bless all the families of the earth.

A. **God's Promise.** A mandate is better than a mere command. God initially extended His mandate in the form of a promise, instead of as a direct imperative command. This promise gives emphasis to what God would do far more than what Abraham was expected to attempt. Instead of ordering Abraham to do a job with step-by-step directives, God emphasized the outcome that He wanted to see among all of earth's peoples. When we consider how many millions of people have been involved in the fulfillment of this promise, what better way could God have used to convey His purpose to the entire faith family that would eventually co-work with Him for thousands of years?

B. **The Progressive Fulfillment of God's Promise.** God reveals His intentions more clearly at each stage of fulfilling His promise, each a successively greater fulfillment. John Stott describes a triple fulfillment. First, it was partially fulfilled in Abraham's day and throughout the period of the Old Testament. Second, it was fully portrayed in the life of Jesus. Finally, the promise will be perfectly fulfilled at the end of the age. It is even now being fulfilled as Christ builds His Church.

C. **God's Promise Reveals a Missionary God.** Through His promise and its fulfillments, we can see the living God as the God of history, the God of covenant and the God of mission.

Read Stott, "The Living God is a Missionary God," pp. 3-9 (all)

The Lord had said to Abram,
"Leave your country, your people and your father's
household and go to the land I will show you.
I will make you into a great nation and I will bless you;
I will make your name great, and you will be a blessing.
I will bless those who bless you,
and whoever curses you I will curse;
and all peoples on earth will be blessed through you."

—Genesis 12:1–3

Read Genesis 12:1-3 carefully. Draw a circle around the different expressions of purpose or outcome beyond Abraham's life. Underline the command(s). Double underline the different parts which are explicitly a promise to Abraham.

Describe some of the details of the triple fulfillment of God's promise to bless the nations.

Progressive Fulfillment of God's Promise

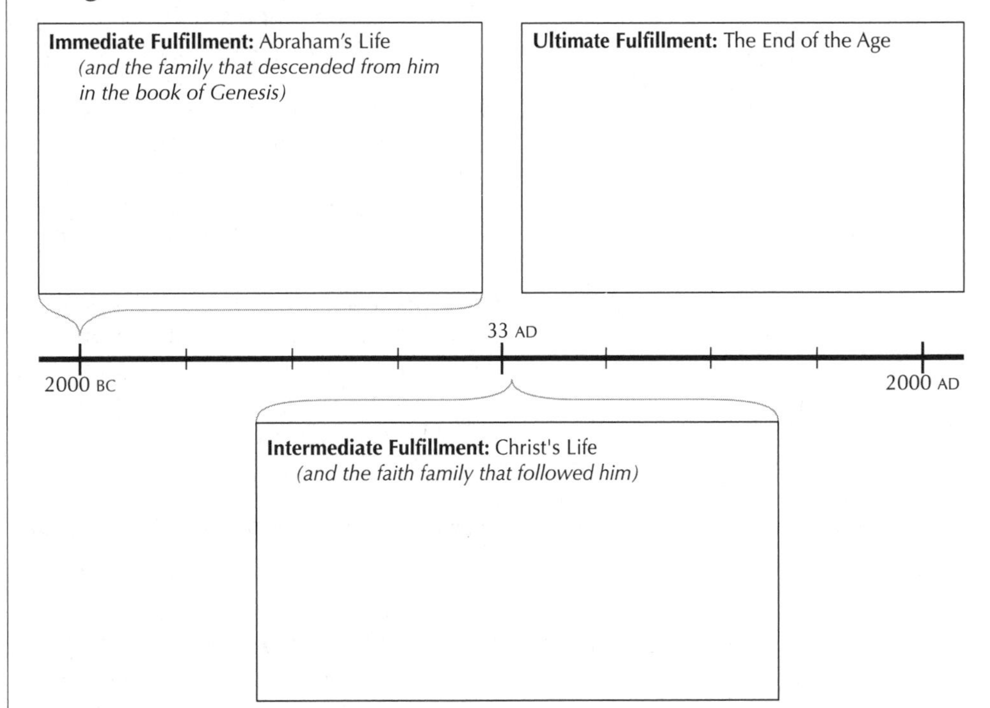

II. God's People Formed to Participate in His Purpose

Even though the promise emphasized that God Himself would do a marvelous thing among the nations, Abraham and his descendants were not to be passive spectators. Walter Kaiser shows Israel's missionary calling in scripture.

A. Not Passive, But Active Communicators of Blessing. The statements of promised blessing came with a clearly connected purpose: "so that you will be a blessing" and "so that in you all the families of the earth will be blessed" (Gen 12:2,3). The express purpose for God's choice of Abraham was for him and his family to play the key role in His global purpose.

B. True Significance. In contrast with the people of Babel, who wanted to "make a name" for themselves (Gen 11:4), God assured Abraham that He would make Abraham's name great. The way of highest significance in life does not lie in acquiring security and self-made prestige. As with Abraham, significance lies in being a blessing to the nations. We are blessed to be a blessing. Far more than a duty—it is our destiny.

Read Kaiser, "Israel's Missionary Call," pp. 10-13a

C. Participating with God as His Priesthood. God's covenant at Sinai reveals His purpose for His people. This is not an isolated verse of Scripture. The Exodus and the covenant made at Sinai were together the most definitive occasion of Israel's history. God's people were constituted for a purpose. Peter makes it clear that God's intentions remain the same in New Testament times and beyond. First, God's people are to be distinctive, a holy people of unique value among the peoples of the world. Second, God's people are to be His priesthood, declaring God's glories to the world.

D. Proving His Purpose. The songs of the Hebrew people reflect their understanding of God's mandate upon them to bring blessing to the nations. Psalm 67 shows that Israel knew the nations were watching them as a spectacle of what God wanted to bring forth among all nations. The destiny of the nations—not some, but all the nations—is to sing praise to God.

God's purpose is the resolute focus of this Psalm: "God blesses us" with the purpose "that all the ends of the earth may fear Him." God's ultimate purpose is that the nations would glorify Him in open recognition of two things: His redemptive, life-giving blessing (Ps 67:1-2,6-7) and the supremacy of His kingship (Ps 67:4).

Read Kaiser, "Israel's Missionary Call," pp. 13b-16

III. What is God's Purpose?

As we will see in later lessons, God pursues a global purpose that will reconcile all things to Himself. Specifically, God is on mission to be loved, served and worshiped by people from all humanity. To accomplish that end, God acts with a determined purpose that will not only affect all peoples but also defeat evil spiritual powers. God's purpose is a singular purpose with three distinct directions: *toward* God, *for* people and *against* evil.

A. Toward God. God desires that worship will come to Him from every nation. Therefore, world evangelization is ultimately for God.

B. For People. God intends to bring redemptive blessing to every people. He will redeem a people from every people.

C. Against Evil. God will overcome evil powers in order to liberate people and, ultimately, to bring all things under His everlasting and complete governance. This kingdom reign is the substance of the blessing He brings to the nations.

God's Purpose Summarized:

For His glory in global worship,
God purposes to overcome evil
by redeeming a people
who will love and obey Him within every people.

IV. God's Purpose in Poetry

Kaiser mentioned Psalm 67. Another way of seeing the structure of Psalm 67 is an "hourglass" form with repeating ideas being placed in a parallel position. It was a form of poetry common to the ancient world.

Psalm 67
[1] *God be gracious to us and bless us,*
and cause His face to shine upon us. Selah.
[2] *That Your way may be known on the earth,*
Your salvation among all nations.

[3] *Let the peoples praise You, O God.*
Let all the peoples praise You.

[4] *Let the nations be glad and sing for joy;*
for You will judge the peoples with uprightness
and guide the nations on the earth. Selah.

[5] *Let the peoples praise You, O God.*
Let all the peoples praise You.

[6] *The earth has yielded its produce.*
God, our God, blesses us. [7] *God blesses us,*
that all the ends of the earth may fear Him.

- **For People: Blessing**. Verses 1-2 and verses 6-7 contain parallel themes of God blessing His people in order to make His salvation known to all the world.
- **Toward God: Glory in Worship.** Verses 3 and 5 are obviously similar, describing the "God-ward" aspect of God's purpose in the worship of all the peoples.
- **Against Evil: His Kingdom.** In the central position, verse 4 is the "pivotal" idea that makes the rest come about. What will cause the nations to rejoice is God intervening to judge on behalf of all peoples. The idea of judgment will be explored more in Lesson 3. Judgment in this text is not simple prosecution or punishment for wrongdoing. It speaks of God's forceful dealings to confront and overcome evil. The verse states that God will not only deal redemptively against evil, he will also bring about a relationship that guides the nations to live under His kingdom rule. This may be one of the most beautiful single-verse expressions of the kingdom of God in the entire Bible.

V. The Story of Blessing

Richard Bauckham surveys the astounding beauty and power of blessing as a theme running through the entire story of the Bible. He describes the mission-motivating dynamic of the ultimate expression of God's blessing: the word concerning the life, death and resurrection of Jesus. Those who are blessed by this word become a blessing to others.

A. Creation and Curse. Bauckham follows the theme of blessing from creation and how God ultimately overwhelms the curse, which came as a consequence of sin, with the blessing of Christ.

B. The Gospel in Genesis 12. Bauckham quotes Galatians 3:8, "The Scripture, foreseeing that God would justify the Gentiles by faith, preached the gospel beforehand to Abraham, saying, 'All the nations will be blessed in you.'" This text says that the gospel is foreshadowed and summed up in God's promise of blessing.

C. God's Full Purpose. As you read, notice how Bauckham mentions the same three directions of God's purpose. The "gospel" announced so early to Abraham eventually overcame the curse and aftermath of *evil*, bringing a flourishing of life and salvation to *people* in order to bring praise to *God*.

1. **Toward God:** "Those who experience blessing from God in turn bless God, which means that they give all that creatures really can give to God: thanksgiving and praise."
2. **For People:** Blessing has to do with every kind of abundance and salvation.
3. **Against Evil:** "The secret of the promise is Christ's bearing of the curse so that the blessing may prevail."

Read Bauckham, "The Story of Blessing: Prevailing Over Curse," pp. 38-39

Conclusion of Key Readings for this lesson. 

VI. God's First Promise Displays His Final Victory

Long before Abraham, God had already promised to vanquish evil and to redeem people. Stanley Ellisen helps us step back to see the background for the promise to Abraham. An earlier promise is found in Genesis 3:14-15, which is often called the "proto-evangel" (first gospel).

A. Two-Fold Problem. Ellisen summarizes the challenge of evil as being a two-fold problem:

1. **A satanic counter-kingdom** arose, bent on usurping God's reign by stealing the allegiance of people and then deceiving and destroying them.
2. **Humans in rebellion** abdicated their regal position as appointed caretakers of the earth, and ironically, in a bid for greater power, succumbed to the lie of Satan's counter-kingdom, which resulted in the slavery of sin and death.

B. God's Two-Fold Strategy for a Single Purpose. His strategy and His purpose are prefigured in the "proto-evangel," in what Ellisen calls "two crushings." God pledges that a human figure will entirely destroy the devil, "crushing" him. In the same breath, God states that Satan will wound that human figure, prefiguring the redemptive suffering of Christ.

1. **Strategy Concerning Satan:** God wages a war of liberation upon the satanic counter-kingdom, thwarting the darkness in order to rescue humankind, and ultimately destroying every work of Satan (the "Kingdom Program" according to Ellisen).

2. **Strategy Concerning People:** God redeems a people from every people, bringing them under the rule of Christ through the cross and resurrection of Christ (the "Redemptive Program" according to Ellisen).

It's important to see that God overcomes both problems together in one mission: He redeems in order to rule, and He rules (gains victory) in order to redeem. Those two strategic emphases have one single, overriding purpose: God's greater glory in worship.

- **God's Ultimate Purpose:** To draw loyal worship from every people, displaying His greater glory and manifesting His fullest love.
- **God's Two-Fold Strategy:** While God's purpose ultimately concerns His glory, He has worked decisively and relentlessly with an integrated strategy *against* Satanic evil and *for* people.

Read Ellisen, "Everyone's Question: What is God Trying to Do?" pp. 17-20 (all)

Consider how God has been advancing His global purpose during your lifetime. How has evil been overcome to a greater extent? How have people been redeemed to serve God? How is God coming to be honored in places where He has never yet been known?

God's Purpose Summarized:

For His glory in global worship,
God purposes to overcome evil
by redeeming a people
who will love and obey Him within every people.

VII. Blessing as Transformation

We return to the unfolding story of God bringing blessing to all the peoples of earth. We have seen in the promise to Abraham God's intention that we become a blessing to the nations. But what does it mean to "be a blessing"? How is done? What does it look like when it happens? Sarita Gallagher and Steven Hawthorne follow the story of blessing in Genesis. The logic of their article is simple: Whatever God meant by "be a blessing" in the promise of Genesis 12 can be seen in the rest of the book of Genesis.

A. Blessing as Both Spoken Endowment and Tangible Fulfillment.

1. **Spoken Endowment.** Blessing is not a common idea in many Western societies. To speak or impart a blessing is to endow the person or thing that is blessed with a potency of life to flourish in an intended fullness. Speaking blessing was considered to be a transaction of life-giving power and not a mere utterance of words.
2. **Tangible Fulfillment.** In the Genesis account we see many instances in which the tangible fulfillment of blessing is seen. When this takes place the person is considered to be blessed. We see three related categories of blessing:

- **Material Wealth and Physical Abundance.** God brought great wealth, by ancient Near East standards, to Abraham and his descendents.
- **God's Presence.** God's presence was recognized by those observing Abraham and his family.
- **Peace with Neighboring Nations.** The examples in the Genesis account suggest that where God brings blessing, there is a beginning of peace between feuding brothers or nations.

Read Gallagher and Hawthorne, "Blessing as Transformation," pp. 34-36a

B. To Be a Blessing. It is one thing to see the incredible range of goodness that blessing entails. It's quite another to see how a person or a people might become a blessing to others. Although Abraham and his descendents were less than a blessing at times, the Genesis story tells of several instances when God brought blessing on other nations and families through them.

1. **Abraham, Isaac and Jacob.** God helped Abraham rescue his neighbors in Sodom and Gomorrah. Abraham interceded for the entire city of Sodom at a later time. Abraham prayed for God to restore the ability to bear children to Abimelech's household. Isaac dug wells that provided enough for him and the surrounding nations. Jacob's labor in Laban's house was obviously the work of God.
2. **Joseph.** The story of Joseph is the crescendo of Genesis and could well offer a prophetic portrait of the crescendo of history. God gave Joseph the ability to interpret a specific dream and then helped him store up enough grain to help many survive a famine that "spread over the face of the whole earth" (Gen 41:56). "The people of all the earth came to buy grain from Joseph" (Gen 41:57). As the famine increased, Joseph not only helped the people of Egypt survive, but he set them up with sufficient supplies to restore normal agricultural cycles. The people declared, "You have saved our lives!" (Gen 47:25).

C. Fulfillment in Later Descendents. The promise that he and his family would be a blessing to the nations was repeated to Abraham three times, then directly to Isaac, and yet a fifth time to Jacob. As the promise was repeated, the language shifted so that it became obvious that much of the promise's fulfillment would take place beyond the lifetime of Abraham, Isaac or Jacob, but instead, in their descendents.

D. Fulfillment in Christ. In the book of Galatians, Paul makes it clear that the promise of the blessing of the nations, the very "gospel" announced early, was fulfilled in one pre-eminent descendent of Abraham: Jesus Christ. But Paul also says that all who trust in Christ become joined with Christ and thus become sons and daughters of Abraham's family. This means that believers in Christ should consider themselves to be descendents of Abraham and heirs of God's promise to bless them so that they will become a blessing to the nations.

Read Gallagher and Hawthorne, "Blessing as Transformation," pp. 36b-38a

E. **Promise Becomes Mandate.** If we are mandated to be His agents of blessing among all the peoples of earth, just what does it mean for the nations to be blessed? And how are we to pursue it?

1. **Relational Blessing.** The blessing of the nations means much more than evangelism, but it certainly can mean no less than the evangelization of every people. As the invitation to belong to God's family by trusting in Christ is extended to every people, we can expect children of Abraham to multiply in every people. As in the book of Genesis, the presence of God upon those who follow Him is the beginning of all the more tangible aspects of blessing that God desires to bring. This means that evangelization has a special priority: It leads to every other kind of goodness that God desires to bring about among the nations.

2. **Material and Social Blessing.** "We should expect God to bring forth every kind of blessing, such as economies that flourish with justice and righteousness, agricultures and industries that abound with plenty for all, and peace throughout communities and between peoples and races. We can expect that God will enable His people to wage war with disease, to break the vicious cycles of poverty, to provide water in desert lands and to be present with healing in the midst of catastrophe."

3. **Not the "Prosperity Gospel."** Take note that Gallagher and Hawthorne distinguish the material abundance of blessing in Genesis from the "prosperity gospel" commonly taught in some circles. They say, "Advocates of the so-called "prosperity gospel" may have more in common with [a magical] worldview which reduces blessing to a method of obtaining wealth from God" (p. 35d). Prosperity gospel teaching can come close to viewing God's blessing as a reward for properly performed "faith" procedures. In its extreme forms, some Christians see blessing as God re-allocating the financial wealth of the nations to come upon Christians, instead of seeing Christians as God's agents of blessing upon the nations.

F. **Blessing as Transformation.** The idea and promise of blessing may give us biblical substance to the sometimes competing agendas calling for "transformation." In the biblical idea of blessing, we find the marvelous power of God at work alongside the vigorous and strategic action of His people. But we are not expected to engineer solutions to every problem or create utopian perfection.

G. **Joseph: The First One to Be Sent.** The model of Joseph helps us understand how we can co-work with God to bring life-giving blessing. He is the first in Scripture who was said to have been sent by God (Gen 45:5).

Read Gallagher and Hawthorne, "Blessing as Transformation," pp. 38b-41

VIII. The Whole Bible as the Greater Mandate

A. **Mandate for Mission.** The biblical mandate for mission is not limited to a few Bible verses. We should never rely on a few apparent proof texts to justify a cause. We must look beyond isolated verses to see the mandate throughout the entire story of the Bible. Along the way we'll note many references of God's concern for the whole world. And of course, we'll examine the relatively few passages in which God gives an explicit command for missionary activity. But we will see the huge mandate for world mission best as we walk through the entire story of the Bible.

Read Stott, "The Bible in World Evangelization," pp. 21-22c

B. **Message, Model and Power for Mission.** The Bible reveals what God has been doing and what He wants done, and how we can accomplish God's purpose in His ways.

Read Stott, "The Bible in World Evangelization," pp. 22c-26

Conclusion of Certificate Readings for this lesson.

After studying this section you should be able to:

- Describe how Isaiah's "Servant Songs" show God's purpose.
- Express God's concern for all He has created and how that concern relates to Christian mission.

IX. The Biblical Foundation in the Story

The most crucial foundation for mission is the biblical story itself. When the diverse stories are allowed to find their natural connection to each other, using the very themes that we have been exploring, a fascinating epic story emerges—a story of God triumphing over His enemies to rescue people from every nation for His glory. Ralph Winter offers a summary of the biblical story as a "prequel" to the history of the gospel's advance.

A. **The Single Drama.** The entrance of the kingdom of God is the central story of the Bible and of all subsequent history. Every part of the Bible has some connection to the saga of God reconquering and redeeming the earth. It follows, then, that this is still the dominant story unfolding in human history.

B. **The Plan of Blessing.** Winter distinguishes blessing from blessings. God speaks of the power of His blessing (singular), which includes blessings and gifts, as having to do with the conferral of a family identity, responsibility and destiny. Such blessing in biblical times was regarded as very desirable, but it carried obligation and responsibility to fulfill a family purpose.

Read Winter, "The Kingdom Strikes Back," pp. 209-210d

X. The Biblical Foundation in Five Themes

Johannes Verkuyl presents five themes running throughout the Old Testament that substantiate the idea that Jewish people "from their earliest days had heard and understood their call to witness directly as well as by their presence."

A. **The Universal Motif.** To enjoy this section you need to open your Bible and scan some of the passages.

1. **Table of Nations.** Look over Genesis 10, which lists the peoples who were scattered at Babel in Genesis 11. The nations are a key part of the biblical drama. God is always concerned with the whole of humanity.

2. **Election of Israel.** The election of Abraham and Israel reveals that God's eye is on the nations.

3. **Breakthrough During Exile.** Roughly 400 years before Christ, God scattered the Jewish people among the nations. After seventy years, some were gathered back to the land again in what some biblical authors consider a second Exodus. Verkuyl points out that the Jews' vision for the world matured during the time of exile.

B. **The Motif of Rescue and Liberation.** That God redeemed Israel was foundational. That God would redeem the nations was a louder theme of the prophets and psalmists as the generations unfolded. Isaiah's "Servant Songs" presented God's purpose to bring salvation to the nations (42:1-12; 43:1-13; 49:1-13; 52:13-53:12).

C. **The Missionary Motif.** Verkuyl offers his view about the frequent charge that Israel was only to be passively present among the nations and God would do the rest. Note that parts of the Bible itself were written in language and forms that would have been meaningful to the surrounding nations.

D. **The Motif of Antagonism.** God is at war with His enemies in order to rescue His servants. This corroborates what Ellisen stated about God's program to defeat evil. Notice particularly how the blazing zeal of God against His enemies is linked to the grand vision of the coming kingdom. God's warfare is linked to His ambition for His glory to be revealed, which is actually a fifth motif.

E. **The Doxological Motif.** "Doxological" refers to God's greater glory. The word "doxological" comes from the Greek word for "glory." This theme is barely mentioned by Verkuyl, but he does mention it.

Read Verkuyl, "The Biblical Foundation for the Worldwide Mission Mandate," pp. 42-45c

XI. Creation Care and Mission

A. **The Earth is the Lord's.** The Bible speaks of God's ownership, enjoyment and glory in His creation. Humans are not the only creatures with relationship toward God. God actually made a covenant in Noah's day with the earth and its creatures. Several scriptures speak of created things praising and glorifying God. Creation is intrinsically good, and we can speak of a sanctity of creation without suggesting its divinity. The purpose of creation is God's glory.

B. **Hope for the Redemption of Creation.** Wright outlines the hope of a new heaven and a new earth. Instead of motivating us to dismiss creation care, this adds an important dimension of motivation and hope to our ecological ethics.

Read Wright, "Mission and God's Earth," pp. 27-30d

C. **Creation Care and Biblical Mission.** But in what sense do ecological ethics constitute Christian mission? Wright offers some points of connection between the two:

1. **The Continuing Mission of Humanity.** Wright describes the initial mission of humanity: "to rule over, to keep and to care for the rest of creation." There is considerable debate as to how fully humankind can or should continue its initial mission and how that mission may or may not be identified with Christ's clear mandate to disciple the nations. No one doubts that some measure of the initial mission of humanity is incumbent upon people everywhere. Although the mission Christ gave His church is related to the initial mission of humanity, the two missions are not the same. If we distinguish them from each other, we will see each more clearly and find ways to fulfill them together.

2. **The Embodiment of God's Compassion and Justice.** The point here is that by caring for creation, we emulate God's own compassion and express His own justice. This can be seen as something related to, but different from, Christian mission.

3. **Contending with False Ideologies**. Involvement with creation care can help Christians contend with contrary ideologies and support the spread of the gospel.

4. **Creation Care Springs from the Mission of God.** According to Wright, "holistic mission" cannot be considered fully holistic if it excludes creatures which will ultimately be part of the reconciliation of the entire universe, which is God's greater mission.

Read Wright, "Mission and God's Earth," pp. 30d-33

2 The Story of His Glory

Studying this lesson will help you:

- Show how several of the main events of the Bible's story contribute to the unfolding of God's purpose to glorify Himself on a global scale by the worship of all nations.
- Describe how God pursued His global purpose by establishing a great reputation for powerful, faithful and loving dealings with His people. Describe why God's name is associated with this story.
- Explain how the story of Jonah shows God's ways of sending His people to the nations.
- Explain how both an expansive and an attractive force have always been used by God to advance His mission purpose.
- Recognize God's mission purpose found in the "Lord's Prayer."
- Explain the sentence: "Missions exists because worship doesn't."
- Explain how worship both reveals and delights God, and expresses His love for people by bringing them near to Him in obedient love.
- Explain some of the biblical grounds for seeing worship that expresses specific cultures of diverse peoples as being valuable to God.
- Explain how hope for God's glory and kingdom can be integrated with compassion for people's needs as a more compelling and sustainable motivation for mission.

Most of us learned the Bible using a story-by-story approach. Lessons from these stories were usually applied to our personal concerns. Because of this we may have wrongly assumed that the Bible is a loose collection of stories with no overriding, integrating purpose. Furthermore, we may quite selfishly conclude that the Bible is all about our personal lives. The reality is that the Bible is far more about God than it is about people. With God at the center and the end of it all, the Bible can be seen not as a disjointed collection of ancient stories and statements, but rather as a single driving saga. This story is still unfolding today.

This all-encompassing story of the Bible is about what God began and what He will finish. As we behold God at work throughout the Bible, we will encounter His zealous passion. Christ wants us to share in His passion in order to enter His mission.

A well-known mission leader once declared, "Let my heart be broken by the things which break the heart of God." We'll explore some of the matters which strike the heart of God with grief, but we'll do it later in the course. At this point, we'll start with what thrills God. Let our hearts first be rejoiced by the things which rejoice the heart of God!

passion Passion is the heart set free to pursue that which is truly worthy. Those who set their hearts on what is most worthy—the glory of God—live with joy-filled abandon. Their hearts are both seized and satisfied with the ambition for Jesus to be ardently worshiped. That love comes to dominate and integrate all other desires so that they live in the freedom of single-minded purpose.

I. The Story of His Glory

The story of the Bible is a story about God more than it is about people. In order to see how the biblical stories come together into a single prolonged story, we'll need a fresh grasp of three biblical terms:

- **Glory:** intrinsic worth, substance, brilliance and beauty.
- **God's Name:** Beyond the function of reference and revelation, the public reputation and open renown of God.
- **Worship:** that which glorifies God by recognizing His glory and by honoring Him with the offerings of the lesser, but worthy glories of the nations. Worship not only delights and reveals God, it fulfills God's love for people by bringing them to a place of their highest honor before Him.

Double Direction of God's Glory. God's mission purpose throughout the story of the Bible can be seen in the double direction of God's glory:

God reveals His glory *to* all nations
in order to receive glory *from* all nations.

World evangelization is the fullest expression of God revealing His glory *to* the nations with the purpose of God receiving glory *from* the nations.

Read Hawthorne, "The Story of His Glory," pp. 49-52b

A. **Abraham: A People For His Name.** Abraham opens the story by openly honoring God's name. His life provides a preview to the later history of the faith family: He made God's name known in worship. God made His name great by dramatic redemptive power. The result was an occasion of multi-national worship with the messianic figure of Melchizedek presiding. Abraham was blessed to be a blessing—with further purpose—in order that the nations would bless God Himself with their grateful worship.

B. **The Great Display.** God makes Himself known by name to the nations at the Exodus. The subsequent establishing of Israel in the land and the opening of the temple made His purpose even more clear.

1. **The Exodus:** the pivotal moment when God revealed Himself globally by name, distinguishing and honoring His name above any other god.
2. **The Conquest:** God's way of establishing the purity of worship to Himself.
3. **The Temple:** God's way of signaling that people from every nation could encounter and worship Him personally.

Read Hawthorne, "The Story of His Glory," pp. 52c-57a

C. **The Great Delay.** Just when it looked as if Israel was going to make God's name widely known among the nations, Solomon led the way in idolatry. Idolatry profaned, or made common, the name of international renown that God had sanctified, or exalted, in the view of the nations. Then began centuries of up and down struggles with idolatry. God finally removed the people from the land, sending them among the nations into a time of captivity known as the Exile.

Look up the verses and describe the reputation God seeks for Himself by filling in the last column. The first three rows are filled in as examples.

God's Fame Among the Nations		
	Name-Tag Name Function: Reference Words used to refer to God.	**Fame Name** Function: Reputation The public report for God's global renown.
Melchizedek—Genesis 14:1-20 In the presence of Abram, the king of Sodom and other kings	**God Most High**	**Genesis 14:20** "... who has delivered your enemies into your hand."
Jethro—Exodus 18:7-12 After the delivery from Egypt	**The LORD (Yahweh)**	**Exodus 18:11** "Now I know that the LORD is greater than all the gods..."
Gibeonites—Joshua 9:3-10 Canaanites pretending to be a people from a distant land who heard of God's name	**The LORD your God**	**Joshua 9:9-10** "... because of the fame (literally name) of the LORD your God, for we have heard the report of Him and all that He did in Egypt."
Moses—Exodus 33:15-34:8 At Sinai after God said that he would pass by Moses and proclaim His name	**The LORD God**	**Exodus 34:6-7** Write what God proclaimed to be His name:
Moses—Numbers 14:1-21 After God said He would destroy the people, Moses prayed, arguing on the basis of God's name	**The LORD**	**Numbers 14:14** What the nations had heard: **Numbers 14:15-16** What the nations would conclude if God destroyed the people: **Numbers 14:17-18** What Moses knew God wanted as His reputation among the nations:
Jonah—Jonah 3:4-4:2 The truth about God that Jonah did not want to disclose to a Gentile nation	**God (Elohim)**	**Jonah 4:2** Compare to Moses above:
Malachi—Malachi 1:11-14 God describing how pure whole-hearted worship reveals His kingly glory	**Lord of Hosts**	**Malachi 1:14** "...I am a great ____________ and my ____________ is to be ____________ among the ______________."

D. God's Persistence and Renewed Promise. God never ceased to pursue His original promise and purpose. The people were brought again into the land, the temple was rebuilt, and a Messiah was expected. God's word about this restoration is clear; it was all for the fulfillment of His global purpose. Many other expressions of the psalmists and prophets clarify God's purpose to be worshiped.

Also the foreigners who join themselves to the LORD,
To minister to Him, and to love the name of the LORD,
To be His servants, every one who keeps from profaning the sabbath,
And holds fast My covenant;
Even those I will bring to My holy mountain,
And make them joyful in My house of prayer.
Their burnt offerings and their sacrifices will be acceptable on My altar;
For My house will be called a house of prayer for all the peoples.

— Isaiah 56:6–7

Read Isaiah 56:6-7 carefully to see the context of the statement "For my house shall be called a house of prayer…." Note the references to prayer in verse 7. What kind of prayers are described? Who is offering these prayers? Jesus did not just quote this verse. He taught about it during what was likely the most public hour of His ministry (Mark 11:17). What kinds of prayer did Jesus want to see?

This passage is often used to encourage prayer on behalf of the nations. This is fine, but it may miss the point of Christ's passionate teaching and temple-cleansing: the hope that the nations *themselves* will pray in full-hearted worship.

E. The Glory of God in Christ. Jesus fulfilled God's purpose to reveal His glory to the world in order to receive glory from the nations.

1. **Prayers For the Name.** By the prayer He taught and the prayers He prayed, we can see how Jesus aimed His entire life at fulfilling the ancient purpose of making God's name known. For God's name to be "hallowed" or "sanctified" is for His namesake to be distinguished, exalted and honored. No prayer could be more basic to the mission purpose of God.

2. **A House of Worship From All Peoples.** The text in Isaiah that Jesus quoted in the temple makes it clear that God rejoiced to receive worship arising *from* nations other than Israel. The temple was destined to become a place of worship that all peoples could easily access in order to meet God, bringing Him their prayerful worship.

Read Hawthorne, "The Story of His Glory," pp. 57b-60a

What did God do for His glory at each of the successive points of the story? Either finish writing out the verse in the spaces provided, or add another note describing God's actions and intentions.

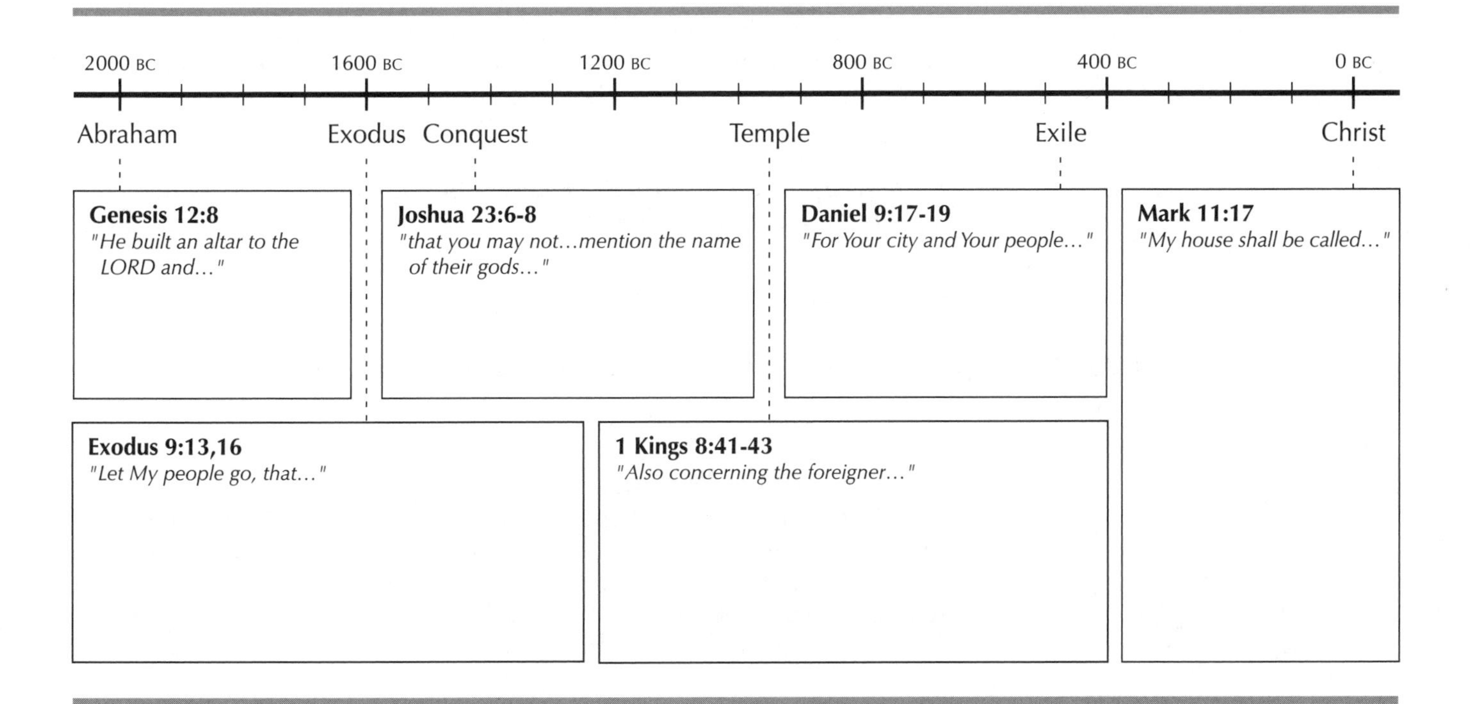

II. Fulfilling the Missionary Task

How was Israel supposed to fulfill her mission mandate? It might appear that Israel was only to play a passive role, attracting the nations to God's worship. Some have concluded that there was not an active mandate to go to the nations until the days of the New Testament. Look again at the biblical record to see the steady, relentless plan of God—both sending His people to the nations to declare the truth of His name, as well as attracting the nations to join His people in worship.

A. **Two Forces.** Jonathan Lewis describes two mechanisms, or forces of mission, which were constantly at work.

1. **Expansive or Centrifugal.** Found throughout the story of Scripture is the outward-bound dynamic, which Lewis calls the expansive force. Others have called this the centrifugal force of missions, or a "go" structure of mission.

2. **Attractive or Centripetal.** There is also found throughout the Bible the inward-bound dynamic, which Lewis calls the attractive force. Others have called this the centripetal force of missions, or a "come" structure of mission.

Read Lewis, "Two Forces," sidebar, pp. 80-81

B. Jonah. Jonah is one of several people in the Old Testament that God sent beyond the borders of Israel. Johannes Verkuyl does not consider the sending of Jonah to be an exception, but an example of the self-centered attitude of God's people. Verkuyl believes that, by the Holy Spirit, the book of Jonah speaks to the Church today. Follow his exposition through the eight scenes of Jonah. Take note of how he describes Jonah's anger because God extended mercy beyond the borders of Israel, even though he knew God's namesake was to be globally known as a "gracious and compassionate" God. Notice Verkuyl's description of Jonah's refusal to acknowledge the purpose of God's covenant with Israel for the salvation of the nations.

Read Verkuyl, "The Biblical Foundation for the Worldwide Mission Mandate," pp. 45c-48 (the Jonah section)

Conclusion of Key Readings for this lesson. 

III. Passion For God's Glory

Paul was motivated by the hope that God would be glorified among the nations. How was Paul's mission, as described in Romans 15, a mission that he aimed to finish? Can or should that be our vision today? Steven Hawthorne describes three changes in practice worth considering as we recognize our part in the ongoing story of God's glory.

A. Deepen Our Motive Base. When mission is merely a compassionate response to human need, motivation can be limited to feelings of concern toward people. Some mobilization can be limited to stirring up guilt. But when mission is defined primarily as an enterprise that brings about something for God, and secondarily as that which brings about something benefitting people, then both our motivation and our mobilization can be more balanced. Compassion may actually run deeper. We can be deeply moved by needs while acting boldly for God's highest purpose.

B. Define the Task. Focusing on God's glory helps us see the value of planting churches which will become an expression of the sanctified best of their particular culture. This may be one of the best grounds for planting church movements among every people group. The people group *approach* is not as important as setting our vision on the people group *result*.

C. Integrate Efforts. Which is more important: evangelism or social action? This is a false dichotomy, in large part answered by lifting vision beyond what happens *for people* (which is usually emphasized in both evangelism and social action) and aiming instead at bringing about glory, thanks, praise and honor *for God*. A single vision for God's glory can integrate and motivate efforts to serve people in their present-hour need, as well as save people from eternal loss.

Read Hawthorne, "The Story of His Glory," pp. 60a-62

IV. The Worth of Each Ethnicity

In the final paragraphs of "The Story of His Glory," Hawthorne states that God "yearns for the unique outpouring of love, righteousness, wisdom and worship that can come from every people" (page 62b). What Hawthorne refers to as "the distinctive wonder of each people group" is part of why Psalm 96:7 calls the "families of the peoples" to give to the Lord "glory and strength" (see Hawthorne, page 52b). The beauty and worth of human cultures, even though we now see them distorted and darkened by evil, is something the Bible celebrates with anticipation. In the age to come, although the city of God is illumined by the glory of God (Rev 21:23), it will be adorned with the glories of all the ethnicities of humankind. The nations "will bring the glory and the honor of the nations into it" (Rev 21:26).

Such high regard for culture and the distinctive worth of every tribe, tongue and people can be seen in the creation accounts of Scripture. Miriam Adeney describes how God endowed humanity to create culture and to flourish in distinctive communities. This means that the reality and value of ethnicity is rooted in creation. God prizes and delights in the cultures of humankind, even though now, because of sin, as Adeney observes, "the cultures we create reek with evil." As we seek to fulfill our part of God's mission, we should evaluate and value culture from God's point of view. Mission work can be seen as helping people begin to bring God a measure of the "glory and the honor of the nations."

Read Adeney, "Is God Colorblind or Colorful?" pp. 416b-417d ("A Place in the Story"), and Sauer, "Created to Create Culture," p. 417

V. God-Centered Mission

We've explored how God's purpose for glory unfolds in history. John Piper restates the case for focusing our motive in mission on God's glory in the worship of the nations. Piper says that world evangelization is a secondary, means-to-an-end activity. God's glory is the primary purpose for mission. "Missions exists because worship doesn't." In other words, the reason God gives us our mission is to bring about obedient, love-filled and life-giving worship among peoples and in places where there is none.

A. **God's Passion.** God's supremacy over other gods provides clear rationale for mission. But an even stronger motive is God's inexhaustible enthusiasm that there be praise arising from the nations. Worship is not only the goal but also the fuel of missions.

B. **God-Centered Compassion.** Calling the nations to worship is to seek their best interest. Understanding the redemptive value of worship can energize our acts of mercy even when, at times, feelings of love for others fade. As the nations experience the dignity of worshiping the living God, His call to come near to Him by worship becomes the highlight of all the blessings He bestows. And it becomes the most shareable message in the world.

Read Piper, "Let the Nations Be Glad!" pp. 64-69 (all)

VI. Co-Working With God on Mission

Tim Dearborn's article is one of the most important in the course. Ponder it carefully. He makes one of the most important distinctions that can be made: We can either see our mission as a series of need-meeting projects, energized by an awareness of the problems of the world. Or we can frame our understanding of mission as an invitation to join with God as He pursues His purpose in the world. What makes it possible to pursue mission in the latter way is a vision of God steadily accomplishing His mission through history. So far in the course we have been tracing the story of how God has pursued His glory and His kingdom.

A. **Beyond Duty.** Dearborn explores some commonplace attitudes toward mission motivation. He exposes the inadequacy of being compelled by human needs. If our primary passion is directed to mission activities, mission will inevitably "degenerate into a wearisome, overwhelming duty." Instead, He suggests that there is one singular passion: "When the King and His kingdom are the unifying, controlling source and goal of all we do," then mission becomes an adventure of joy, passion and hope.

B. **God on Mission With His Church.** Dearborn says it is better to affirm that "the God of mission has a Church in the world" than it is to say "the Church has a mission for God in the world." This means that God's mission is always greater than the mission He has entrusted to His Church. In a very real sense, this means that we are not necessary. How does this idea compare with what Piper and Hawthorne have stated?

C. **The Integrating Reality: The King and His Kingdom.** So many competing agendas and divergent needs call for our attention. They usually amount to sad news of unsolveable problems. Instead of adding to this exhausting, never-ending challenge, Dearborn calls us to see the great victory of Christ and the reality of how God Himself establishes His coming kingdom. He has given us a pivotal role, "but the work remains God's."

D. **Signs of the Kingdom.** Take note of Dearborn's statement that the Church is not to be an "underground railway" to heaven. We are privileged to have a part in the great unfolding story of God's kingdom. He desires that we become living signs of His kingdom and bring about signs of kingdom life in the world. How do such signs of God's kingdom bring glory to God?

Read Dearborn, "Beyond Duty," pp. 70-73 (all)

VII. God on Mission

Henry Blackaby and Avery Willis describe God on mission through history. Although the sentences are short and simple, they are profound. Like Dearborn, they describe God's mission as aiming to establish His kingdom, but integrated with God's kingdom they see God's Name being glorified and the world being reconciled to God.

A. **God Initiates Mission.** Examine the examples of God initiating an act of advancing His mission by revealing what He was going to do. In every case, God gave His people something to accomplish, and yet, God was the one who accomplished everything. Why does God choose to do things in this way? Blackaby and Willis assert that God desires a loving but purposeful relationship with His people.

B. Jesus: On Mission With His Father. There are countless calls to understand our mission as an imitation or continuation of Jesus' work in the world. What Blackaby and Willis offer is something very different. Take note of it. Instead of a call to imitate Jesus' activities, they describe what it means to follow Jesus' example as He joined Himself with the Father in mission. The result was that Jesus united "His life with His Father's mission." Consider how you may be hearing God speak as you work through this course. How can you resolve to follow Christ's example so that you can unite your life with God's mission?

Read Blackaby and Willis, "On Mission With God," pp. 74-76a (up until "Knowing and Working in God's Ways")

Conclusion of Certificate Readings for this lesson.

After studying this section you should be able to:

- Describe the mystery of how God is always the author of mission, and yet enlists people as His co-workers in Christ.
- Explain what it means for the earth to be "filled with God's glory" in terms of church planting.

VIII. The Local Church: His Glory Made Visible

Jim Montgomery encouraged many people to multiply churches throughout the world with a vision he called, "saturation church planting." We include this brief excerpt to explore how God intended for local churches to bring Him glory in the communities of earth.

Montgomery defines local churches in terms of the incarnation: Christ is somehow embodied in His people and is able to reveal His glory and life to the world. The idea of Christ being embodied in His people both defines the nature of the Church and the purpose of the Church. Such an understanding of the Church gives compelling motivation for working to see that churches are planted in every community of earth. Wolfgang Simson makes the same vision even more explicit. He says that we should be satisfied with "nothing short of the very presence of the living Christ in every neighborhood and village" of every nation.

Read Montgomery, "His Glory Made Visible," pp. 660-662 (all), and Simson, "The Shopping Window of God," sidebar, p. 661

IX. God's Mission

David Bosch introduces an important phrase. Don't let its significance be hidden by the Latin. The phrase is *missio Dei*, and it means God's mission, or the mission of God. As we have seen, it is important to focus on God as the author of mission. What if it was up to human ingenuity and mercy to engineer the changes that are needed in the world? That generally describes the approach of the world outside the Judeo-Christian tradition. Think about it. Without mission, the world is a pretty bleak place. The only glimmer of hope would be our best speculations about human progress, based on vague ideas of evolution. When these ideas and other ideas are seen to fail, the world becomes ripe with yearning for someone to be sent, for someone to redeem.

It's no wonder that the prayer Jesus prayed was for the Church to be one with God in mission so that the world would come to know that God had sent Jesus. John 17:11-23 is commonly misunderstood as if the world was to be attracted to God because God's people enjoy relational closeness with one another. The context is all about Jesus leaving and sending His followers, even as He was sent. It's very likely that the idea of being "one even as we are one" refers to a collaborative intimacy in mission rather than an essential unity or a task-free relational closeness. In any case, it is good news that God is on mission Himself. It is also marvelous that He would ever condescend to send others on His behalf. In this section we'll seek to grasp some of the wonder of this awesome way of knowing God.

David Bosch occasionally uses technical words, but the meanings are usually nearby. For example, the word "prolepsis" is followed immediately by its meaning, "an anticipation."

A. **God, the Author of Mission.** Bosch explains more about the light of the Servant of the Lord in Isaiah. He points out that mission works in two directions with the Servant. Light flows from the Servant to the nations. And in response, the nations come and are gathered into a larger people by the attractive power of the light. The main point is that God is the author. Israel never appointed itself as a missionary nation. The Jews did not have a habit of sending themselves on errands of salvation. They were called by God to do so.

B. **The "Tender Mystery" of God and People on Mission.** Bosch explains why both mechanisms were at work throughout both the Old and New Testaments. It would seem that the centripetal or attractive force is God's work. A careless reading of the story at this point would lead one to conclude that centrifugal or expansive mission is man's work. This is a crucial mistake. To highlight the error, he uses the almost ridiculous phrase, "God and Man as Competitors?"

To sum up the issue: If God is the author of only centripetal, or attractive mission, then that seems to imply that people need to undertake the initiative for centrifugal mission. The mistake is compounded when everyday zeal is added to the mix, or American pragmatism that assumes we can do anything if we just put our mind to it. Mission is not to be treated in this spirit. Mission is a "tender mystery" of God and people co-working, though God is always the author. Take special note of the series of paradoxes which illustrate this "tender mystery."

This is not an inconsequential issue. There are two extremes to avoid. If God is the sole initiator, not enlisting any collaboration from people, then there is resignation: Let be what will be. On the other hand, if God's mission is a command waiting for someone to finally be obedient, then there are waves of fanaticism: It all depends on us.

C. **More Than a Command.** This marvelous co-working of God and His people is exactly why the Great Commission is not stamped on every page, but almost presumed throughout the New Testament. Bosch says, "Mission in the New Testament is more than a matter of obeying a command. It is, rather, the result of an encounter with Christ. To meet Christ means to become caught up in a mission to the world." Bosch is not saying that the Great Commission does not have tremendous force. He is saying that the entire Bible supports the Great Commission in greater ways than finding parallel statements from God issuing direct imperative commands.

Read Bosch, "Witness to the World," pp. 78-82 (all)

3 Your Kingdom Come

Studying this lesson will help you:

- Explain how the gospel of the kingdom announces what God has done and is now doing to overcome evil.
- Recognize and use biblical concepts related to the theme of the kingdom of God.
- Explain the surprise of "the mystery of the kingdom" in terms of the Messiah coming not once, but twice.
- Explain how Christ intended the missionary enterprise to extend His "D-Day" victory of the cross and resurrection.
- Explain the mission significance of a "two-tier" timeline of history, in which a present evil age persists even though it is invaded by a coming kingdom age.
- Explain how Matthew 24:14 gives hope and focus for completing world evangelization.
- Explain how Jesus pursued his life-work guided by a vision of the kingdom of God as a fight against evil to bring mercy on the nations.
- Explain how prayer can be seen as rebellion against the status quo.
- Pray with hope and strategic purpose for God to restrain evil powers in order for people to hear the gospel and to hope for lasting change.

To accomplish God's mission, or to enter it at all, we must be convinced that God is not merely managing evil—He is destroying it. Without such hope, we will not likely enlist ourselves in the spiritual war that we see raging. We are likely to explain away the present hurricane of darkness, acquiescing to it as if it were a passing outbreak of bad weather. But we know better. The Bible is clear about the extravagant price God has already paid to reconcile people who were His enemies. The Bible clearly shows God's determination to dismantle every evil power, with present-hour manifestations of the forthcoming triumph.

Jesus had one prevailing theme in His teaching: the kingdom of God. He used that theme to call people to follow Him. He used that language to enlist His friends to follow Him further—into the final stages of the global war against evil.

Christ's focus on the kingdom of God challenges us with matters of huge significance in this war. It is no small thing to establish communities of kingdom life as outposts of light in the midst of spiritual darkness. Because of the surpassing certainty of the inbreak of the kingdom, it is not rare to find Christ's servants loving their own lives so little that death does not threaten them. These people pray and labor for nothing less than His kingdom coming on Earth as it is in heaven. Such a pursuit of Christ's kingdom is the heart of all true hoping. It is the soul of all praying. The kingdom of God is the core of all mission.

hope God has called us to live our lives as a bold act of hope. To hope is not merely to wish for small improvements of personal circumstances. Hope expects all things, large or little, to be overwhelmed and filled with the immense glory of Christ. Thus, true hope pursues global glory and total triumph over evil. Lives of hope can face great evil with relentless courage, since there is no telling how soon God will break through with ultimate victory.

We've already identified God's ultimate purpose to be a crescendo of glory from all peoples. We've traced the outlines of His purpose for worship through the major turning points of the Bible's story. Now we'll focus more closely on the way God liberates people from a kingdom of satanic darkness to serve Him as worshiping priests from all nations.

I. Basic Kingdom Concepts

A. The Meaning of "Kingdom." We commonly use "kingdom" to designate a king's geographical domain or people belonging to such a realm. The Bible uses the term in a different and dynamic way: "Kingdom" is the right to rule, rather than royally-owned real estate.

B. The "Kingdom of God" is the exercise of God's kingship, His authority, His right to rule based on His might, power and glory.

Read Ladd, "The Gospel of the Kingdom," pp. 83-85b

II. Basic Kingdom Conflicts

A. The Mystery of the Kingdom. Jesus used the idea of "the mystery of the Kingdom" to describe a time of mercy for the nations before final judgment. The surprise that defines the mystery is that the expected kingly Messiah figure was to come not once, but twice. He will come in a blaze of glory in His final coming as the Son of Man (Dan 7). But this is preceded by His first coming in humility and in a hidden form as the Suffering Servant of God (Isa 42; 49; 53).

1. **The Old Testament Perspective** saw the kingdom coming as a single cataclysmic event of judgment on God's enemies, beginning a time of God's peace and power.

The Vision of the Kingdom

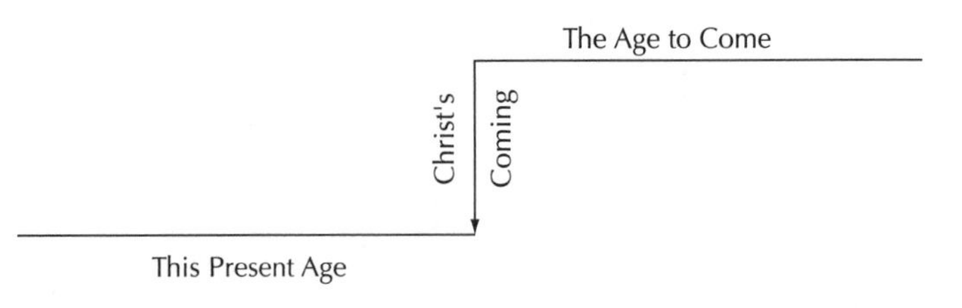

The Messiah Brings God's Day of Peace and Power

2. **God's Kingdom Comes in Two Stages:**

   - **With Jesus' First Coming:** The kingdom has already arrived! But it operates in a more hidden way, breaking satanic power, delivering people of all nations from the grip of evil's power and offering the many blessings of God's rule. This was not envisioned in the Old Testament perspective.
   - **At the End:** It will come openly, in all the world's view, crushing all earthly powers, destroying every attempt to usurp God's rightful rule, and purging all sin and evil from the earth. This fulfills the Old Testament perspective.

The Mystery of the Kingdom

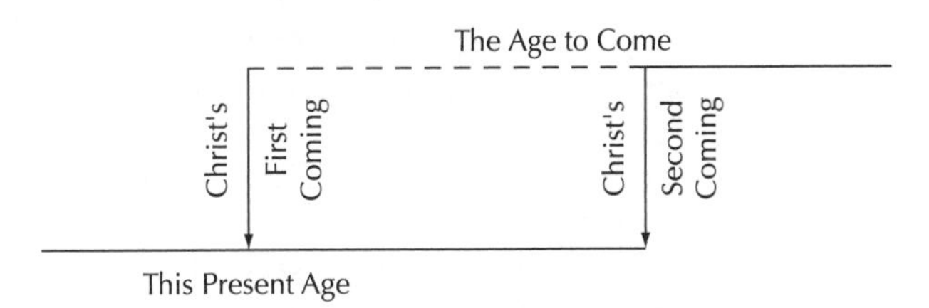

The Messiah Comes Twice

B. The Victory of the Kingdom. God's kingdom is a progressive victory over satanic dominion in order to rescue people of all nations from the power of darkness, and ultimately, to undo the curse over all creation.

This "present evil age" has already been invaded by "the age to come" of God's kingdom. Satan has already been *defeated,* but he is destined to be *destroyed* in "the age to come." We are now living in the overlap of the ages. We work between the "already" of Jesus' first coming and the "not yet" of His second coming. The time between the two comings is fundamentally a time of conflict resulting from the overlap of the ages. The missionary task of the Church (evangelizing the nations) is the primary reason for this interim period. The kingdom victory is accomplished in three great acts:

1. **Christ's First Coming: Breaking Satan's Power.** Jesus' mission on earth by His life, death and resurrection.
2. **Between His Comings: Undoing Satan's Works.** Jesus continues His mission, working with and through His Church.
3. **Christ's Second Coming: Destroying Satan's Kingdom.** Christ comes in full glory.

Read Ladd, "The Gospel of the Kingdom," pp. 85b-88d, and Blue, "D-Day before V-E Day," sidebar, p. 90

III. The Mandate of the Kingdom

George Ladd finds enormous mandate force in Matthew 24:14. We emphasize this verse not because we are predicting a specific time of Christ's return, but to emphasize that God apparently intends to wait until all peoples have had opportunity to respond to an adequate testimony of the gospel of the kingdom.

A. Message of the Kingdom. The gospel of the kingdom declares and displays God's triumph over the three enemies that have been the ruin of people throughout history: death, Satan and sin. They have each been *defeated* by His first coming and they will each be *destroyed* at His final coming.

The gospel of the kingdom announces what God has already done and is now continuing to do to conquer the enemies of sin, death and the devil. God intends to bring substantial healing and transformation in the present day and eternal life in the eternal kingdom. The gospel of the kingdom is not only an announcement, it is a promise of what God will do to reconcile all things under the kingly headship of Christ.

B. The Mission of the Kingdom. Matthew 24:14 is the only verse in scripture in which Jesus gives his disciples a specific description of what *must* be accomplished *before* his second coming and the end of the age. World evangelization is an explicit condition for His return. The gospel of the kingdom must be proclaimed in all the world. Only then will the end come. What constitutes an adequate "witness" or who constitutes "all the peoples" by Christ's understanding cannot be discerned with precision. Should we not take seriously any significant barrier between peoples which may block the flow of the gospel so that none of "the peoples" mentioned in Matthew 24:14 are bypassed? Should we not labor to establish the fullest "witness" possible—an ongoing community of obedience under Christ's Lordship?

1. **Meaning to History.** This truth, that God is holding history open in order for the Church to complete her task, gives meaning to history and gives enormous significance to the obedience of the Church.

2. **Motive of the Kingdom.** If it is true that the coming of the Messiah is in some way contingent upon the Church proclaiming the gospel of the kingdom to all peoples, then we have great motivation: Final victory awaits the completion of the task. No greater hope can be conceived. Ladd asks and answers the question, "Do you love the Lord's appearing? Then you will bend every effort to take the gospel into all the world."

Read Ladd, "The Gospel of the Kingdom," pp. 88d-95

IV. The Prayer of the Kingdom

The essence of intercessory prayer as taught by Jesus is to argue a case in God's court. It is not a matter of explaining or acquiescing to evil, but rather fighting against it. Leading theologian David Wells exposes some common assumptions, held deeply on a worldview level, which affect our view of prayer.

A. The Worldview Beneath Prayer. Wells challenges us to reconsider our sense of failure in prayer. We may fail to practice prayer because we really don't believe it will make a difference. It is commonplace to resign ourselves to the present state of the world's woes as if the evil we see and experience is God's intended plan. Wells declares that a biblical Hebrew/Christian worldview refuses to accept that the evil we find on earth is God's will and plan. Jesus charged His followers to "rebel" against the status quo by intercessory prayer.

B. The Kingdom Prayer.

1. **His Name.** We are to pray that God's name will be honored wherever the truth about God is suppressed or denied (understanding "hallowed" or "sanctified" as the revealing and honoring of God's name).

2. **His Kingdom.** We are to ask that His kingdom rule will become effective even where it is defied and that His will be accomplished even where it is opposed by His enemies.

Read Wells, "Prayer: Rebelling Against the Status Quo," pp. 159-162 (all)

Conclusion of Key Readings for this lesson. 

V. The Messiah on Kingdom Mission

Imagine Jesus reading His Bible. What would He have come to understand about God's purpose and His own part in it? There's no question that when Jesus began His ministry, the kingdom of God was more than a mere topic of His teaching. The reality of the kingdom of God set the stage for all that Jesus did, said or prayed. He knew that He was the key figure in the global struggle between good and evil. He knew that He had been sent into the kingdom war. When Jesus sent His followers, He gave them a clear picture of the drama of God at war to redeem the nations.

A. The Day of the Lord. Cornell Goerner shows how the Book of Malachi helped shape the vision and ministry of both John the Baptist and Jesus.

1. **God's Day of Judgment.** Malachi had warned Israel that God's judgment would fall on them first rather than the nations, who were perceived to be God's enemies. Why judgment on Israel? Because of God's desire to be worshiped by all nations (Mal 1:10-11). Israel had failed to fulfill the most rudimentary regimens of worship and fearing God's name (Mal 2:1-3; 4:1-6).

2. **John's Warning of the Kingdom.** Malachi described a classic expression of the Old Testament vision of God's judgment arriving in a single stroke of destructive power against God's enemies. John the Baptist warned people of a vast coming judgment.

3. **Jesus' Word of the Kingdom.** Jesus continued this same message, calling for repentance because the turning point in history was at hand ("The time is fulfilled, and the kingdom of God is at hand; repent and believe in the gospel." Mark 1:15). As John and others looked on, they expected that the Messiah would boldly confront the leading priests and governing powers after the model of Malachi (Mal 3:1-5), even to the point of throwing off the Roman Empire's control.

Read Goerner, "Jesus and the Gentiles," pp. 112-114a

B. The Surprise: A Day of Mercy for the Nations. Patrick Johnstone sheds important light on one of the opening acts of Jesus' ministry. Find it in Luke 4:14-30. Open your Bible to this passage, as well as to Isaiah 61:1-2, as you read Johnstone's suggestions about how the original language could be translated. Ponder the possible meaning that could be attributed to Jesus' abrupt stop in the middle of a line of Hebrew poetry. What was the popular idea of "the day of vengeance" concerning the nations?

Recall the background we examined about the apocalyptic war, which expected an outbreak of God's judgment on the nations. The townspeople were thinking of the "day of vengeance" in the final line of the prophecy as a long-awaited end to Roman oppression. By leaving off that final phrase, Johnstone says that Jesus was in effect changing the scheme of the end-times. He was declaring that God was giving a time of open-ended mercy. Just when the people had begun to grasp what He meant by interrupting the reading, Jesus confirmed their thoughts by pronouncing, "Today, this scripture is fulfilled."

They understood that Jesus was opening a time of mercy. These were "the gracious words" that were coming from his lips. But Jesus did not just leave it to their imagination to think that God was prolonging a time of kindness only for the nation of Israel. Jesus made it clear that God's mercy was directed toward the nations. It was this statement that provoked them to attempt to kill Him.

Read Johnstone, "A Violent Reaction to Mercy," sidebar, p. 120

Goerner calls attention to this incident in Luke 4. Jesus demonstrated from the earliest days that God's kingdom purpose was for all the nations. Goerner says that Jesus did not "aspire to world dominion." He rejected methods of power, instead choosing a "path of suffering and redemption."

Read Goerner, "Jesus and the Gentiles," pp. 115a-115c

C. The Surprise Messiah. As Ladd described earlier ("The Gospel of the Kingdom," p. 86), Jesus surprised and disappointed John the Baptist. Instead of a conquest over high political powers, Jesus declared that the present day was the time for healing the downtrodden and preaching the gospel to the poor. It soon became clear to His followers that Jesus' healing and preaching to the poor was just the beginning of an engagement with spiritual evil and a proclamation of the gospel to the poor throughout the nations. What kind of Messiah was He? Many of Jesus' day must have asked the same question that John did, "Are you the Expected One or shall we wait for someone else?" (Matt 11:3).

Three models of the Messiah, or the Expected One, were commonly known in Israel. The first was the Son of David, who was expected to be a great military leader, rallying Israel in miraculous fashion to overcome all her enemies, much like David of old (Ps 89:20-29 and many others). Two other models were found in the Old Testament: The Son of Man and the Suffering Servant.

1. **The Son of Man.** Jesus used this messianic title deliberately and frequently. He found it in Daniel, who saw God inaugurating the rule of the Son of Man as king of all peoples and kingdoms. The global ramifications were clear to everyone of His day.

Read Goerner, "Jesus and the Gentiles," pp. 114b-115a

2. **The Suffering Servant.** Jesus did not fulfill the general expectations of the people for a conquering ruler like the Son of David or a cataclysmic firestorm of judgment from the Son of Man. Jesus knew that there was another model of the coming Messiah and the kingdom. It is found in the passages of Isaiah that refer to the Servant: Isaiah 42:1-12; 49:1-6; and 52:13–53:12. These passages tell us that the Servant will suffer; and that His rule will extend to all the nations; and that He will bring the kingdom in unconventional ways among the poor instead of vanquishing the powerful.

...in order that what was spoken through
Isaiah the prophet, might be fulfilled, saying,
"Behold, my Servant whom I have chosen;
My Beloved in whom My soul is well-pleased;
I will put My Spirit upon Him,
And He shall proclaim justice [literally, judgment] to the Gentiles.
He will not quarrel, nor cry out;
Nor will anyone hear His voice in the streets.
A battered reed He will not break off,
And a smoldering wick He will not put out,
Until He leads justice [literally, judgment] to victory.
And in His name the Gentiles [literally, nations] will hope."

—Matthew 12:17–21

Read Matthew 12:17-21. For Matthew to phrase verse 17 in the way that he did shows that the disciples had come to discover much about Jesus' identity in the book of Isaiah. How was this prophecy fulfilled in Jesus' lifetime? Is this one of the prophecies about the Servant (it is located in Isaiah 42:1-4)? How is this prophecy still being fulfilled today? How will the nations be moved to hope?

Designate the location of the following biblical phrases on the timeline to show when they were or will be fulfilled. Sometimes more than one correct answer is possible. From what we've seen of the disappointment of John the Baptist, which of these passages might he have thought were very near? Place yourself on this timeline.

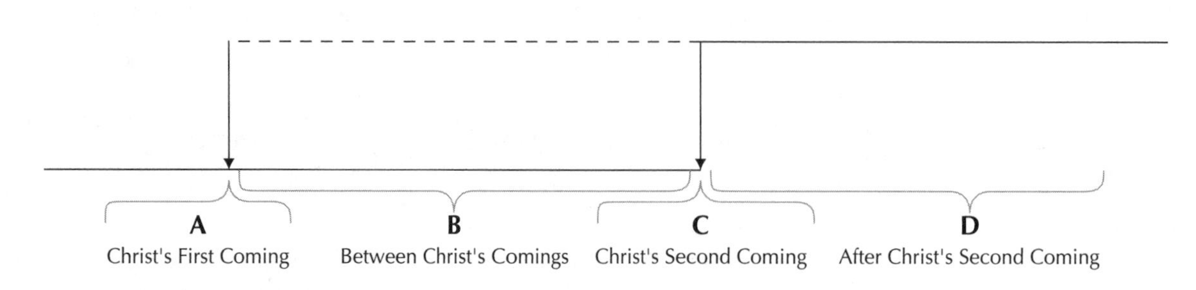

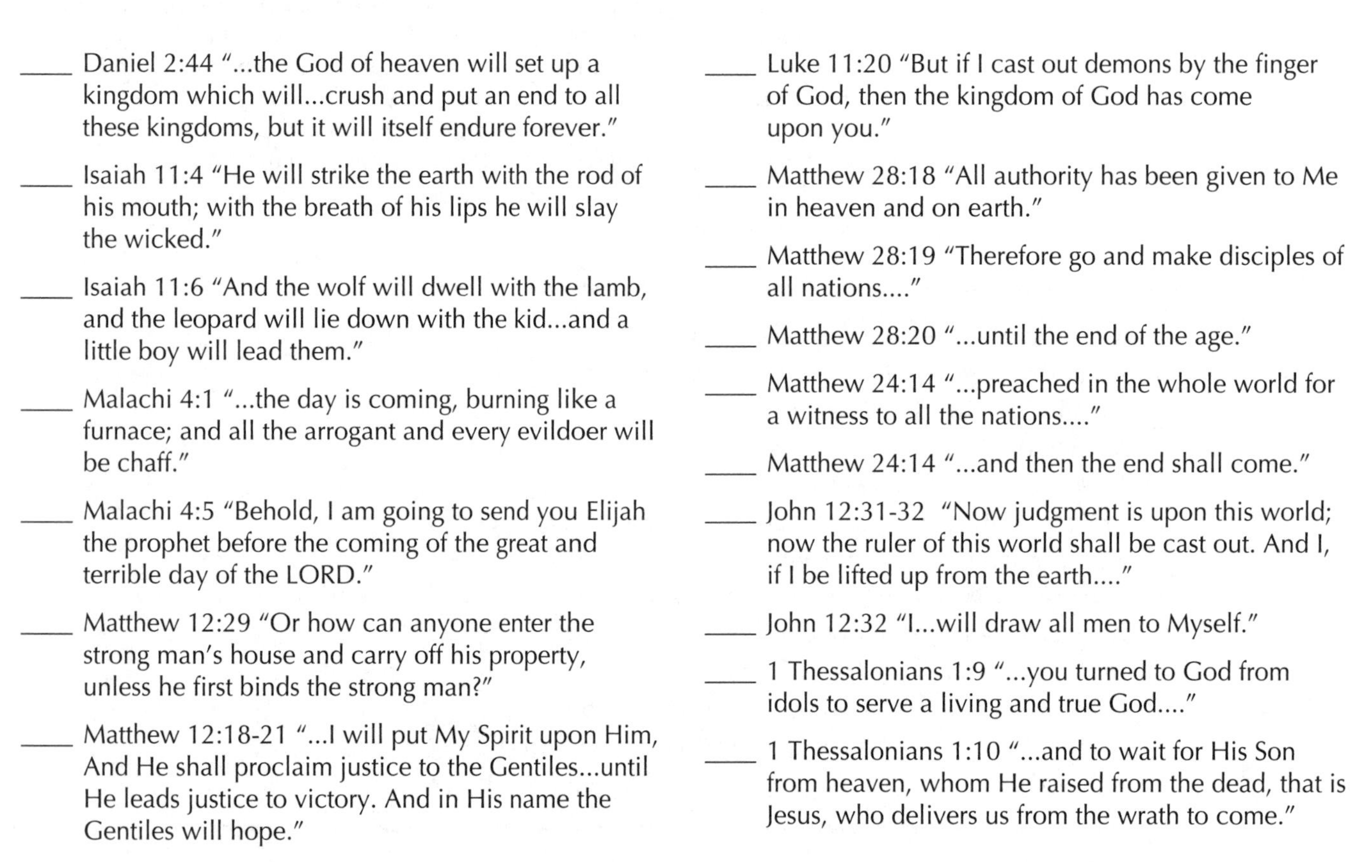

____ Daniel 2:44 "...the God of heaven will set up a kingdom which will...crush and put an end to all these kingdoms, but it will itself endure forever."

____ Isaiah 11:4 "He will strike the earth with the rod of his mouth; with the breath of his lips he will slay the wicked."

____ Isaiah 11:6 "And the wolf will dwell with the lamb, and the leopard will lie down with the kid...and a little boy will lead them."

____ Malachi 4:1 "...the day is coming, burning like a furnace; and all the arrogant and every evildoer will be chaff."

____ Malachi 4:5 "Behold, I am going to send you Elijah the prophet before the coming of the great and terrible day of the LORD."

____ Matthew 12:29 "Or how can anyone enter the strong man's house and carry off his property, unless he first binds the strong man?"

____ Matthew 12:18-21 "...I will put My Spirit upon Him, And He shall proclaim justice to the Gentiles...until He leads justice to victory. And in His name the Gentiles will hope."

____ Luke 11:20 "But if I cast out demons by the finger of God, then the kingdom of God has come upon you."

____ Matthew 28:18 "All authority has been given to Me in heaven and on earth."

____ Matthew 28:19 "Therefore go and make disciples of all nations...."

____ Matthew 28:20 "...until the end of the age."

____ Matthew 24:14 "...preached in the whole world for a witness to all the nations...."

____ Matthew 24:14 "...and then the end shall come."

____ John 12:31-32 "Now judgment is upon this world; now the ruler of this world shall be cast out. And I, if I be lifted up from the earth...."

____ John 12:32 "I...will draw all men to Myself."

____ 1 Thessalonians 1:9 "...you turned to God from idols to serve a living and true God...."

____ 1 Thessalonians 1:10 "...and to wait for His Son from heaven, whom He raised from the dead, that is Jesus, who delivers us from the wrath to come."

Read Verkuyl, "The Biblical Foundation for the Worldwide Mission Mandate," pp. 44a-44b, from "God's Method of Achieving Liberation" to the point where he says "...to become a light to the nations."

Read the following passages in Isaiah: 42:1-12; 49:1-6; 52:13–53:12. Which verses refer to the Servant figure fulfilling God's missionary purpose among many nations? How does this role align with Jesus' teaching about "the mystery of the Kingdom?"

D. **A Different War with Evil.** Gregory Boyd helps us understand more about the way Jesus acted in keeping with how the Jewish people of His day understood the Bible. This worldview was a thoroughly biblical outlook, enhanced by "apocalyptic" writers who emphasized that God was at war against a satanic insurrection. These angelic evil powers had been attempting to thwart God's purposes for Israel to become a blessing to the nations. In the apocalyptic view, this war was coming soon to a climactic finale. With this backdrop we can see Jesus on mission to overcome evil powers in order to liberate people. Furthermore, we can see Christ's followers continuing this same mission.

1. **Jesus as "The Bringer of the Kingdom of God."** Notice Boyd's analysis of how Jesus understood the kingdom of God: "For Jesus, the kingdom of God means abolishing the kingdom of Satan." In this light the actions of Jesus can be seen as deliberate acts of mission to free people from the powers of darkness. Jesus aimed at nothing less than invading the present dark age to establish the enduring reign of God's peace.

Read Boyd, "God at War," pp. 102a-103a, 103d-106d

2. **Continuing the Work of God's War.** Boyd describes how Jesus "commissioned, equipped and empowered" not only His immediate followers, but the entire Church to continue His battle against evil by proclaiming and demonstrating Christ's kingdom. Boyd suggests how centuries ago, Western worldview assumptions may have turned the Church away from the mission of *fighting* evil to a practice of merely *explaining* evil. We are left with the question: Is it possible to carry out Christ's Great Commission without *in some way* fighting against evil?

Read Boyd, "God at War," pp. 106d-108

E. **Following the Messiah in His Mission.** N.T. Wright says that it is wise to consider how the term "kingdom of God" is used as "a flag of convenience" authenticating a multitude of diverse agendas. He says that it is crucially important that we not detach the stories of Jesus' works from the finished work of His death and resurrection.

- If these are considered separately, it is easy to see the work of Jesus' life as nothing more than a good example of social activism.
- On the other hand, if the works of Christ are seen as nothing more than a preamble to His atoning work on the cross, then we miss the launching of His kingdom on earth as it is in heaven.

Either way, we will miss out on His mission. Only when we see His life, death and resurrection together does it become clear that to be joined with Christ is to become engaged with Him in His mission of inaugurating His kingdom.

Read Wright, "To Inaugurate His Kingdom: His Deeds, Death and Resurrection," sidebar, p. 105

VI. Strategic Prayer

John Robb presents prayer as a way to forcefully deal with supernatural evil. He shows how truths about the kingdom of God have been put into practice in prayer, giving biblical as well as contemporary examples.

A. **Socio-Spiritual Forces.** Two complexes, idolatry and strongholds, often dominate the least evangelized settings so that gospel proclamation and even community development efforts have little reception. Idolatry usually enmeshes people into contracts with false gods. Strongholds are false patterns of thought which deny that Christ can be obeyed or, in some cases, that anything at all can change for the better. With idolatry locking up people's sense of allegiance, and with strongholds limiting people to a worldview of hopelessness, the work of prayer is important to prepare the way for the gospel.

B. **Forceful Prayer is Not Magic.** Prayer can be forceful because it invites God into the fray. The temptation is to see ourselves as intrinsically powerful because we are praying. Prayer should never be utilized as if it were a magic formula or a procedure guaranteed to work. Prayer does not so much work—God Himself is at work. Prayer is God's way of involving us with His work. With this balancing wisdom, it is important to pursue prayer in some situations as an act of spiritual violence.

C. **Prayer for Unreached Peoples.** Prayer is particularly significant for unreached peoples. Where Christ does not yet have a following, the strongholds which blind people to the possibility of obeying Christ have rarely been challenged. In such societies, where Christ-obeying churches do not exist, we should not be surprised to see that the worldview of the people is often impregnated with powerful patterns of thinking which resist the gospel. Prayer can be God's way of breaking these fatalistic, hopeless ways of thinking, preparing the way for many to follow Him. God shows Himself to be greater than other gods (sanctifying His name!) by answering prayer, thus breaking patterns of allegiance with dark powers reinforced by idolatry.

Read Robb, "Strategic Prayer," pp. 163-169 (all)

God's Purpose Summarized: For His glory in global worship, and for the blessing of all nations, God purposes to overcome evil by redeeming a people who will love and obey Him from every people.

Now we can better see how the three parts of God's purpose work together:

- **Against Evil:** The kingdom of God advances His purpose against the Satanic counterfeit kingdom in order to rule a kingdom over all kingdoms.
- **For the Nations:** The Kingdom victory opens the way for God to reconcile people to Himself. As Christ's Lordship becomes a reality in the lives of many people, signs of His coming kingdom will bring the blessing promised to Abraham to all nations in this present age.
- **Toward God:** All of this takes place so that God will be served and loved as King by many from every nation.

The mission that God gives to His Church is not a sideline affair. Christ gives us an enormous part to play in bringing forth the fruit of His kingdom victory. In the next lesson we'll explore how Christ grounds the Great Commission on the full measure of authority and power of the kingdom. In Lesson Six we'll explore how all of history after New Testament times can still be characterized by the theme of God's kingdom striking back.

Conclusion of Certificate Readings for this lesson.

After studying this section you should be able to:

- Describe the background of apocalyptic thinking in Jesus' day which shows how His statements and deeds were understood to be an act of war against Satanic powers.
- Explain how the Western worldview is more "truth-conscious" than "power-conscious." Explain the ramifications for ministry among many of the least-evangelized peoples today.
- Explain how the Western worldview can sometimes hinder missionaries from communicating the truths of the gospel.
- Examine the two extremes of Triumphalism and Defeatism as they relate to God's invitation to co-labor with Him.

VII. Worldview and the Kingdom

Peter Wagner describes his journey of growing in practical awareness about working in the power of Christ's victory over evil. Wagner lifts the issue beyond the disputes between Pentecostals/Charismatics and non-Pentecostals/ Charismatics. He cites the valuable exploration of worldview prompted by an article called "The Flaw of The Excluded Middle," by his colleague Paul Hiebert. This challenge to consider worldview opened up a fresh look at the theology of the kingdom. On page 581c, Wagner clearly summarizes contrasting views of the kingdom of God. One view sees the kingdom as entirely future. The other sees the present time as a day of conflict in which God's kingdom is overcoming the kingdom of darkness.

Without questioning the sovereignty of God, Wagner sees that our mission involves acting to oppose that which is contrary to God's will. Just as we are called to do all that may be possible to rescue people who are lost, he suggests that our mission also involves us doing all that may be possible to deal with "the poor, those at war, the oppressed, the demonized and the sick." Such a holistic view of mission does not arise from a more well-rounded view of humans and their needs. It arises from a more complete vision of what God intends to bring forth within the age as a demonstration of His coming kingdom.

Read Wagner, "On the Cutting Edge of Mission Strategy," pp. 574-582 (all)

VIII. The Flaw of the Excluded Middle

We now turn to the article by Paul Hiebert mentioned by Wagner. Hiebert describes his journey in discovering a particular worldview dimension in an Indian village. Worldview assumptions of other cultures can differ greatly from Western ideas and yet correlate quite closely with biblical assumptions. Hiebert describes a problem that he and other Western missionaries have encountered. He offers an analytical framework, from which he asserts that Westerners simply omit an entire tier of power and spiritual beings present in many worldviews. Thus, they fail to see or meet the people's felt needs and miss the drama by which the people frame their self-understanding.

A. **An Analytical Framework.** The framework that Hiebert suggests is a matrix (refer to the matrix diagram on page 410).

- **Organic-Mechanical.** From left to right is the Organic-Mechanical Continuum. "Organic" refers to explanations based on the view that things are living entities, seen or unseen. The "Mechanical" end of the spectrum offers explanations based on impersonal forces such as luck and karma or what Westerners regard as "natural" forces. Mechanical analogies are basically amoral, whereas organic analogies have an ethical dimension since one being's actions always affect other beings.
- **Seen-Unseen.** From top to bottom are different realms or categories classified by how readily they can be observed.

B. **The Excluded Middle.** Western worldviews have usually ignored the middle tier of beings and forces, dismissing them as "not real." What is "real" is precisely the issue of worldview. When missionaries have denied the middle tier and explained things only by what is empirically observable, they have in effect denied the reality or pertinence of the top level. Thus missionaries have inadvertently been a major force in "secularizing" many societies while trying to evangelize them. Use care when you read Hiebert's analysis of the concerns and questions of the middle level (on pages 411c-413a). It can be easy for Westerners, even eager Perspectives students, to disregard these concerns as being of lesser importance. However, these are often the most critical needs and concerns of many peoples of the world.

C. **Implications For Missions.** We need to form holistic theologies that have a complete triple-layered "bandwidth" of history. If we only have room for the upper level of cosmic history (God confined to heaven awaiting disembodied souls) and the lower level of natural history (the created order running autonomously according to scientific laws), then Western theology is severely impoverished compared to the wealth of clear biblical revelation. Biblical revelation is full of references to supernatural beings and supernatural powers intertwined with the affairs of man. Without a clear theology of the middle level, the relevancy and effectiveness of our gospel message for victorious living is diminished.

There are two dangerous extremes to be avoided in forming a theology which includes the middle level. And then there is a better, more biblical way to include this level.

1. **Secularism.** Christianity that denies the realities of the spiritual realm in the events of human life can be a secularizing force. With God confined to the top tier, events are explained by purely mechanical and scientific reasoning, which results in secularism.

2. **Christianized Animism.** Spiritual dynamics can be overused to explain everything. The subtle danger is a form of Christian magic where prayer formulas are used to counter every problem as if they were all caused by spiritual powers. Magic, as Hiebert described in the opening of the article, is a way for humans to control unseen forces through rituals of some sort. Could it be that some of the "spiritual warfare" prayers express a bid for control but lack a fundamental focus on the centrality and supremacy of God? Read these paragraphs carefully. Hiebert acknowledges that much of our struggle is against Satan and fallen angels. There is a place for spiritual warfare accomplished in part by prayers of God's people.

3. **God and His Acts.** The emphasis in Scripture is on God and His acts. The story of what God has done and will do is paramount. The point of prayer is not fundamentally to make things happen, but rather to bring God glory. The point of mission is not to teach how to control God by prayer, but rather to bring about a relationship of worship.

Read Hiebert, "The Flaw of the Excluded Middle," pp. 407-414 (all)

IX. The Mission of God is a War Against Evil

Gregory Boyd presents more about the background of Jesus' mission. A significant transformation of worldview took place during the "Intertestamental period." The Intertestamental period was the time between the final prophet that spoke to Israel (Malachi) and the precursor of Jesus (John the Baptist). Jewish teachers never changed their view of the magnificent supremacy of God at all, but they became convinced that a cosmic war was being fought between a Satanic counterfeit kingdom and the armies of the living God. This view had abundant grounding in the Scriptures (as Verkuyl has already pointed out to us, calling it the "motif of antagonism," p. 45), but was significantly developed during the Intertestamental period.

A. **Cosmic War.** Fallen angels were fighting against God. Had God "lost" or was He allowing a greater victory in the days to come? A middle tier of angelic powers was seen to be wreaking havoc with the complicity of people from many nations. Creation, at least during the "present evil age," was seen as a diabolical war zone. God would, of course, rise as Judge of all the earth at the fullness of time and bring complete defeat of His spiritual enemies. The day of God's climactic inbreaking power, which would inaugurate an era of great peace (Hebrew: "Shalom"), was referred to as "the Day of the Lord" and "the kingdom of God."

B. **Jesus' Mission.** Jesus is presented in the Gospels as overcoming Satan in a global struggle. The struggle with Satan was about the kingdoms of the world and their glory. Jesus' teaching and miracles were portrayed with vocabulary of the day which indicates that Jesus was boldly pressing forward a campaign to break Satan's power in order to free people. As you read Boyd's writing, take note of the careful balance that he injects. For example, Boyd notes that Jesus never endorses the apocalyptic tendency to speculate about hierarchies of angels. Being "saved" has the additional dimension of being delivered from the evil grasp of the enemy. Boyd is careful not to eliminate the meaning of spiritual regeneration from the idea of being saved. At times you'll need to refer to Boyd's footnotes (which are fascinating) to catch all the biblical references.

Read Boyd, "God at War," pp. 100-103d

X. Building For the Kingdom

A. Building the Kingdom or Building *For* the Kingdom. N. T. Wright raises an important concern: When we speak of building God's kingdom, it easily sounds as if we are trying to make it happen by human power and ingenuity. Wright answers this with two points:

1. **A Co-Laboring: God Builds His Kingdom through His Servants.** God indeed makes the kingdom happen. But He ordains that His work comes about through His servants.

2. **A Distinction: The Final Kingdom and the Present Anticipation.** The final coming together of heaven and earth is the new creation for which the resurrection of Jesus was the prototype. In the present anticipation of the kingdom we do not so much build the kingdom as we build *for* the kingdom. Our everyday deeds of service, as well as great multi-generational mission accomplishments, all contribute to what God will bring about in the age to come. Even though our work may bring nothing more than signs of the kingdom of God, our labors in the resurrected Lord are *not* in vain.

B. The Two Extremes of Activism or Dualism. Wright warns against two extremes that result from misunderstanding these points:

1. **Triumphalism** is the assumption that we can and must make all necessary changes to bring about the kingdom of God on earth. This is often related to a form of despair that God is not really at work in the world, but instead, He relies completely on people. Variations of this have been called "the Social Gospel."

2. **Defeatism** works from a dualism rather than a despair. This extreme considers making any changes in the present age to be of little worth.

Both of these extremes can throw us off from pursuing signs of the kingdom by fighting injustice in the present day. How we go about pursuing justice should be based on the life example of Jesus, but it must also be framed around the reality that we co-labor with the risen Messiah. In Him, our labors are *not* in vain.

Read Wright, "Building for the Kingdom," pp. 96-97 (all)

4 Mandate for the Nations

Studying this lesson will help you:

- Explain the strategic value of Jesus working with a few leaders to launch a movement to reach the entire world.
- Explain the strategic value of Jesus' focus on the Jewish people.
- Tell the story of how Jesus taught and modeled ministry to Gentiles.
- Explain the Great Commission, describing Christ's expectation of what is to be completed among all peoples.
- Describe the strategic value of focusing on people groups for completing the entire task of world evangelization.
- Explain how Jesus sends His followers on mission in the same way the Father sent Him on mission.
- Respond to the challenge of pluralism by presenting features of the uniqueness of Christ that mention His works, words, death and resurrection.
- Present the best biblical grounds for explaining the lostness of humankind in response to the ideas of universalism.

We rightly exalt Jesus as personal Savior. But in seeking to honor Christ for the great worth of His death and resurrection, we may have ignored much of the astounding accomplishment of His life. Jesus did far more than provide for salvation, He launched a movement that would actually bring that salvation to every part of the world. In this lesson we'll examine Jesus' life-work and His enduring mandate. He chose His followers and ordered His actions with strategic intent. He said to His Father at the end of His life, "I glorified You on the earth, having accomplished the work which You gave Me to do" (John 17:4).

Christ's mandate to us spells out our assignment to continue the work that He began during His life—until it is complete in every people. It's obvious that we will miss the point of our mission if we fail to understand how He pursued His mission. For those who have embraced His purpose, no phrase becomes more precious than "As the Father has sent Me, I also send you" (John 20:21).

mandate To live under mandate is to be entrusted with a task of lasting significance. Mandates are not commands. By direct commands we assign small errands or daily chores. A mandate, on the other hand, releases authority and responsibility to pursue endeavors of historic importance. God has entrusted to Christ, and with Him to the Church, a mandate to fulfill His purpose for all of history.

I. The Strategic Focus of Jesus

Jesus acted with strategic purpose. He not only modeled God's concern for world evangelization, He also prepared a dynamic, multiplying movement capable of evangelizing the world. H. Cornell Goerner describes the background of Jesus' work and helps us see His strategic intent.

A. Jesus' Concentration on the Jewish People. God had prepared the Jewish people to receive and understand the gospel. Even so, when Jesus came, He faced vicious hostility from the first moments of public ministry. Though many Jews rejected Him, a substantial portion of the Jewish people eventually did receive Him as Messiah. God's desire to make the Hebrew people a light to the nations was indeed fulfilled. However, it was not accomplished apart from a significant effort by Jesus to form His Jewish following into a mission movement.

He began to reveal God's mission heart to His followers by first sending the twelve to "the lost sheep of the house of Israel," adding that they were explicitly not to "go in the way of the Gentiles" (Matt 10:5-6). He then sent the seventy to "every city and place to which He Himself was going to come" (Luke 10:1). Because the number of nations, or peoples, in the mindset of Israel at that time was seventy, it's likely that Jesus was foreshadowing the eventual commission to evangelize every city and place and people throughout the earth.

Read Goerner, "Jesus and the Gentiles," pp. 115d-116a

B. Jesus' Concern for Gentiles. The Gospels report that Jesus was profoundly concerned for non-Jewish people. On dozens of occasions He modeled God's heart for all peoples by deliberate outreach to Gentiles, whom most Jewish people despised. Because His teaching throughout His ministry emphasized the global scale of God's heart, the Great Commission was not a last-minute add-on to His teaching. When we look at the entire record, everything Jesus did and said came to a crescendo in the Great Commission. Goerner and Don Richardson recount the sometimes overlooked stories about Jesus demonstrating concern for the nations.

Read Goerner, "Jesus and the Gentiles," pp. 116b-117, and Richardson, "A Man for All Peoples," pp. 118-121 (all)

C. Jesus' Focus on a Few. Robert Coleman, in his classic work, *The Master Plan of Evangelism*, points out that Jesus selected a few people and developed them as leaders in a movement that would impact the entire earth. Jesus' strategy focused on:

1. **Reproducing Character.** Jesus knew that people would have to be "imbued with His life" in order to reflect and reproduce His character. Thus, He focused on pouring His life into some who would continue to do the same with others.

2. **Reproducing Structure.** Jesus knew that the only way to reach the world was to launch a movement that would reproduce itself. A multiplying church would continue to expand in "an ever enlarging circumference" until the multitudes of the earth had heard the gospel.

   Coleman observes that for the disciples, the purpose of world evangelization was "progressively clarified in their thinking as they followed Him, and finally spelled out in no uncertain terms" in the Great Commission.

Read Coleman, "The Master's Plan," pp. 122-125 (all)

II. The Great Commission

Each of the Gospels, as well as the Book of Acts, includes a direct expression of Christ commissioning His people to fulfill His mission in the world. The expressions in Matthew, Mark, Luke and Acts together show a clear mandate to complete world evangelization. The commissioning in the Gospel of John is different. It focuses on the way that Jesus now sends us in the same way that He was sent by the Father.

- **Mark 16:15-16** is a direct imperative to communicate the gospel to every person in every place. The outcome described is either belief and salvation or disbelief and eternal loss.
- **Luke 24:46-49** includes Jesus' summary of what Scripture promises will take place among all nations. He indicates that His followers are to be witnesses who will proclaim a pardon for sin to all the nations.
- **Acts 1:8** is more of a promise than a command, that the disciples would become His witnesses. But it nevertheless carries mandate force to live out the full intent of Christ that they would be His witnesses in every part of the world (more on acting as witnesses in Lesson 5).
- **Matthew 28:18-20,** commonly known as "the Great Commission," contains the clearest expression of Christ's mandate to complete world evangelization.
- **John 20:21-23** does not contain a direct command concerning the nations. In the context of these words, however, Jesus imparts the Spirit of God and declares that the disciples are sent in the same way and for the same purpose for which He was sent.

Steven Hawthorne's description of Matthew 28 invites readers to place themselves alongside the eleven as they first heard the mandate. The word "all" is used four times in the text.

A. **All Authority.** The commission is based on a transaction of authority from the Father to the Son. What was this authority? When was it given to Jesus? How does this authority enable believers to carry out the mandate? Use what you have already learned about the kingdom of God to reflect on what Jesus meant by this authority transfer. Jesus was referring to the Father awarding Him spiritual authority to subdue every evil power beneath His feet as defeated enemies in order to bring people from every tribe and tongue under His headship as His devoted servants. This kind of authority is required for the mandate which follows.

The main verb in the commission is "to disciple." This word emphasizes enlisting new followers instead of perfecting fully trained, fully taught, and fully tested super-followers living exactly like Jesus. This means that Christ expects more than an understanding of His message. He expects a personal obedience to Him as Lord. The reference to His commands is certainly not legalism. He is pointing to Himself as the one to be obeyed. Calling for obedience to His commands is in stark contrast to the typical teaching of rabbis of His day. Rabbis would never say that their personal commands were to be obeyed. Instead, they would call for obedience to their interpretation of the Torah or commands of Scripture. Jesus is pointing to His unique place as Lord and He mandates that people be trained to live under His Lordship. He is calling for His kingship to become effective in the lives of people within every people.

Read Revelation 5:1-14, Daniel 7:9-14 and Psalm 110 (the most oft-quoted Old Testament passage in the New Testament). How do these passages help you understand Matthew 28:18 better? What difference does it make for everyday obedience to the Great Commission to know that there is such an authority behind it all?

Read Hawthorne, "Mandate on the Mountain," pp. 126-127

B. All the Peoples. The mandate to "disciple the peoples" does not refer to a particular ministry activity. Rather, discipling "all the peoples" must be understood as a once-for-all global goal. Nurturing and training individuals and small groups in basic discipleship skills who will then pass them on to others is a wonderful and necessary activity. However, the original language used in Matthew 28 indicates that there will be a once-in-history achievement of establishing Christward movements within every people group. With this clarity, we can speak of finishing the task of world evangelization.

Christ's commission uses the Greek phrase *panta ta ethne,* which in most English translations is translated vaguely as "all nations." The Greek phrase is more precisely understood in English as "all the peoples." Based on the way the full phrase *panta ta ethne* is used in the New Testament, we can rule out two possible interpretations and affirm a third:

1. **Countries?** Are the *ethne* nation-states or countries? This is probably the most common misimpression of our day. Jesus did not have politically defined countries in mind. The Greek words of Matthew 28 would not have been understood as referring to nation-states by those who heard the mandate in the first century.
2. **Gentiles in General?** Is Jesus referring to Gentiles in general? Another misimpression is that Jesus is simply sending the disciples beyond the bounds of Israel to non-Jewish persons. The way that the phrase *panta ta ethne* is used in other biblical passages will not sustain this view. The word *ethnos* in singular form is never used of Gentiles in general. It always refers to a people group. The plural use of the word can sometimes mean Gentiles, but the full phrase *panta ta ethne* is always used to describe ethnicities defined by race, language or culture.

3. **People Groups.** The interpretation of *panta ta ethne*, with the best support from New Testament usage, is that Jesus has in view the people groups of the world as they tend to understand and define themselves: by language, lineage or socio-cultural factors.

Read Hawthorne, "Mandate on the Mountain," pp. 128-129c

C. **All That I Commanded.** Two activities, baptizing and teaching, define what it means to "disciple all the peoples." With John the Baptist's ministry as a backdrop to Jesus' command, baptism was to mark a loyalty change, a preparation for the Messiah's coming. Baptism forms a community of shared allegiance to God as He has fully revealed Himself—as the Father who sent His Son and gives His Spirit. In this context, "teaching" goes beyond merely educating people to know about Jesus' commands. It refers to the work of training people to live in daily, vital obedience to Jesus. These two facets—proclaimed allegiance to the God of the Bible, and growing obedience to Christ as Lord—are the core of what it means to establish kingdom communities that we have come to call churches.

D. **All the Days.** This phrase clearly reveals that Jesus was issuing a mandate for the entire age and for every believer. It is not a command that any single person can accomplish. It is a mandate that can only be fulfilled collectively. Christ's reference to the culmination of the age gives extra force to the idea that He intends evangelization to be understood as a task to be accomplished in this age, not merely as an optional activity or as an ongoing ethical value.

Read Hawthorne, "Mandate on the Mountain," pp. 129c-131

III. Focus on Finishing the Task

A. **The Priority of Peoples.** The Great Commission defines the task in terms of people groups. In our day, many have recognized that focusing on people groups is important. But we need to be sure that we focus on reaching people groups for the best reason.

It may seem important to place priority on people groups because they are filled with lost people who have not yet heard the gospel. This consideration, while meaningful, is not nearly as significant as approaching people groups from the strategic viewpoint of fulfilling the task of evangelizing all of the world's people groups.

Completing the total task will require that in every single people group, at some point in history, there be a movement of baptized and obedient disciples capable of evangelizing their entire people. Until there are such movements in every people, we have not completed the mandate Christ has given us. This means that it doesn't matter exactly how many individuals populate these people groups. If a people group numbers ten thousand or ten million, the strategic priority is virtually the same with respect to finishing the entire global mandate.

The strategic priority of "unreached" peoples is not that they are the neediest peoples. Although they are often needy in every way, the strategic priority of unreached peoples is that they lack a discipling movement of any kind. They are not the *neediest* peoples, they are the *remaining* peoples in the task Christ has given us.

B. The Great Commission as Historic Accomplishment with the Great Commandment as Constant Imperative. These two imperatives must not be held as equivalent or as being in competition.

- **Both For God.** The two imperatives of loving neighbors and discipling nations have the same focal point: Both are for God. Matthew 28 brings forth disciples who name and obey God. The main point of Matthew 22 is that God would be loved with heart, soul, mind and strength.
- **One Crucial Difference.** But these two important imperatives are *different in one crucial way:* Matthew 28 calls for a historic accomplishment of a task, fulfilled over many generations. Matthew 22 calls for people to love God and people at all times and in all ways.

Neither can happen without the other. The world cannot be evangelized without Christians loving their neighbors. But there will be no love of God and neighbor in many communities without the completion of the task to bring about movements of people committed to obey Christ's commands.

Read Hawthorne, "The Great Commission and the Great Commandment," sidebar, pp. 128-129

Conclusion of Key Readings for this lesson. 

IV. On Mission with Jesus

It may be more important to understand the *way* that Jesus sent His followers than to grasp *what* He sent them to do.

A. As the Father Sent Me. Consider one of the most powerful statements in all of Scripture: "As the Father has sent Me, I also send you" (John 20:21).

1. **The Ways of God.** We can understand this verse to read: "As the Father sent me, so also *in the same way* I am sending you." How did the Father send the Son? The Father loved and listened to the Son. The Son loved and watched for what the Father initiated. Jesus, in dynamic nearness to the Father, continued what God had been doing throughout history. Jesus sends us in this same way.
2. **The Purpose of God.** The verse also means: "As the Father sent me, so also you are sent to accomplish *the same historic purpose* for which I was sent." This is more than mind-boggling. Jesus entrusted ordinary people with the same enormous matters which the Father entrusted to Him. Some have suggested that this articulation of the mandate should be understood as a calling for us to follow the *example* of Jesus' deeds. But in fact, a clear reading of the text and other texts like it in John will show that Jesus is emphasizing the *commingling* of His life with our life in power rather than simply calling for us to imitate His example.

B. On Mission With God. Henry Blackaby and Avery Willis describe how God enlists people to be on mission with Him. Behind their statements are radical ideas! What Blackaby and Willis present is contrary to some high-pressure styles of mobilizing mission involvement. Such guilt-inducing tactics often backfire, causing many people to resent what seems to them to be an unbearable burden of saving billions of lost people. Notice how they give more detail to what Jesus meant by "As the Father sent Me" in John 20:21. Consider each of the seven points concerning God's ways. One of the last sentences of the article sums up much of God's ways of involving us in His will: "He calls every one of His followers to join Him in that relationship of *love, power and purpose.*"

1. **Love.** God's way of sending is relational, rather than utilitarian. When God calls us to be on mission with Him, He always invites us to experience a more intimate love relationship with Him. He is much more focused on that love relationship than on getting certain jobs done. The tasks are indeed accomplished in God's ways, but in the power of a growing experience of close relationship.
2. **Power.** God's way of sending is empowering, rather than acting in a coercive way. He extends invitations rather than obligating demands. He reveals first what He is doing rather than pointing out what is not being done. He speaks to us about His will as we listen. He enables us to respond in trust. He patiently works and waits for us to make adjustments to Him, so that we can do His will for our own good and His greater glory.
3. **Purpose.** God's way of sending is purposeful, rather than being oriented around us. As much as He loves us, He refuses to allow our lives to be oriented around ourselves. God is focused on a historic fulfillment of His global mission. He is determined to honor us with the dignity of being on mission with Him, fulfilling part of His historic purpose.

Read Blackaby and Willis, "On Mission With God," pp. 74-77 (all)

V. The Uniqueness of Christ: Dealing With Pluralism

Mission sounds to many as if it were a campaign of self-authorized religious supremacists. This is understandable if one's operative belief system is framed with the assumptions of pluralism. Pluralism is a philosophical assumption that it is not possible to recognize any one system of thought as absolute truth. Forms of pluralism are prevalent in many parts of the world. Many Christians find aspects of pluralism as attractive as they are confusing.

Advocates of pluralism argue against the missionary enterprise in two ways. First there are some who declare that Christian missions are acts of intolerant bigotry. Secondly, there are those who dismiss the message of Christ because, in their view, it is virtually identical to other religions.

Ajith Fernando helps us respond to the pluralism we find in different parts of the world, as well as the skepticism that may have already affected our own vision. He calls us to look to the uniqueness of Jesus, and therefore embrace a shameless, even joyous conviction that because Jesus Christ is unique, He is supreme. Fernando expands Jesus' own statement that He is the Way, the Truth and the Life.

A. Christ the Truth. Arguments for absolute truth must be grounded on the huge fact of the incarnation. Absolute truth can be known because the Absolute has become concrete in history in the person of Jesus. Jesus' words and works open people to an encounter which is not just a mental grasp of truths, but a personal encounter with the person who is Truth. What separates the gospel from all other religions is the joy of relationship with the person of Jesus and the completeness of His message.

B. Christ the Way. By His statement in John 14:6, Jesus meant that He would become the Way through His death.

1. **The Accomplishment of the Cross.** It is essential to understand what Jesus accomplished on the cross. We have already seen in the previous lesson how God used Christ's death to overcome evil. Fernando lists six more biblical ways of recognizing the uniqueness of Jesus' death. It's breathtaking to consider the global importance of each one.
2. **The Offense of the Cross.** People invariably attempt self-salvation. The cross shouts that this is impossible. This offense of the cross may explain some of the hostility of pluralists to the missionary movement.

Read Fernando, "The Supremacy of Christ," pp. 183-189d

I am the good shepherd;
the good shepherd lays down His life for the sheep...
and I lay down My life for the sheep.
And I have other sheep, which are not of this fold;
I must bring them also, and they shall hear My voice;
and they shall become one flock with one shepherd.

— John 10:11,15b–16

Read John 10:11-16. Reflect on the purpose of Jesus' words about "other sheep." How will they hear His voice? What is the significance of these sheep being formed into "one flock" instead of multiple flocks? Why is it significant that there is a single shepherd figure?

C. Christ the Life. Jesus summons a people from every people. John 10:10 is commonly quoted to affirm Christ's intention to bring fullness of life. Fernando directs our attention further in this same passage (through verse 16), where Jesus is described as the singular life-giving Shepherd. Jesus is drawing together people from every people by His life-giving power, so that there will be "one flock," in Fernando's words, a "new humanity with one Shepherd." This "Good Shepherd" passage is not about personal comfort through trying times—it is a declaration of Christ's global mission. Because the Shepherd figure lays down His life to defeat the marauding thief and to gather sheep from all over the world, there can be only one Shepherd. The Shepherd figure is necessarily unique. The resurrection makes it starkly clear that Jesus Christ is unique, and therefore, utterly supreme.

Read Fernando, "The Supremacy of Christ," pp. 189d-191

VI. To Seek and to Save the Lost: Dealing With Universalism

We've considered the primary focus of world evangelization to be God gaining worshipers for His greater glory. We've suggested that glorifying God is a more important focus of Scripture than saving people from eternal loss. But people do matter! Their eternal destiny must be our concern also. Jesus Himself said that He came "to seek and to save that which was lost" (Luke 19:10). What does it mean to be lost? Who are the lost? How shall we understand the plight of the people who have never heard of Jesus or who have rejected Him? How can we carry this burden in the way God wants?

Universalism is a commonly held idea that God's salvation in Christ will be universally accepted or applied to all persons. Some models deriving from universalism—the so-called "wider hope" theories—assume that people are saved in a general way and damned only by rejecting the gospel. If this is true, then it might be better to keep the world ignorant of salvation in Jesus. But the Bible teaches clearly that people are not lost because they reject the truth, but rather because of sin that has warped them in their own evil.

Robertson McQuilkin affirms the biblical truth that there are two kinds of people: the saved and the lost. It may appear that universalism presents a more compassionate God. But only the biblical God is both loving *and* good. God does not mock His own goodness by declaring people to be good who have chosen evil. Instead, God honors an individual's choice of good or evil, always giving them enough spiritual light that they can choose God's way. God has appointed that people be saved in the light of Christ's name. Jesus Christ is the *only* agency of salvation.

What about those who have never heard? Based on the story of Cornelius in Acts, McQuilkin says that God brings greater light to any who respond positively to the light He has already given them. It is not possible to prove that people have never been saved by following all the light that they had. But neither is it possible to prove that anyone has been saved apart from Christ.

McQuilkin points out how universalism makes a mockery of the cross. If all are saved without hearing or responding to Christ, why did He die at all? It is this compelling thought that underlies his closing illustration of a bridge.

Read McQuilkin, "Lost," pp. 170-175 (all)

Conclusion of Certificate Readings for this lesson. 

After studying this section you should be able to:

- Explain what is meant by the Greek phrase *panta ta ethne* and its significance for world evangelization.
- Explain why the wounds of the cross encourage us to confront the powers of this world without using conventional means of power.
- Explain what is meant by pluralism, inclusivism and exclusivism.
- Describe the ramifications of the confession "Jesus Christ is Lord" for Christians who affirm this statement in keeping with Van Engen's "evangelist" position.

VII. Discipling All Peoples

We've seen that the Greek word translated as "make disciples" requires a direct object in order to make sense. In Matthew 28:14, the direct object of the sentence is the phrase translated "all nations." John Piper examines the Greek meaning behind these words. He does this with such a methodical simplicity that you don't have to be a Greek scholar to grasp the incredible significance of the phrase *panta ta ethne*.

A. Comparing Singular With Plural Usages. The Greek word *ethnos* always means a people group defined by language or lineage when used in the singular. The plural usage rarely refers to Gentiles in general. The majority of the usages by far refer to people groups.

B. Old Testament Cross Reference. Of the five repetitions of the Abrahamic covenant, two of them (Gen 12:3; 28:14) use the Hebrew phrase *kol mishpahot*. This phrase refers to even smaller groupings than the Greek word *ethnos*, such as clans or small tribes. The other three (Gen 18:18; 22:18; 26:4) are translated in the Greek translation of the Old Testament with the phrase *panta ta ethne*. These are the passages that Peter refers to in Acts 3:25.

Piper concludes that the Great Commission defines the task as discipling people groups defined by language, lineage or tribal boundaries. The weight of evidence excludes the ideas that Jesus was mandating an outreach to non-Jewish people in general, or an outreach to politically-defined countries. This is an important distinction since the mandate is given to us as a task to be completed. To complete our mandate, we must understand what we are aiming to accomplish.

Read Piper, "Discipling All the Peoples," pp. 132-136 (all)

VIII. With Christ or Imitating Christ? The Limits of Our Mandate

Deriving our mandate from Christ's example can be tricky. It is easy to find one's own agenda somehow exemplified in some word or deed of Jesus. Lesslie Newbigin, a significant mission leader of a previous generation who anticipated and addressed many of the issues we face today, offered his reflections on the mandate we find in John 20:21.

John 20:21 has sometimes been used to help support a wider mandate to bring about a perfect world. Newbigin points out the triumphalist danger of aiming to produce utopia, but does not allow us to be passive or inactive in the struggles of the world. He uses the word "quietism" which refers to a withdrawal from the world in order to contemplate God.

Newbigin says that as we carry out the mission Jesus imparted, we will necessarily contend with and confront the powers of the world's systems. This does not mean that we are mandated to bring about the kingdom of God in perfect measure, but instead to bring about signs of the kingdom—"the reality of God's reign."

What do you think of his assertion that the ultimate sign of the kingdom of God is the cross? Newbigin says that Jesus' gesture of showing his pierced hands and side as He spoke the words of John 20:21 suggests that the sign of the cross is something to be displayed in the lives of His followers as well. How does this limit or increase our mandate?

Read Newbigin, "The Kingdom of God in the Life of the World," pp. 98-99 (all)

IX. A Paradigm to Encounter Pluralism

Charles Van Engen describes the pluralistic worldview of our day. To speak clearly and biblically about other religions, we need to do something beyond proclaiming our opinion that Jesus is the one and only way. New categories may help us proclaim the astounding claims of Scripture in a relevant way. Without clarity on these issues, we can easily be made to feel that we are religious bigots, foisting our views on people in ways which seem to many to be religiously criminal.

The standard categories force many, including some in the Church, to conclude that if someone believes that Jesus is unique (i.e., the only way to salvation) then they are automatically considered to be offensively intolerant and should be asked to stop pushing their religion on others. In reality, if someone affirms Christ's uniqueness, this does not mean that such a person is a mean-spirited exclusivist. Van Engen's article is helpful for marking out an approach that is faithful to Christ and relevant to culture.

A. **Three Standard Positions.** There are three standard positions on the issue of the uniqueness of Christ and the adequacy of other religions: *Pluralist, Inclusivist* and *Exclusivist*. Evangelizing Christians are usually placed in the exclusivist category. Christians often drift toward a vague, unstated inclusivist position.

B. **An Important Distinction: Faith Does Not Equal Culture.** If faith were just another aspect of one's culture then faith might not be regarded as truth-based, but as an expression of one's culture. However, Christian faith is based on the fact of the historic Jesus. The truth that is the basis of faith is not relative to different cultural environments.

C. **A Fourth Position: Evangelist.** To the three common positions, Van Engen adds another—the Evangelist. It is based on the historic Jesus as reported in the Bible and is summed up in the core confession of the Church: Jesus Christ is Lord. The Evangelist position is:

1. **Faith-Particularist.** This is not a question of whether you are inside or outside any particular church boundaries. The particularist (having to do with that which is unique and distinctive) affirmation is the question of discipleship, "of one's proximity to, or distance from, Jesus the Lord."

2. **Culturally Pluralist.** If faith does not equal culture, then Christians can be eager pluralists regarding culture. This means that they can affirm the value and beauty of any culture. "Everything that does not contradict the biblical revelation concerning the historical Jesus Christ our Lord is open for consideration."

3. **Ecclesiologically Inclusivist**. "Ecclesiological" has to do with churches. The Evangelist position is so focused on Jesus as the Head of the Church that church membership is not seen as the dividing line between the saved and the unsaved. That distinction is left to Jesus Himself. The mission task is to gather people together under His Lordship. His Lordship over all requires a vision of His headship over the Church. This means that there is a diversity of churches which thrive under Christ's headship. The evangelist eagerly welcomes people into the Church because that is where Christ's Lordship is to be enjoyed.

Read Van Engen, "The Uniqueness of Christ," pp. 176-182 (all)

5 Unleashing the Gospel

Studying this lesson will help you:

- Explain how God helped the early Church to be faithful to Christ's mandate to be witnesses.
- Describe what Jesus meant when He said, "You will be my witnesses."
- Describe the crucial importance of the Acts 15 council for understanding how to present the gospel to the nations without presenting cultural obstacles to following Christ.
- Explain why the conversion barrier is greater than the communication barrier in pioneer mission work.
- Explain why Paul's two cross-cultural principles of "become like" and "remain like" are crucial to seeing breakthroughs of the gospel.
- Describe the roles of the Holy Spirit, missionaries and the Word of God in terms of conviction of sin and progressive change toward Christ-like maturity in new church movements.
- Describe the difference and relationship of the apostolic and congregational structures of the Church.
- Learn how a person can develop an "apostolic passion" for the worship of Jesus among the nations.
- Explain the strategic value of suffering and martyrdom in terms of the triumph of truth, the defeat of evil, and the glory of God.

We have seen that whenever God's people have been unfaithful, God has remained persistent in His purpose. Through many generations God is the faithful One, unfolding His plan to bring light to the nations with steady continuity. All of history comes to a breakthrough moment in Jesus.

We have seen how Christ trained His followers. His death broke the power of sin in a decisive way. His resurrection meant the power of His life could be extended to all nations. He commissioned them with power and clear purpose. As Jesus departed, the entire purpose of God seemed to be in the hands of a few ordinary men and women with a spotty track record of faithfulness. What would happen? Would they fulfill God's purpose? Would God's purpose come to a standstill?

Some have judged that these early leaders failed for long years, delaying the advance of the gospel. The real matter is not whether the disciples stopped the progress of missionaries going out to the nations. The wonderful thing to behold is that the nations were not hindered from following Christ. The Holy Spirit was at work, opening "a door of faith" for the peoples and helping the Apostles to hold it open. The crucial moment of unleashing the gospel to advance throughout the nations was the Jerusalem council described in Acts 15.

In this lesson we will see how God launched the World Christian movement. We will discover that the Church is a double structure that endures to this day. We will discover how specific prayer for the needs of entire cities prepared the way for the rapid advance of the gospel throughout entire regions. We will watch how ordinary people chose a strategy of suffering which they learned from Jesus. We will examine the biblical grounds of hope for an enormous ingathering at the end of the age.

witness A witness is what you *are* far more than it is something that you *do.* God arranges for His servants to display what they declare. By public testimony in the face of hostility, ordinary people accomplish far more than merely affirming the truth of Christ. Witnesses establish the value of following Christ. Their persuasive power is not only because their words match their life—their words and their life match those of Christ Himself. It is as if Christ Himself stands to testify before the world.

I. A Local Following Became a Global Movement

Were the disciples slow to extend the gospel from Jerusalem? Steven Hawthorne presents the idea that they were incredibly faithful and swift to obey, as God helped them to be obedient to do what He had given them at that time.

A. **Persistence in Big-Picture Vision.** Jesus gave them orders by the Holy Spirit. The encounter on the Emmaus road prefigured how He continues to speak to His Church even though He may go unseen. At that time He recounted the entire biblical story of His glory and the Kingdom as a backdrop for the specific instructions they were to carry out. The initial assignment was to do a very strategic, and yet dangerous thing: stay in Jerusalem. It's a common misconception to imagine that instead of reaching out to the nations, the disciples stayed home. But Jerusalem was not their home! In fact, by staying, they subjected themselves to great danger.

B. **Boldness in Public Witness.** Staying in Jerusalem was the surest and most public way to encounter the pressure of political and religious powers. Standing this test by their clear testimony is exactly what Jesus meant by the word "witness." The idea of "witnessing" in our day usually means attempting to communicate the gospel to others. But the use of this term was much different in biblical days. To "witness" was to offer prolonged public testimony. The court setting was not a way to get a public venue to preach "sermons." The trials were not really about conveying gospel information. Instead, the ordeal of public trials established the value of following Christ and thus confirmed the validity of the Christ-following movement to the common people.

Read Hawthorne, "Acts of Obedience," pp. 137-139c

C. **Faithfulness to Accelerate Gospel Breakthrough.** One of the most crucial moments in the Book of Acts is certainly the Jerusalem council. The gospel could have very well evolved as a small splinter sect of Judaism. Instead, it became a movement of faith that centered on Jesus and extended the heritage of the Hebrew people. Yet it also encompassed the cultural expression and diversity of every race and language of the world. How God achieved this required of the disciples a perceptive wisdom that we still need today. The issue amounted to this: Did God require non-Jewish people to become Jewish in cultural ways in order to follow Christ?

Read Hawthorne, "Acts of Obedience," pp. 139c-141

D. **The Priority of Gospel Breakthrough.** The Book of Acts highlights both the importance of declaring the Word of God and the greater priority of facilitating a movement of obedience to Christ. The issue of Acts 15 is alive today. Does God intend to divorce people from their home culture? If instead, God desires to draw many throughout an entire community to follow Jesus together, how does the account of the Book of Acts help us facilitate these movements today?

II. The Critical Turning Point

M. R. Thomas, no stranger to the issues of gospel and culture because of his work in his native India, describes the enormous significance of the Jerusalem council of Acts 15. He aptly calls it the "greatest crisis" of the Church. He unfolds the story of how the disciples had to "sort out the universal glory of Jesus from the cultural patterns of Judaism before they could obey the Great Commission and take the gospel to all the nations." Thomas is not the only one to surmise that if the debate had gone otherwise, the movement of Christ-followers would have ended up as one of the hundreds of "splinter sects of Judaism which are now defunct." Thomas explains how the decisions of this Acts 15 council unleashed the gospel to spread "unhindered" (Acts 28:31).

Read Thomas, "The Turning Point: Setting the Gospel Free," pp. 143-145 (all)

From there they sailed to Antioch,
from which they had been commended to the grace of God
for the work that they had accomplished.
When they had arrived and gathered the church together,
they began to report all things that God had done with them
and how He had opened a door of faith to the Gentiles.
— Acts 14:26–27

Acts 14:26-27 describes the return of Barnabas and Paul to Antioch. Think about the expression used for their sending. What did it mean that they had been "commended to the grace of God"? Compare and contrast these two expressions: "work they had accomplished" and "all the things God had done with them." Who did the work? Scan over Acts 13 and 14 to see what "the work" was all about. What did it mean that God had opened "a door of faith"? Had it been closed before then?

III. Both Parts of the Task: Communicating the Message and Facilitating Movements

A. The Wall and the Canyon. Steven Hawthorne distinguishes two parts of the missionary task. The first part is communicating the gospel. The second is facilitating a following of Christ that flourishes in the local society and culture. Overcoming the barrier of understanding to communicate the gospel (the "Wall") is a great challenge for cross-cultural missionaries. But the greater challenges (the "Canyon") are the difficulties faced by would-be followers of Christ to find ways to openly serve and obey Christ while remaining an integral part of their people.

Read Hawthorne, "The Wall and the Canyon," sidebar, pp. 140-141

B. Become Like, Remain Like. Harley Talman tells how he came to understand his role as a missionary much better when he read 1 Corinthians while attempting to bring the gospel to Muslim people. Paul's words to "become like" those he desired to evangelize took on new importance. But Talman went on to recognize the critical importance of helping new followers avoid taking on foreign cultural practices as if they were the substance of the gospel. He realized that it was important to urge believers to "remain like" their people, just as Paul had urged in 1 Corinthians 7.

David Anthony tells a very similar story, visiting some of the same passages. He adds his insight concerning a basic principle which Paul called a "rule" (in some translations of both 1 Corinthians 7:17 and Galatians 6:16), that insured the new churches from becoming cultural mongrels who focus on particular religious traditions. Instead, by following the simple "rule" of encouraging obedience of faith to Christ, rather than meritorious compliance with customs, they brought about "a new creation" in the midst of the existing people.

Read Talman, "Become Like, Remain Like," and Anthony, "A New Creation," sidebar, pp. 146-148 (all)

IV. Bringing Forth Maturity: Helping Others Follow the Holy Spirit

The Great Commission focuses on bringing about movements that obey everything that Jesus commands. How can missionaries encourage radical obedience to Christ without imposing their own cultural ideals as the paragon of Christian maturity? How can missionaries be patient when new believers appear to be in no hurry to repent of sins that seem so abhorrent from a Western viewpoint? How do missionaries collaborate with the Holy Spirit to bring about strong movements of dedicated, life-transforming obedience to Christ?

A. The Challenge: The Initial Point of Repentance. Wayne Dye describes a missionary named Pete who made the issues of polygamy, smoking and betel nut chewing to be central in the initial steps of repentance and maturity. These were behaviors that bothered Pete most. However, they were not items about which the Holy Spirit brought conviction or which the people of that culture regarded as matters of primary importance.

B. The Standard: A Universal Definition of Sin. Scripture does offer universal moral principles. How these are followed may be different in various cultural settings. This does not at all mean that missionaries should embrace situational ethics. There is right and there is wrong. While the essence of the commands and principles are clear, the cultural "edges" are defined differently in different societies. How can missionaries help people follow Christ according to Scripture and in keeping with their culture?

C. The Progressive Change: The Role of the Holy Spirit. The key truth in Dye's article is that God is continually guiding each person into greater spiritual maturity, love and obedience. There are, in fact, many occasions for repentance in the life of any believer. If this is true of an individual believer, it is just as true regarding the journey of a people following Christ together. The growth in righteousness of a church, and therefore of an entire society, is progressive. The role of the missionary starts becoming clearer. Instead of imposing a set of standards, the missionary can help bring about an allegiance to Christ by training leaders to follow the Holy Spirit in accordance with Scripture.

D. An Approach: Allowing the Holy Spirit to Convict and Transform. A six-point list on page 495 outlines a way for missionaries to encourage a Christ-focused obedience.

Read Dye, "Discovering the Holy Spirit's Work in a Community," pp. 493-496 (all)

V. Apostolic Passion

Floyd McClung defines the words "passion" and "apostolic" in a compelling way. Take note of McClung's observations of God as the source of passion. Watch how he says passion can be chosen and cultivated—not as a feeling but as a fulfillment of life. McClung says that no one should assume that God does not want them to be directly involved in apostolic church planting. Instead of negotiating with God for a "safe" assignment, why not delight God by seeking to be directly involved in planting churches where Christ is not yet worshiped? Let God be the one who limits, who says, "Stay." Read the last three paragraphs to yourself out loud (Why not? Just do it!).

Read McClung, "Apostolic Passion," pp. 204-206 (all)

Is apostolic passion, as McClung describes it, an extraordinary sort of Christianity? Or is it for everyone? Do you agree that the beginnings of apostolic passion can be found in any worshiping Christian? How do you aspire to grow in apostolic prayer? In apostolic choices?

Conclusion of Key Readings for this lesson. 

VI. The Apostolic Band

The churches that the apostles and Paul planted were, for the most part, light and lean "house churches" without a great deal of institutional trappings. Such house churches multiplied quickly throughout whole cities. But when God desired there to be a cross-cultural extension of the gospel, beyond the range of existing churches, there came about another Church structure, what some have called "the apostolic band."

A. **The Double Structure of the Church.** Arthur Glasser describes the important emergence of the apostolic band. Such teams set their own membership, charted out their goals, were economically self-sufficient and were not expected to answer to a local church. They were a distinctive structure of the Church in parallel with the congregational parish structure. Glasser argues that the congregational parish structure and the mobile missionary band structure should both be considered the "Church" since both express the life of God's people.

B. **The Strategy of Paul's Band.** It is valuable to recognize that Jewish missionaries had preceded the Church throughout much of the world with the objective of strengthening scattered Jews in the Jewish faith and proselytizing willing Gentiles (that is to make a proselyte, someone who was circumcised and subscribed to all Jewish cultural practices). Paul's strategy was to reach to those, like Cornelius, who wanted to hear about the Hebrew God, but who were unwilling to become proselytes. Paul had great news for Gentiles: They could follow Christ without becoming Jewish! Thus house churches were formed after the pattern of synagogues as an initial structure of what later became the congregational parish church.

Read Glasser, "The Apostle Paul and the Missionary Task," pp. 149-151d

C. **Jewish Forms of Synagogue and Mission Band.** Ralph Winter explores the same double structure of the early Church, noting as Glasser does, that the structures of both congregation and mission were largely borrowed from Jewish traditions of synagogue and missionary band.

Read Winter, "The Two Structures of God's Redemptive Mission," pp. 244-246a

D. **Modality and Sodality.** We're going to get a head start on the upcoming history section by continuing to read Winter's "Two Structures" article. Winter follows how the two structures were expressed after New Testament times within the social organization and culture of the Roman Empire. Local congregational structures recognized bishops with territorial jurisdiction, after the pattern of the Roman magisterial territories. The Roman term used for these territories was "diocese." The mission structures that emerged—the monastic movements—borrowed patterns from Roman military practice. Protestants generally have stereotyped impressions of monasteries as places where ascetic monks fled the world. In reality, the monastic movements were largely responsible for bringing the blessing of the gospel to the world.

Winter applies some simple terms from the discipline of sociology to the double structure of congregation and mission. The two terms are *modality* and *sodality*. We'll use these terms in upcoming lessons.

- **Modality** refers to nurture-oriented congregational church structures.
- **Sodality** refers to task-oriented mission structures.

Read Winter, "The Two Structures of God's Redemptive Mission," pp. 246b-248b

VII. Apostolic Suffering

Paul suffered wherever he planted churches. Paul intentionally took the beating at Philippi, keeping his identity as a Roman citizen undisclosed. Why? It must have been purposeful. He would later tell the same church that they were "graced" by God, not only to believe, "but also to suffer, experiencing the same conflict *which you saw in me*, and now hear to be in me" (Phil 1:29-30). Paul must have known that the church he was planting in Philippi would need to stand boldly through a blast of hostility. His readiness to stand openly for the gospel, without using the privilege of citizenship to dodge the backlash, prepared the church to enjoy "fellowship in the gospel" from that "first day" until "the day of Christ" (Phil 1:5-6). That fellowship in the gospel would always mean a fellowship in the sufferings of Christ Himself (Phil 3:10).

A. **A Strategy of Suffering.** Glasser points out what he calls a cardinal principle: Wherever the gospel is preached and people are gathered into congregations, there will always be people suffering for Christ in a way that fulfills what is lacking in Christ's afflictions. These afflictions do not bring atonement, as only Christ's death has done. These sufferings are, however, a factor in overcoming the spiritual powers that blind people to the gospel.

Read Glasser, "The Apostle Paul and the Missionary Task," pp. 152c-153

VIII. God's Strategy in Apostolic Suffering

More people suffer persecution for Christ today than at any other time in history. Suffering is particularly intense in places where the gospel is advancing among unreached peoples. Josef Tson defines suffering as something not self-inflicted, but nonetheless voluntary. Martyrdom is God's gift to some "to die for the sake of Christ and His gospel." What is God's purpose in martyrdom? Suffering and sacrifice are God's methods of overcoming rebellion and evil. Most notably, Christ has not changed His strategy of answering hell's hatred with suffering love. "His method is still the method of the cross."

In Lesson 1, we described God's purpose in this way: *For His glory in global worship, and for the blessing of all nations, God purposes to overcome evil by redeeming a people who will love and obey Him within every people.* Tson says that suffering is part of God's way to defeat Satan and destabilize his kingdom. Tson also says that suffering enables the truth to come to redemptive clarity so that God is recognized and glorified.

Suffering and martyrdom are in line with God's purpose at the end of the age. Then we should "think it not strange," as Peter puts it, that many of our brothers and sisters in Christ are encountering phenomenal suffering. The best formulated strategies for advancing the gospel will take this factor into account. Tson sees three things achieved by this suffering. As you read, it will help you a great deal to look up the passages that he refers to. Some of them are passages that are not often brought to our attention.

A. **The Triumph of God's Truth.** When an ambassador speaks the truth in love and meets death with joy, eyes are opened to the gospel. Christ's own death had this effect on one of His executioners.

B. **The Defeat of Satan.** When martyrs meet their death without fear, they demonstrate that Satan's ability to control us by fear is broken. Tson suggests that an important dimension to Satan's defeat and shame in the heavenlies was revealed in the account of Job. Paul echoes this purpose when he says that he was "a spectacle to the world, both to angels and to men" (1 Cor 4:9).

C. **The Glory of God.** In a powerful paradox, the shame of death brings about God's glory. According to Church tradition, both Paul and Peter had this destiny.

Read Tson, "Suffering and Martyrdom: God's Strategy in the World," pp. 195-198 (all)

IX. To Enter Suffering By Prayer

Brother Andrew's comments are rich with seasoned wisdom. Why have so many Christians been willing to suffer? The report of "the vanished church" today might parallel the report that Nehemiah heard in his day. Examine Nehemiah's response as an example for engaging in the work of the gospel in hostile environments. Andrew notes that Nehemiah's example combines a zeal for the glory of God with a deep compassion for the well-being of people.

Read Andrew, "If I Perish," pp. 193-194 (all)

X. The Power of the Spirit and the Hope of Christ

The last three paragraphs of the Lausanne Covenant beautifully summarize the significance of the Spirit's outpouring for the Church. The hope of the Holy Spirit visiting, filling and renewing His Church should stir us to pray and to anticipate days of working together in His power. The hope of Christ's coming should motivate us to rededicate ourselves to fulfilling the mission He has given us.

Read "The Lausanne Covenant," pp. 768b-768d

Conclusion of Certificate Readings for this lesson. 

After studying this section you should be able to:

- Describe how the Church is formed by reconciliation, and it results in reconciliation.
- Define a church in biblical ways using the concepts of community and Christ's kingdom.
- Explain why describing the Church as a living thing is significant for mission activity.
- Describe some of the biblical grounds for hope of a tremendous ingathering at the end of the age, in the midst of a time of great hostility to Christ.

XI. The Local Church on Mission

Paul did not regard the apostolic bands to be sufficient to fulfill God's work in the world. He fully expected God to work through the churches. The ministry of the churches was a matter of God's grace by spiritual gifts. A large part of the local church's fulfillment of its mission was by maintaining a fruitful symbiotic relationship with the apostolic bands. As you read this, consider the value of local churches today flourishing in relationship with mission structures. Take special note of why Paul wrote the book of Romans. It was not written as a treatise of doctrine so much as it was written to motivate the churches in Rome to become "a second Antioch."

Read Glasser, "The Apostle Paul and the Missionary Task," pp. 151d-152c

XII. The Church in God's Plan

We have seen God's purpose unfold throughout history and come to a mighty culmination as churches are planted in every people group. To many, this is not joyous news. Many have had disappointing or painful experiences with churches. These people are not going to eagerly support or even clearly understand mission efforts which talk about multiplying churches among unreached peoples. It's foundational to grasp what the Church is all about.

Howard Snyder guides us through a short study in the book of Ephesians to discover the purpose of God's brand new life form on the planet: the Church. Please keep your Bible open as you work through this article. Read the verses that come from Ephesians.

A. **God's Purpose: Reconciliation Under the Son.** Snyder proposes a radical idea of reconciliation. He asserts that God's plan all along has not been to repair the earth or to simply rescue people from hell. God has been determined to bring about something better than what has ever come about before. God's purpose all along has been to enjoy a huge household. He is "the Father, from whom every family in heaven and on earth derives its name" (Eph 3:14-15).

Bringing things together under Christ's headship is a double idea. It suggests a submission to Christ's magnificent lordship. It also opens the way for people to finally join together in joyous fellowship as a family. Reconciliation is not a sentimental affair of hand-holding and having nice feelings about one another. Reconciliation is the formation of something new—far more than it is the restoration of that which was broken. Jew and Gentile were made to be "one new man" by Christ's reconciling power. Can you imagine what is on display in the heavenlies before the angelic enemies of God?

Every time a church is planted, there is another acceleration toward the grand finale of a family of all peoples enjoying God's life in face-to-face glory. Never get used to the wonder of the Church!

B. The Biblical Vision: A Life and Love Affair With Christ. Different images are important to consider. Each of them helps church members and church planters grasp who they are and what they are a part of. Each of the images that Snyder mentions is a living thing. Even the temple is made of living stones. The Church is alive with the life of God. When we come to consider church planting, it matters greatly that we are basically tending a life form that can reproduce. Missionaries do not need to force or fake the Church. It is alive by resurrection power.

1. **Cosmic/Historic Perspective.** God has been working on His Church for millennia. The Church has a great honor from God. She has been placed at the center of all that God wants to do on the earth. That is no small thing. It wouldn't necessarily have to be that way.
2. **Charismatic Rather Than Institutional Terms.** The Church exists by grace (Greek word, *charis*) and is built up with the gifts of grace (Greek word, *charismata*). This is why we must view churches as living organisms and relational communities instead of programmed marketing devices.
3. **Community of God's People.** The definition of the Church that lies at the heart of our mission is this:

   The Church is the community of God's people.

   Defining or organizing churches in any other way bogs down the work of evangelization as well as frustrates every other work of the Kingdom. This definition is the reason why the most effective missionaries are multiplying churches which are very simplified. They understand that they are God's household, so it's natural for them to meet in houses. They know themselves to be the Body of Christ, so it's natural for them to form churches as small cells. It really doesn't matter what external form the Church takes on, but the churches flourish when communal interdependency and the centrality of Christ's Lordship are emphasized. The Church is not the kingdom of God, but it expresses the King's will. It is the community of the King.

Read Snyder, "The Church in God's Plan," pp. 154-158 (all)

XIII. Apostolic Hope

Robert Coleman starts at Pentecost, where this lesson began, to draw our attention to the global outpouring of God's Spirit in the midst of tumultuous days at the end of the age. In the midst of these days of great trouble, there will be a profound cleansing of the Church and the largest ever ingathering of people to the Church. Note that Coleman sees Christ's return coming after a global harvest of huge proportions so that "the nations of the earth shall come and worship before the Lord." Anticipating Christ's return is a summons to action to accomplish the central task of world evangelization. The hope of global revival becomes a call to advance the gospel, to unite in prayer, and to live in vibrant expectancy.

Read Coleman, "The Hope of a Coming World Revival," pp. 199-203 (all)

6 Expansion of the World Christian Movement

Studying this lesson will help you:

- Tell the "broad-stroke" story of how God's blessing has continued to extend to all peoples throughout 4,000 years of history.
- Describe the expansion of the gospel to different geographic areas and cultural basins in the West during each of five 400-year periods since Christ.
- Explain how the gospel advanced even when God's people were disobedient with reference to different mechanisms of mission involving people coming or messengers going, both voluntarily or involuntarily.
- Recall some key mission leaders, their strategies and the movements that resulted from their efforts.
- Describe the two functional structures of the Church through the centuries using the terms "modality" and "sodality."
- Explain the different challenges and responses to the gospel as it expanded east into Asia in contrast to what transpired as it expanded west.
- Describe the sociological evidence that prolonged missionary presence is associated with positive measurable improvements in the quality of life.

We have seen how the plot of the entire Bible unfolds steadily toward the fulfillment of God's global purpose. But what happened after Acts 28? Most of us have a vague idea of early believers enduring the catacombs as Rome burned around them. Then, in the popular understanding, the medieval dark ages blanketed the Christian movement with crusades and chaos until the Reformation. If this is really all that happened, then God's promises to bless the nations were more hype than hope. After the first century, did God get frustrated with His followers for long centuries and abandon His intention to see the gospel go to the ends of the earth? Has God only recently awakened to bright possibilities of missions in the modern world? Is God an opportunist, achieving great things when the situation seems ripe, but allowing eons of darkness to roll by without action?

The core question is this: Is there continuity to history? Many historians say no, explaining any apparent significant succession of events as only a mirage. Believers in Christ, however, have only to recall that Jesus Himself announced the kingdom of God by declaring, "the time is fulfilled!" (Mark 1:15). That statement alone should be enough to awaken us to the reality that there is a magnificent purpose in all of history. All of Scripture throbs with the steady pulse of God's purpose through the years. The kingdom of God has come and will come with even greater power. The God of all nations is the God of all generations. He can be fully followed by those who know Him as the God of all history.

Why delve into the archives? It's not a matter of memorizing the dates and names of past popes and rulers. It's a matter of tracing the hand of God as He fulfills His purpose. Those who follow history from God's perspective are not disappointed. They are the ones who can sort out the unfolding "plot" from that which is interesting but peripheral.

In this lesson we'll follow how God's blessing extended successively from one region and people to another. We'll see the drastic consequences for the Christian movement when the blessing of the gospel of God was not extended. We'll set the record straight about the wider impact and spread of the general blessings of the kingdom of God throughout the world.

momentum It's often hard to sense the accelerating pace of God's work in history. Many live encased in the present moment and tend to miss the momentum of the mighty God of the ages. But would God tell us so much of His story and His purposes without intending for us to follow Him through history? Those who know God's history can better lay hold of God's intended destiny.

I. The Drama Moving Through All of History: The Kingdom Strikes Back

Human history could be summarized using one dominant theme. Ralph Winter finds this keynote theme in the Bible. He sees the theme of the kingdom of God as the primary drama throughout "a single ten-epoch 4,000-year unfolding story."

A. **Ten Epochs Through 4,000 Years.** Dividing history into ten 400-year periods is a device to help us remember and follow the developing story. Even though fascinating patterns and recurrent themes do emerge, Winter does not mean to imply that history follows rigidly patterned 400-year cycles.

B. **The Counterattack on Evil.** In addition to the kingdom of God, another dominant theme is God's war against evil. God intervenes in the suffering of people under the domain and the devices of evil. History is God's invasion of Satan's domain, undoing all of his works and freeing people to glorify His name. It is a costly war. Again and again in God's redemptive story, His servants suffer even as Christ suffered in the same struggle.

C. **Redemption by Blessing.** Winter's description of blessing is one of the best. He distinguishes between the common Western idea of *blessings* (plural) as material or social benefits, and the Hebrew idea of *blessing* (singular) as relational realities which confer responsibility and obligation as well as privilege. Blessing is a distinctively familial idea. By extending His blessing, God is establishing an enormous family, an array of households of faith which together display His kingdom and His glory. This is the blessing that God's people were to become as well as pass on to others.

D. **Four Mechanisms of Mission.** Not every epoch is marked by God's people faithfully launching out in cross-cultural mission. During much of history there seems to be very little, if any, such obedience. Does this mean God's story slows down and stops? Not at all! Winter points out that God manages to see that the blessing continues to spread even when His people are unwilling to extend it. To see this wonderful continuity throughout history we need to recognize four mechanisms of mission. These concepts expand on the distinction of centripetal (coming) and centrifugal (going) mission explored in Lesson 2. These four mechanisms demonstrate how God presses His mission forward with or without the full cooperation of His chosen people:

1. **Voluntary Going**
2. **Involuntary Going** (without initial missionary intent)
3. **Voluntary Coming**
4. **Involuntary Coming** (occasions of forced settlement among God's people)

Read Winter, "The Kingdom Strikes Back," pp. 209-211d

MECHANISMS	OLD TESTAMENT	NEW TESTAMENT	EARLY CHURCH TO 1800	MODERN MISSIONARY ERA
Voluntary Going Centrifugal (Expansive)	• Abraham to Canaan • Minor Prophets preach to other nations near Israel • Pharisees sent out "over land and sea"	• Jesus in Samaria • Peter to Cornelius • Paul and Barnabas on their missionary journeys • Witness of other Christians in Babylon, Rome, Cyprus, etc.	• St. Patrick to Ireland • Celtic peregrini to England and Europe • Friars to China, India, Japan, America • Moravians to America	• William Carey and other missionaries of the 1st Era • Hudson Taylor and the 2nd Era missionaries • 3rd Era to present
Involuntary Going Centrifugal (Expansive)	• Joseph, sold into slavery in Egypt, witnesses to Pharaoh • Naomi witnesses to Ruth because of famine • Jonah—the reluctant missionary • Hebrew girl is taken off to Naaman's home • Captive Hebrews in Babylon witness to captors	• Persecution of Christians forces them out of Holy Land all over the Roman Empire and beyond	• Ulifas sold as slave to the Goths • Exiled Arian bishops go to Gothic areas • Christians evangelize their Viking captors • Christian soldiers sent by Rome to England, Spain, etc. • Pilgrims and Puritans forced to the Americas and discover their mission to the Indians	• WWII Christian soldiers sent around the globe return to start 150 new mission agencies • Ugandan Christians flee to other parts of Africa • Korean Christians flee to less-Christian South, later sent to Saudi Arabia and Iran, etc. to work
Voluntary Coming Centripetal (Attractive)	• Naaman the Syrian came to Elisha • Queen of Sheba came to Solomon's court • Ruth chose to go to Judah from Moab	• Greeks who sought out Jesus • Cornelius sends for Peter • Man of Macedonia calls to Paul	• Goths invade Christian Rome, learn more of the Christian faith • Vikings invade Christian Europe, are won to the faith eventually through that contact	• The influx of international visitors, students and businessmen into the Christian West
Involuntary Coming Centripetal (Attractive)	• Gentiles settled in Israel by Cyrus the Great	• Roman military occupation and infiltration of "Galilee of the Gentiles"	• Slaves brought from Africa to America	• Refugees from Communism • Boat people, Cubans forced out, etc.

II. The Second Half of the Story

Winter summarizes many of the events and themes of the last 2,000 years. As you read the following selection, take note of the names of the five most recent epochs on the timeline.

A. **Advance Both Cultural and Geographic.** Winter characterizes the advance of the gospel as an "invasion" of specific "cultural basins." A cultural basin is a large system of people groups, languages, cultures and political systems. Sometimes the advance and the blessing of the gospel flow to, and then through, a specific cluster of peoples over many centuries, as with the Celtic peoples. In other cases the gospel's advance can be described better by the geographic extent of Christianity's growing edge. Watch for both cultural and geographic expansion of the Christian movement.

B. Dismissing the BOBO Theory. A popular impression is that the Christian faith somehow "Blinked Out" after the apostles and then "Blinked On" (BOBO) again much later at the Reformation. The truth is that since the early Church, there have always been people of vibrant faith.

C. "Flourishings" or "Renaissances." Near the close of the epochs were often times Winter calls "flourishings." These seasons of flourishing, or renaissance, were times when the gospel brought stability, abundance and strength to entire social structures. These times expressed part of the blessing of the kingdom of God.

III. Period One: Winning the Romans (A.D. 0-400)

A. Mechanism. The gospel advanced by all four mechanisms. The "voluntary-go" pattern was reflected by Paul's missionary band. The "involuntary-go" pattern was seen in the dispersion of Christians during times of persecution.

B. Advance. The gospel flowed along trade routes as well as throughout the social strata. During the early centuries, Christianity was a religion without a nationalistic political identity. As such, it appealed to many throughout the empire—and beyond. Once it became the official imperial religion, Christianity began to carry the political and cultural stigma of being Roman. This slowed down the advance which was already underway in areas beyond the Roman Empire, particularly where Rome was despised or feared. Winter suggests a new way to look at what might be regarded as heresy. There were different flavors of Christian faith that differed very slightly in the details but gave people a way to espouse their own brand of Christianity. Thus, areas hostile to the Roman empire were more likely to embrace what the Roman empire/church considered heresy, such as Arianism (even though Arian theology had been official in Rome for 60 years).

C. Flourishing. Winter mentions, at a later point in the article, a cultural "flourishing" of the peoples and lands that had become Christian. If Roman Christians had "used" some of the wealth and power of the A.D. 310 to A.D. 410 period to reach out, the fate of Roman society might have been much different and the gospel might have advanced more rapidly.

Read Winter, "The Kingdom Strikes Back," pp. 211d-216c

IV. Period Two: Winning the Barbarians (A.D. 400-800)

A. Mechanism. The Barbarian tribes invaded the Roman Empire and became even more thoroughly evangelized. This period was an expression of the "voluntary-come" mechanism. Later in the period came the first establishment of monastic orders. Most of the monastic tradition should be recognized for sustaining and extending the faith in and around the monasteries. Some, however, became expressly missionary, following a "voluntary-go" pattern. Notable among these were the Celtic or Irish *peregrini* (wandering evangelists), and their Anglo-Saxon followers, among whom were Columban, Boniface and Patrick.

B. Advance. Barbarian tribes, such as the Goths, Visigoths, Vandals and Anglo-Saxons, invaded most of Western and Central Europe. Though Rome lost half its empire, the Barbarian world gained the Christian faith in the process.

C. **Flourishing.** Charlemagne, himself a descendant of a Germanic barbarian tribe, facilitated a rise of education and economic development that temporarily pulled Europe out of leaderless chaos. Under the strong influence of the monastic centers of his day, Charlemagne promoted the mission centers of monastic life that had spread and held the faith throughout Europe. Under his influence, the "Carolingian Renaissance" broke the medieval "Dark Ages" into two distinctive periods. As much as Charlemagne boosted the faith, his efforts to evangelize the attacking Vikings from the north were too little and too late.

Read Winter, "The Kingdom Strikes Back," pp. 216c-219c

V. Period Three: Winning the Vikings (A.D. 800-1200)

A. **Mechanism.** The Viking conquerors were themselves conquered by the faith of their captives. Once again, an "involuntary-go" pattern is observed.

B. **Advance.** The gospel spread to Scandinavia and other north European areas.

C. **Flourishing.** The Gregorian Reform was made strong by the Cluny, the Cistercian and allied spiritual movements. The expression of mission then went awry, as described in the next epoch.

VI. Period Four: Winning the Muslims? (A.D. 1200-1600)

A. **Mechanism.** Once the Vikings capitulated to "the counterattack of the gospel," they became leaders in the greatest perversion of mission in history: the Crusades. Using a deeply flawed "voluntary-go" pattern, they destroyed and conquered territory without any success in extending the blessing of the gospel to the Muslims, sometimes referred to as the Saracens. At the same time, a new type of monasticism arose which was truly missionary in nature. This resulted in the movement of Friars who traveled all over Europe with the gospel. However, just when it looked as if the Friars would bring blessing to lands beyond, the Black Plague struck. The Friars were hit especially hard. Winter theorizes that God employed Satan's intent of removing the messengers of the gospel as a judgment against those who chose not to hear.

B. **Advance.** The Crusades were an abortion of advance. The beginnings of colonial expansion brought some advance of Christian faith, but not of Protestant faith.

C. **Flourishing.** The Renaissance and the Reformation were times of flourishing. The Reformation created a drastic and dramatic decentralization of Christianity as it grew with vitality in many places. The Catholic, or Latin, variety of Christianity, with its growing monastic mission structures, developed alongside colonial expansion. The newly established Protestant movements were caught up in theological reformulation and remained virtually without mission structures that could reach beyond their own people.

Read Winter, "The Kingdom Strikes Back," pp. 219c-224c

VII. Period Five: To the Ends of the Earth (A.D. 1600-2000)

A. **Mechanism.** The Catholic expansion continued and then was suddenly stunted around 1800, when Napoleon ransacked Europe and atheism, deism and humanism grew more popular. At the same time, the "voluntary-go" mechanism of the Protestant mission movement finally became launched.

B. **Advance.** Protestant missionaries reached across the globe. The Protestant movement first advanced to the coastlands with or without colonial expansion. Then came another wave to the inland areas. Finally, the focus fell on reaching all the *peoples* of the earth.

C. **Flourishing.** Western civilization, with all of its wealth and corruption, may be the greatest flourishing of all. However, Winter poses the question: If we insist on keeping the blessing instead of sharing it, will God act so that we, like other nations before us, will lose some of the material benefits of God's blessing in order that God's purpose to bless all the nations will be fulfilled?

Read Winter, "The Kingdom Strikes Back," pp. 224c-227

Conclusion of Key Readings for this lesson. 

VIII. Advance to the East

In the first millennium, the gospel spread farther eastward than westward. In the east, however, the gospel encountered major intercultural state religions, such as Zoroastrianism, Buddhism, Hinduism and Taoism. By contrast, as the gospel moved throughout the Roman Empire in Europe and Africa, it encountered smaller, local, "ethnic" religions, which offered less resistance. In lands to the east, Christianity spread widely, but in almost every case, Christians remained a minority until the last few generations. Scott Sunquist lists five major advances, of which the first and last have been the most effective:

1. **Persian Advance** (first millennium)
2. **Franciscan-Mongol Interlude** (1206-1368)
3. **Jesuit Advance** (1542-1773)
4. **Protestant Advance** (1706-1950)
5. **Asian Indigenous** (1950-present)

Read Sunquist, "Asian Christianity: Facing the Rising Sun," pp. 239-243 (all)

IX. Mission Strategy

R. Pierce Beaver adds more color and depth to some of the historical figures we have mentioned. He explores different approaches to mission strategy in times preceding William Carey. As you read about each of the following figures and periods, consider the different approaches that missions used to advance the gospel. When exploring the mission work of previous centuries it is important to acknowledge the actions which were setbacks or that brought more damage than blessing. At the same time, it's important to recognize the lasting strategic value of many of the efforts. We have much to learn from the seasoned wisdom of earlier experiments and advances.

The list below highlights some important cross-cultural communication issues that we'll explore later in the course. Allow the accounts to whet your appetite to read beyond what the *Perspectives* course can provide. Pay particular attention to four broad areas of mission strategy:

- **Adaptation.** Ways that the local culture was respected and valued or the message adapted in gospel communication.
- **Civilizing.** Contextualization of the resulting movements. To what degree were the resulting churches allowed to reflect their local culture? Or were they instead brought into alignment with the missionary's culture?
- **Conquest.** Missionaries in some cases followed colonial or imperial powers. Did they intend to bring peoples under the political sway of their home countries? Were they perceived as facilitating control by foreign powers?
- **Development.** Missionaries often introduced significant ways of meeting basic human needs. At times these efforts were considered a civilizing service or possibly part of an economic conquest.

A. **Boniface.** Beaver characterizes this key figure of the monastic movement as exhibiting "a true sending mission." He went to convert tribes rather than extend a political domain. To encourage group conversions of entire tribes, he used what we have come to call "power encounter." An example of Boniface using a "power encounter": He cut down the sacred trees of other gods to expose their impotence, confronting them with the power of Christ. He established churches, monasteries and schools. Ultimately, however, he was perceived by those he reached as an instrument of imperial expansion.

B. **The Crusades.** Tragically, the Crusades warped mission into conquest. The effect of the Crusades reverberates to this day in most of the Muslim world. The Crusades highlight two other notable monastic figures, Francis of Assisi and Ramon Lull, who sought to preach the gospel to Muslims instead of violent conquest.

C. **Colonial Expansion.** Portuguese, Dutch, Spanish, French and British imperial expansion was often linked with mission but in very different ways. Methods often hinged on whether to first "Christianize" or "civilize."

D. **Strategists of the 17th Century.** Sunquist already mentioned something of the innovative aspects of Jesuit mission strategy as the gospel was taken to the east. The experiments and experiences of Jesuits have often determined the missiological climate that missionaries face today. The Jesuits not only encountered strong resistance in Japan in spite of their innovative methods, they also affected modern Japanese resistance to the gospel. Some of the creative approaches of Robert de Nobili and Matteo Ricci are still considered as models by missionaries today.

Read Beaver, "The History of Mission Strategy," pp. 228-231a

X. The Two Structures of God's Redemptive Mission

We'll now resume reading Winter's article, "The Two Structures of God's Redemptive Mission," which we began studying in Lesson 5. Winter states that the Church has grown and extended itself in mission by following forms found within the social structure of the day as well as forms found in the Bible. Throughout history, even though superficial details change, when we speak of the "Church" we see two fundamental structures: the congregational structure and the mission structure. Winter introduces the sociological terms "modality" and "sodality" to help identify these structures at different points of history.

- **Modality** structures are inclusive, nurture-oriented, structured fellowships (for example, a church congregation or a secular town).
- **Sodality** structures are second-decision, task-oriented, structured fellowships (for example, a mission society or a military force).

Both structures exist in civil and religious societies. Both are found in the Bible. Both are legitimate and necessary in God's redemptive mission. Sodality structures nourish and extend the church. Modality structures strengthen and support the mission band. They work together in an important symbiosis.

A. **Redemptive Structures Prior to and During the First Century.** The congregational structure followed the synagogue patterns of the day. The mission structures had precedent in the Jewish rabbinical mission efforts, but they soon became highly dynamic missionary bands, similar to Paul's small groups that traveled and planted churches.

B. **Early Development Within Roman Culture.** Local congregational structures recognized bishops with territorial jurisdiction, after the pattern of the Roman magisterial territories. The Roman term used for these territories was "diocese." The mission structures that emerged—the monastic movements—borrowed patterns from Roman military practice. Protestants have generally stereotyped impressions of monasteries as places where ascetic monks fled the world. In reality, the monastic movements were largely responsible for bringing the blessing of the gospel to the world.

C. **The Medieval Synthesis.** The survival of the parish church structures came to depend largely on the more committed devotion of the monastic movement. Several of the largest mission endeavors of Christian history arose from the monastic movement. As monastic movements became inadvertently wealthy, however, local rulers demanded and took control of their leadership, resulting in spiritual decline and decay.

Read Winter, "The Two Structures of God's Redemptive Mission," pp. 246b-250b

D. The Protestant Recovery. Earlier we asked why Protestants celebrated the gospel but failed dismally to extend it. For nearly 200 years there was virtually no mission outreach. Winter, along with Latourette and other scholars, points to what may be the greatest error of the Protestant movement: the Reformers abandoned sodality structures. Because monastic life was rejected, there was virtually no interest in preserving or extending the mission structures. William Carey called for Christians to "use means" to complete the commission of Christ. By "means" he meant organized mission structures. He called for the formation of mission societies. Once Protestants organized sodality structures, whether denominational or interdenominational, the numbers of Protestant missionaries exploded.

While they were ministering to the Lord and fasting,
the Holy Spirit said,
" Set apart for Me Barnabas and Saul
for the work to which I have called them."
Then, when they had fasted and prayed
and laid their hands on them, they sent them away.
So, being sent out by the Holy Spirit,
they went down to Seleucia
and from there they sailed to Cyprus.
— Acts 13:2–4

How distinct was Paul's missionary band from the Antioch church? Examine the two aspects of the "sending" of Paul's missionary band in Acts 13. In verse 3, the Greek word for "they sent them away" has more to do with releasing and setting loose. The following verse, "being sent out by the Holy Spirit," contains a different, more forceful Greek word for sending that suggests something like military command.

Was the missionary band *commanded* by the church, or *commended* to God's care and control? How did their prayer and fasting play a part in recognizing the composition of the team? How does the expression "ministering to the Lord" suggest that their mission vision was directed toward and for God?

E. Contemporary Misunderstanding. Protestant missions were organized initially without denominational backing. Gradually, the once-independent structures became increasingly regulated and eventually were dominated by denominational leaders. This brought both health and problems to the mission expansion. As a result, a later wave of mission structures called "faith missions" was launched, which was actually a second surge of non-denominational initiative (what we will call Second Era missions in Lesson 7). Some strong, highly regarded denominational leaders have recognized the importance of some mission structures which were not tied to any denomination. But on the whole, there has been dubious support of mission structures. At times there has been critique and open doubt expressed concerning the legitimacy of sodality structures. The result on mission fields has predictably been a failure to encourage newly planted churches to form mission structures and send their own missionaries. The now vast phenomenon of non-Western missionaries has grown with relatively little missionary support.

Read Winter, "The Two Structures of God's Redemptive Mission," pp. 250b-253

XI. The Fruit of the Movement: Transformation

The key idea throughout this lesson is the continuity of history. God has been relentlessly unfolding His purposes throughout the generations and centuries. Not all times are equal. There are periods of decline and apparent inactivity. But God's mission purpose has never been fully dependent on human activity. We identified the nature of mission history as a prolonged struggle, virtually a spiritual war. We've seen how God has used different mechanisms and movements. We presented God's purpose as that of fulfilling His promise to bless the nations. Have the nations been blessed? Is God accomplishing His purpose? What has been the outcome? According to a popular view, Christianity has been a source of hindrance and damage to the best interests of societies all over the world. This view is not correct. Although there have been many disappointing and destructive things done in the name of Christ, the overall positive impact of the person of Jesus Christ on the societies of the world has been incalculable.

A. Does Christian Mission Bring Blessing or Harm? The ongoing controversy surrounding Christian missions usually alleges that Christian mission has always been the handmaiden of colonialism and a destructive force upon indigenous cultures. Robert Woodberry challenges these ideas, usually sourced in anecdotes and fiction, with verifiable sociological data. If the net result of the presence of missionaries is that societies are harmed, we would expect conditions to be worse in settings where missionaries have been working longer or in greater numbers. But Woodberry says that the data shows exactly the opposite. In situations where missionaries have been present and have been at liberty to work, societies are better off in areas of human thriving such as literacy, educational enrollment, infant mortality, life expectancy, economic development, freedom from corruption and political democracy.

Read Woodberry, "The Social Impact of Christian Missions," pp. 286-290 (all)

B. The Ideal and Goal of the Kingdom. According to the famous historian Kenneth Scott Latourette, the ideal and goal of the kingdom of God had vastly shaped history subsequent to Jesus. Latourette documented the increase of the World Christian movement in various bursts of increasing magnitude and frequency (see the chart on p. 225 which displays Latourette's "resurgences" and "recessions" next to Winter's 400-year periods). In Latourette's view, the Christian movement entered its greatest expansion ever in the last century. The movement exploded just as he thought it might. Latourette not only told the story of the ongoing movement of Christianity, he also summed up the fruit of the movement. From Latourette's two-volume work entitled *A History of Christianity*:

> From individuals who have been inspired by Christ and from the Church has issued movement after movement for attaining the Christian ideal. That ideal has centered around the kingdom of God, an order in which God's will is done. It sets infinite value upon the individual.... Its goal for the individual cannot be completely attained this side of the grave, but is so breathtaking

that within history only a beginning is possible. Nor can it be reached in isolation, but only in community. In Christ's teaching, love for God, as the duty and privilege of man, is inseparably joined with love for one's neighbor.

The ideal and the goal have determined the character of the movements which have been the fruits of Christianity. Although men can use and often have used knowledge and education to the seeming defeat of the ideal, across the centuries Christianity has been the means of reducing more languages to writing than have all other factors combined. It has created more schools, more theories of education, and more systems than has any other one force. More than any other power in history it has impelled men to fight suffering, whether that suffering has come from disease, war, or natural disasters. It has built thousands of hospitals, inspired the emergence of nursing and medical professions, and furthered movements for public health and the relief and prevention of famine.

Although explorations and conquests which were in part its outgrowth led to the enslavement of Africans for the plantations of the Americas, men and women whose consciences were awakened by Christianity and whose wills it served brought about the abolition of slavery. Men and women similarly moved and sustained, wrote into the laws of Spain and Portugal provisions to alleviate the ruthless exploitation of the Indians of the New World.

Wars have often been waged in the name of Christianity. They have attained their most colossal dimensions through weapons and large scale organization initiated in Christendom. Yet from no other source have there come as many and as strong movements to eliminate or regulate war and to ease the suffering brought by war. From its first centuries the Christian faith has caused many of its adherents to be uneasy about war. It has led minorities to refuse to have any part in it. It has impelled others to seek to limit war by defining what, in their judgment, from the Christian standpoint is a "just war." In the turbulent middle ages of Europe it gave rise to the Truce of God and the Peace of God. In a later era it was the main impulse in the formulation of international law. But for it the League of Nations and the United Nations would not have been. By its name and symbol the most extensive organization ever created for the relief of the suffering caused by war, the Red Cross, bears witness to its Christian origin.

The list might go on indefinitely. It includes many other humanitarian projects and movements, ideals in government, the reform of prisons and the emergence of criminology, great art and architecture, and outstanding literature. In geographic extent and potency the results were never as marked as in the nineteenth and twentieth centuries.

Kenneth Scott Latourette. "A History of Christianity," (Peabody, MA: Prince Press, 1997) pp. 1470-1471.

Conclusion of Certificate Readings for this lesson. 

After studying this section you should be able to:

- Describe some of the features of social transformation that have resulted from mission efforts.
- Describe how the goals and methods of the Protestant mission movement have changed over time.

C. **The History of Transformation.** The fruit of changing society toward the peace and justice of God's kingdom was not a matter of passive hope. The missionary movement has been an almost constant force for positive change. Paul Pierson tells the story.

1. **Monasticism.** Look again at the tremendous heritage of the monastic movement. This movement, properly understood, has been salt and light in God's hand throughout many centuries.
2. **Forerunners.** The Church has had tremendous impact on the nations when the core values of the gospel bloomed and bore fruit over time. The Puritan, Pietistic, Moravian and Wesleyan movements each brought a greater focus of biblical hope for transformed personal and community life. It's not surprising that a vision for evangelization went hand in hand with a vision for profound social transformation.

3. **A Striking Contrast of Reality and False Report.** William Carey is recognized as the father of modern mission. What is not often known is the phenomenal breadth of his endeavors and the incredible changes that are still continuing because of his work. In contrast is the stereotype of missionaries who ruin cultures. Pierson mentions some of the truth about the falsely maligned missionaries to Hawaii.

4. **A Striking Comparison.** Not every place that Christianity has touched has been transformed to the same degree. There are, of course, many factors contributing to the different impact that the gospel has had in different places. One key factor is the vision and labor of missionaries to include local leaders in an intentional transformation of community life.

Read the section, "A Striking Comparison," p. 283b-283d, to imagine the dramatic differences in just one situation. There had been minimal influence from the Catholic Church on both sides of the river. What factors were part of the different outcomes on the different sides of the river? What does this suggest about the need for integrated community development?

5. **The Different Routes Toward Fruit.** Missionaries have labored in education, health care, agriculture and ministries for oppressed people, particularly women and slaves. Pierson does not so much provide a summary as a sample of the contributions of Christian missions. He is offering just a few very specific examples of a huge movement. The impact of the Christian movement has been so pervasive that it may be impossible to ever trace the entire impact. But it's safe to say that there has never been a greater source of betterment of the human situation than the global Christian movement in terms of education, health care and the status of women and slaves.

Read Pierson, "A History of Transformation," pp. 279-285 (all)

XII. Strategies of Mission

We return to Beaver's survey of mission strategy. But first we should consider the value of examining old strategies of bygone centuries. Why not get busy working on today's urgent needs? The history of strategy is bursting with practical significance for anyone who plays any part in the missionary enterprise. Some of God's servants in the past accomplished amazing things by incredible displays of love, wisdom and sacrifice, while others have floundered, even with admirable intentions.

If your part in mission is primarily to support others who are frontline missionaries, your acquaintance with these issues will give you a wider panorama of vision, enhancing your decisions and encouragements. If you eventually work in cross-cultural mission yourself, even for a short term, an awareness of strategic breakthroughs and blunders can help you make a contribution of lasting value.

A. Early Protestant Missions

1. **New England Puritans.** The American mission experience to reach the "Indians" began with what seemed to be an attempt to "civilize" them in special towns prior to "Christianizing" them. Evangelism by extracting converts from the larger tribal societies ended up forming a separated people who could not "pass on the contagion of personal faith." The "Praying Indian" towns may have been set up to protect the Christian Indians from both pagan Indians and pagan colonists. However, the "Praying Indian" towns were eventually burned down by unruly settlers from Europe. Notable figures in this chapter of mission effort were John Eliot and David Brainerd.
2. **Danish-Halle Mission.** An early, famous Protestant sending mission from Europe attempted some of the most innovative approaches to contextualize the message and assume effective roles to communicate the gospel. Two leaders stand out: Bartholomew Ziegenbalg and Frederick Schwartz.
3. **Moravians.** Beaver describes the Moravians' efforts to respect local cultures. They expected that the resulting movements would be different from their own. They taught new believers skills which established them economically.

Read Beaver, "The History of Mission Strategy," pp. 231b-233a

B. The Great Century of Protestant Missions

The 19th century has been referred to as "the Great Century" because of the phenomenal advance of the gospel in every geographic area of the globe. We'll continue to read Pierce Beaver's summary of mission strategy which provides fascinating details about this period. To help you follow the story through the first 18 centuries of mission strategy, we had pointed out four themes in Section IX: adaptation, "civilizing," conquest and development. Now as we read Beaver's comments about the 19th century, we will focus on these three themes:

- **Contextualization.** Because of a low view of the value of other cultures, the idea of "civilizing" the different societies to Western ideals was assumed.
- **Control**. Models of "conquest" were dismissed, partly because the colonial era had largely subjugated the unevangelized regions. Conquest was replaced by the far more subtle issue of control.
- **Transformation.** Development efforts multiplied. Beaver uses the term of "transformation."

1. **Mission Structures.** Operating mission structures was a new endeavor for Protestants. Confusion from the sending church structures about control of the mission operation dampened much of the early effectiveness. The issue of control from the European homelands was so great that mission structures were dominated by sending churches. William Carey's efforts were hindered by this confusion.

2. **Mission Objectives.** The general aim was individual conversions, church planting and social transformation.

   - **Christianization or Civilization?** Local cultures were seen as primitive and superstitious. The approach of changing their culture as an initial effort to prepare the way for "Christianization" eventually gave way to the idea that the gospel itself would have a transforming power upon the culture. William Carey and the "Serampore Trio" provided a valuable pattern in pioneering the idea of independent churches and emphasizing the power of the gospel in transforming society.

   - **Stations or Churches?** The mission station approach had pressed converts into a social and economic dependency on missionaries. Carey aimed for an educated, independent leadership and laity gathered in churches. Mission leaders Rufus Anderson and Henry Venn exerted great influence to break up the mission station structures and assumptions. Venn and Anderson proposed the famous "three-self" formula to describe the independent churches that they wanted their missionaries to aim for, but they may not have been sufficiently influential in their day. Near the end of the 19th century there was another emergence of colonial paternalism. This led to a hasty "evolution" of authority from the mission structures to the native churches at the earlier part of the 20th century.

   - **Transformation and Education.** William Carey went further than most of his counterparts in later generations by envisioning a highly educated leadership. Different views on transformation were related to different theological assumptions about the kingdom of God at the turn of the century. Missionaries worked industriously to establish medical and educational systems.

3. **Comity and Continuity.** The practice of "comity" exemplifies the long heritage of unity in mission efforts. Such recognition of diverse parts of the Church paved the way for national and international missionary conferences which have continued to this day.

4. **Transition to a New Age of Mission.** Beaver mentions Roland Allen's ideas as a radically different strategy. Compare his summary of this strategy to what Carey, Venn and Anderson pressed toward. Allen articulated a new level of simplicity in strategic intent that was devoid of colonial infrastructure. Note how Beaver describes the churches which result from Allen's theory as "spontaneously missionary." Then the very next paragraph mentions that several mission organizations were dissolved. Which dynamic was at work? The onward surge of mission or the dissolution of mission structures? This confusion is a telling example of the two minds of Protestant mission at two very significant transitional periods. We'll examine these transitions in greater detail in Lesson 7.

   Beaver's assessment of a radical new strategy may actually be a simplification of church and mission structures, and a hope for tremendous transformation which was not dependent on Western colonial culture and power. Beaver's final statement of the "central task of the Church" refers to the mission calling of the Church in general. In Lesson 9 we'll identify an essential missionary task which can be completed, which opens the way for every kind of flourishing of the blessing of the kingdom of God.

Read Beaver, "The History of Mission Strategy," pp. 233a-238

7 Eras of Mission History

Studying this lesson will help you:

- Recall the approximate dates, emphasis, leaders and student movement associated with each of the three eras of Protestant mission history.
- Explain the four stages of mission activity.
- Explain the tensions of the transitions between the eras.
- Recognize the interplay of secular and Christian events in history, and how they have influenced Christian mission priorities.
- Use the E-Scale to describe the cultural distance of missionaries from their intended hearers.
- Use the P-Scale to describe the comparative socio-cultural distance of would-be followers of Christ fom existing churches.
- Describe the increase of the non-Western missionary force in recent years.
- Define "people blindness."
- Describe the shift of Christianity to the Global South.

We have surveyed the expansion of the World Christian movement through the major epochs of the last two millennia, focusing on the steady growth from one cultural sphere to another. In this lesson we'll focus on how that steady expansion became an explosion during the last 200 years.

The pace of growth is accelerating so quickly that more people have followed Christ in the last 100 years than in all of the previous centuries combined. And there are more people alive today who call themselves Christians than all of the previous generations put together. The majority of those who name the name of Christ are from the Global South. Christianity has become a truly global movement, with its most vibrant and growing churches flourishing in the Global South.

At times this phenomenal expansion has nearly brought itself to a halt. Whenever the harvest is great, the crowds of new Christians make demands upon missionaries for nurture, training and discipling. This deflects the attention of missionaries away from other regions or peoples that have yet to hear. Were it not for the many determined leaders whose minds were set on finishing the entire task of world evangelization, the movement might have stalled long ago. We'll examine some key figures and features that have kept propelling wave after wave of workers to the least evangelized places.

Why dig into these episodes of history? Because we stand at a critical moment. The entire World Christian movement is beginning again to penetrate the final frontiers. But legitimate demands of home and nearby churches can deter us from pushing forward with strategic wisdom to finish the remaining task.

Perhaps the most thrilling phenomenon today is that missionaries are not only *going to* every part of the world—they are *coming from* every part of the world. Missions and churches of the Majority World in Latin America, Asia and Africa are the new vanguard of missionary sending.

finishing Some set their hearts on finishing what God has begun. They are the ones who come to know the expanse of God, who is the Beginning and the End of all that lasts. It should be no surprise that these finishers are actually the ones who *begin* the things that matter. They order their steps with strategic simplicity, not hesitating nor hurrying, but tenaciously continuing to do whatever it takes to finish the task God has given them.

I. The Stages of Protestant Expansion

During its first 200 years, the Protestant movement did nearly nothing to bring the gospel to the nations. After mission structures were launched, and with years of painstaking effort, the first wave of Protestant missionaries began to see the fruit of their labors. Much of the early success preoccupied missionaries with the care of new converts. The demands of nurturing the growing churches often hindered missionaries from pushing on to lesser evangelized areas. While many were dealing with the needs of younger churches, other visionaries recognized new mission frontiers and called for new ventures.

A. **Four Stages.** Most mission efforts pass through four stages of development in the relationship between the mission agencies and the national church they plant. Understanding these stages will help us recognize why churches and missions often pursue different mission priorities. Missionaries themselves struggle to prioritize allocation of limited resources. Crucial decisions rest on "identifying the maturity level" of the new church and weighing its demands against the priority of evangelizing the unreached.

1. **Pioneer Stage**—First contact with a people group.
2. **Paternal Stage**—Expatriates train national leadership.
3. **Partnership Stage**—National leaders work as equals with expatriates.
4. **Participation Stage**—Expatriates are no longer equal partners, but participate only by invitation.

Mission-Church Relations: Four Stages of Development

Stage One: Pioneer
Requires gift of leadership, along with other gifts.
No Believers—missionary must lead and do much of the work himself.

Stage Two: Parent
Requires gift of teaching.
The young church has a growing child's relationship to the mission. But the "parent" must avoid "paternalism."

Stage Three: Partner
Requires changes from parent-child relation to adult-adult relation.
Difficult for both to change, but essential to the church's becoming a mature "adult."

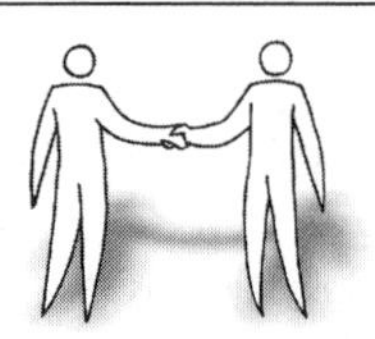

Stage Four: Participant
A fully mature church assumes leadership.
As long as the mission remains, it should use its gifts to strengthen the church to meet the original objectives of Matt 28:19-20. Meanwhile, the mission should be involved in Stage One elsewhere.

Adapted from "Four Men, Three Eras, Two Transitions, Modern Missions," in *Perspectives on the World Christian Movement*, Third Edition, 1998.

B. **Three Eras.** When Ralph Winter first framed the Three Eras of Protestant mission, he characterized them as three bursts of activity, each focused on advancing the gospel in unreached parts or populations of the world. Yvonne Wood Huneycutt summarizes the Three Eras.

1. **The First Era: To the Coastlands.** William Carey did more than any other person to lift the vision of Protestants to the importance of fulfilling the commission of Christ. But Carey also saw the crucial need to form mission structures. Carey's *Enquiry* had widespread influence, awakening mission interest in Europe and in other parts of the Protestant world. Most mission structures of this era emerged from Europe with ties to denominations. The location of Carey's mission to Serampore, India was typical of many of the mission efforts of that day. First Era missions primarily operated in the coastal trade cities of the colonial powers; thus, the generalization that they focused on the "coastlands." Two important features of this era: an astonishing readiness to sacrifice and keen insight into mission strategy.

2. **The Second Era: To the Inland Areas.** Hudson Taylor was one of the most influential leaders of the next era. He called for efforts to complete the task of evangelizing the inland areas of China that were largely untouched by the gospel. Eventually he felt he had to launch a mission structure in order to carry out this focus. The newly formed mission was typical of the many "faith missions" which arose during this time, which were independent of denominational control. The recruits of this era sometimes ignored much of the developed missiological wisdom of the earlier era but eventually planted churches in almost every geographic region. By 1940, the reality of the establishment of churches in every part of the world was celebrated as the "great new fact of our time." To many, world evangelization appeared to be virtually finished. Some missions began to bring missionaries home from mission fields, presuming that the day of missions was over.

3. **The Third Era: To the Unreached Peoples.** This era was set in motion by Cameron Townsend and Donald McGavran, and clarified by a fifth figure: Ralph Winter. Townsend focused attention on the linguistic groups lacking a Bible translation, and McGavran pointed out bypassed social groupings. The two approaches were ethnolinguistic ("horizontal" groupings viewed by linguistic or ethnic differences) and sociocultural ("vertical" groupings taking into account the subtle cultural traditions and prejudices). These two ways of viewing the mission turned the question from "where?" (or in what place mission was being done) to the question of "whom?" (or for what people was mission being aimed).

   McGavran focused on studying people movements, which drew attention to people-specific mission, churches and priorities. By focusing on the languages that lacked translations, Townsend turned attention toward the linguistically defined groups that had not been evangelized. But it was Ralph Winter who brought the insights of McGavran and Townsend together, using McGavran's idea of people groups and extending Townsend's idea of which people lacked sufficient testimony to follow Christ. Winter identified which people groups had already been evangelized to the point that the gospel would continue without outside help, and which people groups would require a special mission effort to bring about a sustainable movement to Christ. Ralph Winter and others developed the term "unreached peoples." Many new service and mobilization mission structures emerged. Non-western or Majority World mission agencies are beginning to surpass the numbers and influence of earlier missions. McGavran often declared that the present hour was the sunrise, and not the sunset of missions.

C. Two Transitions Between Eras. Each of the explosions of Protestant mission vision for the frontiers has roughly proceeded through the four stages of development (pioneer, paternal, partnership and participation). However, the overlap of these eras has resulted in confusion regarding the appropriate strategy. Because of the success of the previous era, many missionaries were recalled. At the same time, others envisioned new frontiers that demanded new workers. The pressing need in pioneer fields is for missionaries to complete their roles in the pioneer and paternal stages. After that point, many missionaries need to move on to other unreached peoples or strategically serve in the partnership and participation stages, encouraging the national church toward developing its own pioneer missions.

Two Transitions Between Protestant Mission Eras

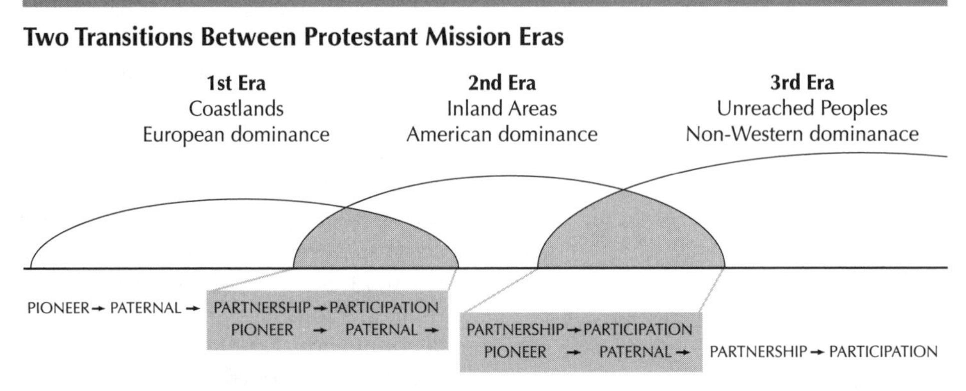

Periods of conflict and confusion of mission priorities during overlap of the Eras

Huneycutt explains that the present transition has additional complexity because of the welcome rise of Majority World missions. Majority World mission efforts are displaying the same kind of bold, finish-the-task vision of earlier eras, with resolute focus on finishing the task of evangelizing earth's remaining unreached peoples. But missions from the Majority World are facing two broad issues which tend to prolong conflict or confusion about mission priorities:

1. **Widening the Mission?** Huneycutt says that Majority World missions will find it challenging to prioritize the initial planting of churches among all peoples. The need to mobilize churches to carry out the responsibility of working toward justice and righteousness in their own societies seems to be a competing priority. There is no question that working toward justice and the transformation of society should be considered part of the mission of existing churches. The issue is how finishing the global task of world evangelization will be prioritized.

2. **Narrowing the Mission?** Huneycutt points out another area of confusion that is especially pertinent to Majority World sending structures. Many of these missions are based in countries such as India, Indonesia or Nigeria, which have many unreached people groups within their borders. The natural sense of responsibility for people groups within one's own country can become a limiting factor if peoples in other countries are never considered. Christians of every country share the responsibility to see the entire world evangelized. Says Huneycutt, "The Majority World has not been given a minor commission, but a Great Commission."

Read Huneycutt, "New Pioneers Leading the Way in the Final Era," pp. 377-381 (all)

II. Three Mission Eras

In 2008, Ralph Winter wrote an article based on his earlier observations about the eras of Protestant mission. In the new article, called "Three Mission Eras," he covers the same 200-year period of history and the same three historical eras. This time, Winter focuses more on how American events, religious and secular, have influenced the mission movement to take on different priorities. Winter's earlier focus on the three eras was on the advance of the mission movement among the unreached (the first two eras being geographical advance, and the third era identifying the unreached people groups remaining in every region). This new article is far more concerned with the priorities of mission as it advanced over each period. Winter also extensively highlights the impact of Christian events on secular developments, and vice versa.

A. **The First Era,** which brought Protestant missionaries to the "coastlands," was fueled by profound evangelical awakenings in the USA and Britain. According to Winter, there was a more substantial balance of mission focus in this era. He refers to this particular balance of mission focus as "kingdom mission." While the evangelical movement at home flourished, keeping churches packed with awakened, sincere believers, evangelicals were also reforming society and confronting many evils of the time. Note that men like John Wesley, the great British evangelist and reformer, William Wilberforce, who worked to abolish slavery in Britain, and William Carey, were all inspired by what is called the First Evangelical Awakening.

The Second Evangelical Awakening had possibly an even greater impact in the USA, bringing about what Winter calls "the most extensive positive transformation any country has ever experienced in history." This was a time of tremendous spiritual optimism in America.

William Carey, influenced by the First Evangelical Awakening, pioneered mission work in India with concern for both evangelism and socio-cultural transformation. Winter observes that the mission work of the entire first era, of which Carey is identified as the pioneer, tended to be characterized by this more balanced approach to mission.

B. **The Second Era,** which Winter characterized by mission efforts pushing beyond the already-evangelized coastlands to the still-unreached "inlands," began around the time of the American Civil War. It was followed by massive immigration to America and was further impacted by Darwin and "higher criticism" of the Bible coming from Germany. These influences especially impacted the more educated ranks, while evangelists like D. L. Moody continued to evangelize the working class. The Christian movement in America began to be far less optimistic about broadly impacting the evils in society and focused more exclusively on evangelism, which Winter calls "church mission."

This era is marked by a polarization between mission priorities. According to Winter, one focus was toward people, getting them saved and into church fellowships. The opposite pole was primarily focused on the advance of God's kingdom against evil. Those who focused primarily on evangelism tended to view social action as a distraction to getting people saved and the Church established. On the other side, those who worked toward social transformation tended to neglect building the Church. It was in this atmosphere that J. Hudson Taylor went to China and heard God's call to push inland. His concern was that missionaries to China ought only to evangelize. He later broadened the range of activities in his mission, but he well represents the mood of this era.

C. **The Third Era,** beginning in 1935, was pioneered by Cameron Townsend and Donald McGavran. Both of them, in different ways, brought attention to the fact that many ethnically unique groups of people remained unreached by the gospel. In this era, the unreached people groups of the world were identified as the "final frontier" of the gospel.

Winter notes that during the third era, there has been some recovery from the "Fundamentalist/Modernist" controversies that dominated the first half of the 20th century. Winter offers evidence that evangelicals are once again becoming more optimistic about the impact of the kingdom of God on the evils of this world, and calls this a return to "kingdom mission." Winter hopes for an era in which the Church's good works go well beyond the call to do individual good works, in order to pursue organized efforts dealing with major global problems, such as the eradication of disease, similar to the abolition of slavery in the days of Wilberforce.

Read Winter, "Three Mission Eras," pp. 263-278 (all)

Conclusion of Key Readings for this lesson. 

III. The New Macedonia

In 1974, Ralph Winter addressed the Lausanne Congress on World Evangelization in a way that brought much-needed light to the confusion of the second transition. By calling for a new thrust of mission to the bypassed people groups, Winter helped many recognize the malady which he called "people blindness." Winter later titled his paper "The New Macedonia," after the call for help in Acts 16:9. The influence of this address has been widespread and longstanding. You will read only a portion of it here.

A. **To Finish the Task.** Winter identifies three different kinds of evangelism, distinguished by the cultural distance that the evangelist spans in communicating effectively with intended hearers.

1. **The "E-Scale"** has been a widely used reference tool for describing and comparing evangelistic difficulties and needs.

   - **E-0:** Evangelism of people who are part of Christian families and peoples. It is basically catechism and renewal. No real cultural barriers are crossed.
   - **E-1:** Evangelism of people outside the church but within one's culture. Only one barrier is crossed: the "stained-glass" membership boundaries of the church. This kind of evangelism is the "most powerful" because people are far more likely to understand what is being communicated in ways that they can pass on to others like themselves.
   - **E-2:** Evangelism of people from different but similar cultures. Two barriers are crossed: the "stained-glass" barrier and an additional cultural distance sufficient to require separate church fellowships.

- **E-3:** Evangelism of people from radically different cultures. To emphasize the greater cultural distance of an evangelist attempting to communicate to a very different and potentially hostile environment, it is supposed that evangelists attempt to cross at least three barriers in E-3 efforts. For example, for Americans to work with Saharan nomads it would require crossing the "stained-glass" barrier, a language barrier and a major lifestyle barrier. E-3 is the most difficult kind of evangelism.

2. **Cultural Rather Than Geographical Distance.** Winter uses Acts 1:8 as a rough parallel to the distinctions of the E-Scale. Geography does not matter nearly as much as the breakthrough to culturally different people groups.

B. The Master Pattern of Evangelism was, according to Winter in 1974, "first for special E-2 and E-3 efforts to cross cultural barriers to establish strong, evangelizing denominations, and then for that national church to carry the word forward on the really high-powered E-1 level." E-3 evangelism is essential so that the more powerful E-1 evangelism can be done by the newly planted churches.

C. People Blindness refers to a limited outlook that fails to notice the sub-groups within a country. The blindness is a significant barrier to developing effective mission strategy. Society should be seen, as McGavran suggested, as a complex mosaic of peoples. God loves and values each people group within the larger mosaic of society.

Read Winter, "The New Macedonia," pp. 347-351 and 353a-354a (beginning with "However, the truth about the superior...")

E-Scale

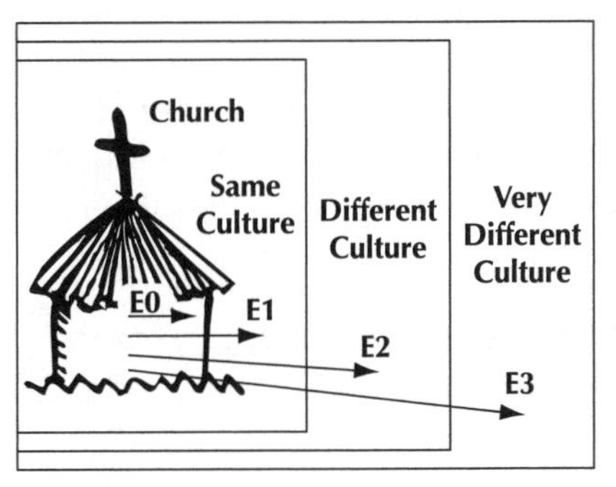

P-Scale

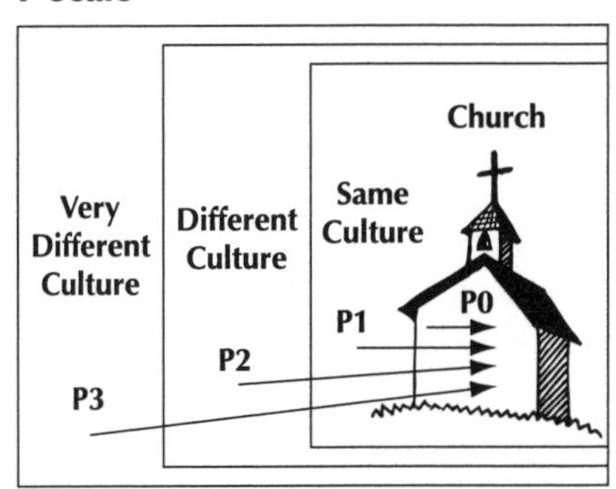

D. The "P-Scale" was also developed by Winter, years after the Lausanne Congress in 1974. The P-Scale looks at evangelization from the vantage point of unevangelized peoples. It evaluates the cultural distance that potential converts need to move in order to join the church most relevant to their own culture. It's important to grasp the difference of the E-Scale and the P-Scale. The E-Scale gauges the cultural distance crossed by those who do evangelism. The P-Scale looks at the cultural distance that those who are evangelized would be required to cross in order to be part of an existing church. The P-Scale and E-Scale correspond to the barriers dubbed the "Wall and the Canyon" by Hawthorne, on pages 140-141.

- **P-0:** Identifies church members who need spiritual renewal. No distance lies between them and following Christ according to the customs of their church. It is more a matter of revival.
- **P-1:** Identifies people who live in cultures which have a culturally-relevant local church movement capable of evangelizing them.
- **P-2:** Identifies people who live in a culture that has no church relevant to their people group, but there is a church in a "near" culture. To follow Christ, the potential convert would have to cross both a culture barrier as well as the "stained-glass" barrier by adopting the social and cultural values of a local church within a people other than their own.
- **P-3:** Identifies people who live in a culture without a relevant church. There are no nearby cultures similar to their own within which churches have been established. To follow Christ, they would have to surmount significant cultural and social boundaries.

IV. The Bridges of God

Donald McGavran is one of the previously mentioned pioneers who set in motion the Third Era of Protestant missions. We will read an excerpt from his influential book, *The Bridges of God*. His lasting contribution is the call to evangelize entire peoples who are culturally isolated from the gospel.

A. Western Individualism. McGavran says that Western individualism has long obscured the way that most people throughout history have ever become Christian. (In the full text of the book, McGavran substantiates this point with examples from many parts of history.) Because peoples are not readily seen, people movements are often not recognized.

B. Peoples and Multi-Individual Decisions. McGavran defines what is meant by "a people" and describes the dynamic of group decisions to follow Christ.

C. People Movements. These movements—marked by a group decision to follow Christ but also to retain its identity and social relationships as a people group—should intentionally be sustained and nurtured to maturity. Achieving "a people movement to Christ" is McGavran's original phrase. This is another way to describe the essential missionary task as mentioned by Winter.

Read McGavran, "The Bridges of God," pp. 335-338a

V. Expecting a Great Harvest

Patrick Johnstone, author of the early editions of the well-known prayer volume, *Operation World*, summarizes the phenomenal hope of completing world evangelization. He provides another look at the biblical basis for that hope and then sums up the increase of the gospel over the centuries.

A. The Spread of Christianity Through History. Note that the period of most rapid expansion, from 1800 to the present, is the same 200-year period as the "Three Eras." In his graph, "The Spread of Christianity," Johnstone introduces David Barrett's model of "Worlds A, B and C" as ways of looking at the earth in terms of individuals being exposed to the gospel. "World A" is rapidly disappearing. This is what you would expect to see as evangelizing churches are planted within every people.

Worlds A, B and C (exposure to the gospel)	E-Scale (kind of evangelism required)
World C: All individuals who would identify themselves as Christians.	**E-0:** Evangelism of those who would call themselves Christians or who are participating in a local church though not yet true believers.
World B: All non-Christians who live within societies where they have heard or are likely to hear the gospel during their lifetime.	**E-1:** Evangelism of non-Christians within the same culture as the evangelist.
World A: All non-Christians who are "unevangelized" (not adequately exposed to the gospel) and are likely to remain so without a pioneering effort by Christians to bring the gospel to them.	**E-2:** Evangelism of non-Christians within cultures that are similar to the culture of the missionary. **E-3:** Evangelism of non-Christians within cultures that are very different from the culture of the missionary.

B. Two Millennia of Evangelizing Peoples. Johnstone also gives us a similar view of the world in terms of ethnolinguistic peoples. Again the number and percentage of peoples that are unreached continues to shrink as missionaries of the Three Eras have gone to the nations. Some day there will be no more P-2 or P-3 non-Christians beyond the reach of evangelizing churches (represented by the black area in the chart on page 217). This is what we mean by the term "world evangelization." On the other hand, the number of unreached peoples is constantly expanding as we discover that most ethnolinguistic peoples are actually clusters of smaller peoples!

C. Discipling the World's Peoples. Johnstone shows a breakdown of the world's ethnolinguistic peoples according to those which are predominantly Christian; those which are not predominantly Christian but have had a "missiological breakthrough;" and the people groups which are still "pioneer fields" requiring mission endeavor. Even though there are thousands of ethnolinguistic people yet to be evangelized, we can rejoice that work has already begun in more than half of them!

Read Johnstone, "Expecting a Harvest," pp. 382-386 (all)

VI. The Growing Non-Western Mission Force

Beram Kumar and Bruce Koch describe the maturity, vigor and diversity of the non-Western mission force.

A. Already Effective. Kumar highlights how non-Western missionaries are already especially effective because of trends such as migration and increasing government restrictions. Non-Western missionaries have been particularly effective in the midst of crisis and disaster relief and in settings in which only trans-national tentmaking teams can function well. Kumar calls for an increase of partnership between missions of the West and their non-Western counterparts as "equal and able partners." He anticipates a "powerful end-time harvest" as these partnerships increase.

B. Already More Missionaries From the Non-West. There is a difference between foreign and cross-cultural mission. *Foreign mission* means working in another country. *Cross-cultural mission* does not only take place in foreign countries. Many non-Western missionaries do cross-cultural work in their home countries. Some estimates of the numbers of Western and non-Western missionaries only considered whether the missionaries were foreign. When the totals of missionaries from the West and from the non-West include both foreign and domestic cross-cultural workers, it becomes clear that the number of non-Western missionaries is growing at a much faster rate than many realized—as much as eight times faster than those from the West during the 1990s. It is projected that the number of non-Western cross-cultural missionaries surpassed those from the West sometime around 2005.

Read Kumar, "No Longer Emerging," and Koch, "The Surging Non-Western Mission Force," pp. 369-370

Do you not say,
"There are yet four months,
and then comes the harvest?"
Behold, I say to you, lift up your eyes, and look on the fields,
that they are white for harvest.
Already he who reaps is receiving wages
and is gathering fruit for life eternal;
so that he who sows and he who reaps may rejoice together.
For in this case the saying is true,
"One sows, and another reaps."
I sent you to reap that for which you have not labored;
others have labored, and you have entered into their labor.
— John 4:35–38

Jesus took His followers on a training mission to Samaria. He wanted them to see the immensity of the harvest as well as the interdependency they would need to complete the task. Read Jesus' words in John 4:35-38. What does it mean to "enter the labor" of another person? Have you ever done this? Is it possible for you to take part in the huge harvest ahead without involving the partnership of other generations or cultures?

VII. The Coming of Global Christianity

Philip Jenkins says that in the last century, the "center of gravity" of Christianity (that is the bulk of the number of followers), gradually shifted to the south, away from the northern areas of Europe and North America. Already the largest Christian communities are in Africa and Latin America. Looking ahead, it is important to note that the increase of numbers is only one aspect. The changes of the coming decades will be much more sweeping than an increase in numbers. Expect many different patterns, styles and forms of Christianity to be practiced. In Todd Johnson's words (on page 391c), we should expect "new cultural forms of Christianity" or "Christianities."

Read Jenkins, "The Next Christendom: The Coming of Global Christianity," sidebar, pp. 390-391

Conclusion of Certificate Readings for this lesson. 

After studying this section you should be able to:

- Describe a "people movement."
- Recognize features of the "Mission Station" approach in modern mission efforts.
- Recognize features of "Christward movements" in modern mission efforts.
- Explain the significance of the Student Volunteer Movement's watchword.

VIII. Farewell to "The Great Century"

We return to McGavran's assessment of the strategic approach in the first two eras of Protestant mission. We need to understand this pattern very well so that we do not inadvertently slip into an approach which fits the colonial era. Western individualism, when combined with a sense of cultural superiority, can sometimes divert well-intentioned missionaries into repeating a subtle form of the mission station approach. Many of the early workers of the Second Era ignored both the hard-won wisdom of First Era missionaries, as well as the lessons to be gained from mistakes.

A. **Across the Gulf of Separation: Exploratory Mission Station Approach.** Missionaries encountered great cultural differences. The usual approach was to establish a mission station and draw converts in a "gathered colony" style. The pattern of conversion was extraction from family, culture and relationships. Evangelism was slow and often reached some of the least influential of the community. McGavran does not criticize missionaries for beginning their work in this way. In his view, it fit the colonial era as the best possible strategy.

B. **The Fork in the Road: Mission Station or People Movement?** McGavran describes the mission station approach as a road on a flat plain which branches toward a steep high road of the people movement approach. Great hopes for large movements were often frustrated because of the vicious cycle of extracting converts out of their people. This led to a meager response, which in turn produced a mentality that abandoned the vision of large people movements following Christ. In contrast, there were several significant occasions of people movements. These were usually not sought by the missionaries and, in fact, were often resisted by them.

C. **Resulting Churches Contrasted: Gathered Colony vs. Christward Movements.** Gathered colony churches are dependent on missionaries. On page 341, McGavran describes how missionaries were somewhat successful during the First and Second Eras, but came to be inundated by demands of pastoring and governing the institutionalized churches, schools and hospitals that were established. There was often a vested interest in the status quo and little sustained effort to evangelize beyond the immediate vicinity of the mission station. In contrast, the Karen and the Chura case studies on page 342 exemplify the dynamism of people movement churches. Take note that in both cases, an early convert from their people was far more influential than the foreign missionary. In both cases, missionaries (even the notorious Adoniram Judson!) were doubtful of the value and appropriateness of these movements. God blessed the movements anyway. McGavran's point is that missionaries must now recognize the beginnings of such God-given movements and seek to enhance them.

Read McGavran, "The Bridges of God," 338a-344c

IX. Student Power in the Three Eras

The three great waves of Protestant missionaries did not suddenly appear out of thin air. Their work was always birthed and marked by sustained united prayer and the mobilizing zeal of students. Ralph Winter has observed that a student movement was associated with each of the eras.

A. **First Era Fuel: The Haystack Prayer Meeting.** Samuel Mills, impacted by the Great Awakening, joined other students in a gathering that met by a river, and during a storm, they took refuge under a haystack. This particular meeting was the initial impulse for much of the early American missionary enterprise. They formed "The Society of the Brethren" with the goal of mobilizing others for missions.

B. **Second Era Fire: The Student Volunteer Movement.** Howard says that no single factor has wielded a greater influence in the worldwide outreach of the Church in modern times than the Student Volunteer Movement (SVM). Their watchword was "The evangelization of the world in this generation." Key leaders were John R. Mott, Robert Speer, Robert Wilder, Samuel Zwemer and A. T. Pierson. Howard describes the features of the SVM's decline because present-day movements of mission mobilization could repeat the same mistakes.

C. **Third Era Fusion: The Student Foreign Missions Fellowship and Inter-Varsity.** The SFMF was formed specifically to continue and extend the mission mobilization vision of the SVM. A few years later, the SFMF became the Missionary Department of Inter-Varsity Christian Fellowship, widely known for the Urbana student missionary conventions. The U.S. Center For World Mission (USCWM) and other mobilization structures continue mobilization of students, lay people and local churches. Mobilization of missionaries in non-Western countries is being done by a multitude of diverse movements.

Read Howard, "Student Power in World Missions," pp. 305-311 (all)

X. New Sending Movements

On pages 371-375, you'll find a collection of seven brief summaries, describing the exciting rise of sending movements from different parts of the world. Get acquainted with the truly global movement that you are a part of. As one person put it, mission is no longer, "from the West to the rest."

Choose any two of the seven reports on pp. 371-375.

8 Pioneers of the World Christian Movement

Studying this lesson will help you:

- Describe the commitment and zeal of "First Era" missionaries.
- Describe how Carey, Taylor and Townsend mobilized others to complete world evangelization.
- Explain the rationale that William Carey used to argue that the Great Commission was a binding mandate for believers in the present day.
- Explain why it is important for the global Church to understand the present state of the world in terms of evangelization.
- Explain how Carey's motto, "Expect great things from God. Attempt great things for God," helps explain the attitude and actions of the mission movement pioneers.
- Explain why Hudson Taylor founded a mission agency.
- Explain why Cameron Townsend began translating the Bible.
- Describe the ways that women have been an important part of mission efforts throughout history.
- Explain how the Moravian community is exemplary to the Church today in areas of motivation and persistence.

In this lesson we will meet some of the key figures of the past 200 years. These people did not wait for someone else to go first; they opened the way for others. The only word that accurately describes them is "pioneers."

Why should we examine the lives and words of these pioneers? One reason is that they gave us something: a world almost evangelized—a nearly complete task. It would be foolish for us to respond to the needs of the world as if it had been our idea to evangelize it. God Himself began it all, and worthy people throughout the generations have each finished their part. Some knew that they were laying down their lives so that others would complete what they began.

One notable pioneer, David Livingstone, said to an assembly of people who had gathered to hear him tell of his ventures in Africa: "I go back to Africa to try to make an open path. Carry out the work which I have begun. I leave it with you."

All of the people you will meet in this chapter were people of prayer. They prayed that others would join them. No doubt they prayed for those who followed them years later. Is it possible that you are the answer to their prayers?

In this lesson we'll learn how one of the Second Era leaders specifically called his contemporaries to continue the task that earlier missionaries (from the First Era) left to them. We'll read the original writings of some of the key instigators of the Three Eras of Protestant mission history. We'll get acquainted with some of the women who have carried an enormous part of world evangelization. Pioneers are not solitary heroic figures. They form or are followed by apostolic movements. The Moravian movement is an example of such a pioneer fellowship.

faithful Faithful people know they are being trusted. Zeal to fulfill that trust distinguishes the faithful from those who are merely dutiful. The dutiful perform what is required, and so they are sometimes daunted in the face of sacrifice. The faithful remain dedicated to the One who entrusts them despite the high cost. Sacrifice is a light thing for them, because they have already entered into some of the joy of their Master, who commends them for being not only good, but also faithful.

I. Continuing What Earlier Generations Began

Samuel Zwemer was a leader in the Student Volunteer Movement and worked for many years in the Muslim world. Discover what he means by "inverted homesickness," "apostolic ambition," "the pioneer spirit" and "the unoccupied fields." Learn the context for memorable statements, such as, "The prospects are as bright as are the promises of God" or "I never made a sacrifice." Zwemer challenged people in his day to consider unoccupied fields. How does this compare to the call to labor among unreached peoples? Is this an identical challenge?

Read Zwemer, "The Glory of the Impossible," pp. 329-334 (all)

II. Pioneers of the Movement

In the last lesson we read the words of Donald McGavran, one of the four key leaders mentioned by Winter as being largely responsible for spearheading the Three Eras of Protestant missions. We've selected some key writings of the other three leaders. As you read, take note of several common factors. First of all, each of them displays a confidence that world evangelization will be completed. They also call for others to be involved in specific parts of the world as a strategic step toward completing the entire task. Each of them displays an awareness of the demographic details. Their efforts are grounded in Scripture, which they are convinced is the Word of God. Finally, each leader calls for prayer.

A. **William Carey.** Probably no piece of literature has motivated so many in such crucial ways as Carey's *Enquiry*. He offered a challenge to do at least as much as commercial ventures were doing, and to follow as far as commerce would go, by traveling to distant lands in order to proclaim the gospel. His exposition of the commission of Christ exposed the inadequate but common view that Matthew 28:18-20 pertained only to the first apostles and was no longer applicable.

Read Carey, "An Enquiry into the Obligation of Christians to Use Means for the Conversion of the Heathens," pp. 312-318 (all)

Consider Carey's motto:

"Expect great things from God.
Attempt great things for God."

At what points in your life have you chosen to follow God in this way? What happens when either half of the motto is followed without the other half? Is there any other way to experience great things?

B. Hudson Taylor. In the following selection, Taylor recounts the development in his sense of calling to serve as a missionary and how he felt motivated by the hope of Christ's appearing. He describes how he pursued China as a field and how he prepared for that service. He radically simplified his lifestyle because it enhanced his ministry to the poor. He then describes how and why he began the China Inland Mission.

Read Taylor, "The Call to Service," pp. 319-322 (all)

Conclusion of Key Readings for this lesson. 

C. Cameron Townsend. Several friends argued against Townsend's first vision to translate the Bible for a tribal group (one group of many thousands that would follow). He showed incredible resolve to launch a new kind of mission for an overlooked kind of people. Take note of the biblical grounds he found for establishing the mission and the biblical basis for his expectation that every tribe and tongue would be reached.

Read Townsend, "Tribes, Tongues and Translators," pp. 327-328 (all)

For the Son of Man has come to save that which was lost.
What do you think?
If any man has a hundred sheep, and one of them has gone astray,
does he not leave the ninety-nine on the mountains
and go and search for the one that is straying?
— Matthew 18:11–12

Matthew 18:11-12 was important to "Uncle Cam" Townsend. He said, "That verse guided me." Jesus asks his listeners to think about the story. Having just stated His life purpose as resolutely focusing on the lost, it becomes clear that Jesus is revealing the rationale for His own sense of priority. How might this verse shape your priorities or guide you?

III. The Present Hour

Each of the pioneers we've highlighted worked to discover how far the gospel had spread in their day. They were particularly looking to see the remaining, overlooked parts of the task. In the same spirit, Jason Mandryk summarized the "State of the Gospel" shortly after the turn of the millennium. Enjoy this readable and exciting manifesto to fulfill the task.

A. **Global Christianity.** We no longer see Christianity as primarily a Western phenomenon—Our faith is truly global. Evangelical Christianity is growing much faster than any other religion—Our faith is truly prolific. Christianity flourishes in thousands of cultures on all continents—Our faith is truly diverse.

B. **Christianity in the West.** While there are encouraging signs, Christianity is in decline in Europe and other places considered Western. Whether America follows Europe in this decline remains to be seen.

C. **Christianity in the Majority World.** Over 60% of those who consider themselves to be Christian or Christ followers are not from the West. Mandryk provides a few summary representations of each of the continental areas of the Majority World.

D. **The State of Global Mission.** Mission from the Majority World has dramatically increased. No longer is mission "from the West to the rest." Some of the most effective missionaries are being sent from the Majority World in ever-increasing numbers.

E. **The Remaining Task.** While there are Christians in every country and every geographical area, there remain billions of unevangelized people. Even though "every human being is a valid mission field," Mandryk says it's not hard to identify where the greatest concentration of unreached peoples are. He highlights the five countries of Pakistan, India, China, Nepal and Bangladesh as containing the most unreached peoples.

   At the same time, there is an imbalance of sending. By Mandryk's analysis, 27% of the world's population should be considered "unevangelized." Only 2.5% of the world's foreign missionary force is allocated to these unreached, while 80% of the world's foreign missionaries go to peoples that are already predominantly Christian.

F. **To Get the Job Done.** Mandryk highlights five essentials to finish the Great Commission soon:

   1. **Priorities** shaped by the reality of the task.
   2. **Sacrifice** to lay down careers, time and perhaps our lives.
   3. **Partnership** with churches and movements all over the world.
   4. **Unity** in working in multicultural teams.
   5. **Prayer** that is united, informed and persistent.

Read Mandryk, "State of the Gospel," pp. 361-368 (all)

IV. Women in Mission

Marguerite Kraft and Meg Crossman recount the tremendous record of women in missions. The women of earlier generations present us with marvelous examples to be admired. Kraft and Crossman tell the story in a way that effectively challenges faulty notions regarding the value and role of women in the mission enterprise. The patient leadership that women have offered in the past continues today. Women and men can find in this brief account many practical insights for how the entire Body of Christ can continue to work together to complete the task.

A. **Before the Protestant Reformation,** women had always been a part of mission efforts. The monastic tradition gave women a way to exert leadership in mission.

B. **The Beginning of the First Era.** A significant slowing down of women missionaries took place because of the policy that single women could not be sent alone, following the assumption among Protestants that missionaries should be married. Still, the women went.

C. **The Beginning of the Second Era.** In the United States, women's participation in missions during the Second Era was spurred by the Civil War, which wiped out a whole generation of men. Women, forced to emerge in leadership, began to organize their own mission boards. Gradually, however, the boards were absorbed into other mission structures and women lost the opportunity to direct the efforts.

D. **Women Excel.** There is no mission task that women have not accomplished. Women are uniquely suited for several specific endeavors. In many tasks and roles, they are essential.

E. **A Mostly Female Force.** For most of Protestant mission history, as much as two-thirds of the mission force has been female. Recognizing the wide range of roles in which women are excelling may release an even greater number and enhance the effectiveness of women in mission.

Read Kraft and Crossman, "Women in Mission," pp. 294-298 (all)

What attitudes or expectations regarding women does this article reveal or challenge? What women do you know who are currently living out this heritage? What areas can you see for further involvement of women or partnership with women?

V. Moravians: A Pioneer Movement

Colin Grant enables us to examine the Moravian movement in which we will clearly see that mission obedience is not a matter of individual heroics. Pioneering is always accomplished by working together.

A. **Spontaneous Obedience.** As Grant describes it, the Moravians were the first clearly Protestant mission "order." They lived as a community of obedience. Such a shared sense of obedience to Jesus meant that not a few mission heroes were supported by people of lesser commitment. Everyone shared a ready eagerness to obey as directed by the Holy Spirit.

B. Passion For Christ. Singular devotion to Christ did not sideline Moravians into passive contemplation. Worshipful passion for Jesus moved them into powerful mission obedience.

C. Courage in the Face of Danger. Moravians articulated their mission motivation in this way: "May the Lamb that was slain receive the reward of His suffering." Since Christ suffered and died, they did not think it was out of line for his servants to enter into difficult or painful situations.

> On October 8,1732, a Dutch ship left the Copenhagen harbor bound for the Danish West Indies. On board were the two first Moravian missionaries; John Leonard Dober, a potter, and David Nitschman, a carpenter. Both were ready to sell themselves into slavery to reach the slaves of the West Indies. As the ship slipped away, they lifted up a cry that would one day become the rallying call for all Moravian missionaries, "May the Lamb that was slain receive the reward of His suffering."
>
> *David Smithers, used with permission.*

Most of the early missionaries went out as "tentmakers," working humbly, by colonial era standards, among the people they were trying to reach, in trades such as artisans, craftsmen and farmers.

D. Tenacity of Purpose. The perseverance of the Moravians may have been cultivated in their diligence in prayer. The Moravian movement sustained a 24-hour-a-day prayer meeting for over one hundred years, seeking God's intervention for spiritual awakening and world evangelization.

E. Responsibility of the Church as a Whole. The approach of the Moravian Church may not be out of reach of many of our churches today. A sense of shared ownership filled the entire community.

Read Grant, "Europe's Moravians: A Pioneer Missionary Church," pp. 291-293 (all)

Conclusion of Certificate Readings for this lesson. 

After studying this section you should be able to:

- Describe African American involvement in missions before and after Emancipation.
- Characterize the status of world evangelization informed by the progress of various approaches.

VI. African Americans in World Missions

David Cornelius recounts the little-known history of African Americans in world mission. The relatively small number of African Americans in foreign missions may seem to suggest that this part of the Church has not been responsive to the Great Commission. But the actual story reveals a substantial heritage of stalwart obedience.

A. **Early Pioneers Before Emancipation.** Just about every denominational stream of the African American church has a history of mission obedience. It was in the hearts of African Americans, even while they were slaves, to obey the Great Commission.

- **Freedom Used for the Gospel.** Several of the pioneers of this period worked for decades to purchase their freedom and then used that freedom to serve as missionaries.
- **Back to the Fatherland.** They were sent most often to Africa and other places where African Americans were originally enslaved, such as the Caribbean.
- **Another Pioneer Named Carey.** One outstanding African American missionary was Lott Carey. He organized the African Baptist Foreign Missionary Society, the first organization established by African Americans for mission purpose.
- **Sacrifice and Partnership.** The mission ventures were funded with great sacrifice. There were requests for financial assistance from wealthier white Christians. Some were honored, others were turned down.

B. **After Emancipation.** African Americans suffered illness and death in Africa in the same way as did their white counterparts. The Baptist Foreign Mission Convention spearheaded many efforts. Decline came around the turn of the century as a result of hardships on the field and the diversion of attention to problems in America. Jim Crow laws mandating segregation and slowing the progress of African Americans toward economic and social prosperity made the struggle for human rights in America a high priority for many of the best leaders. For African Americans, the definition of missions came to include efforts for racial justice, hence the need for the term "international missions."

C. **Recent Resurgence.** There is a renewal of interest in international missions among African Americans.

Read Cornelius, "A Historical Survey of African Americans in World Missions," pp. 299-303 (all)

VII. Calling to Purpose or Compelling by Need? Or Both?

Hudson Taylor's most influential writing was *China's Spiritual Need and Claims*, in which he summarized facts from China and framed them as a call to action. Taylor wants his readers to consider "the state of these unsaved" and then consider if they are doing their "utmost to make Him known." This is powerful logic with some measure of biblical ground. It is, however, different than the approach we've taken in this course.

Our approach frames our mission as part of God's mission, as revealed in the entire story and statements of God's purpose in all of Scripture. We take very seriously the mandate Jesus gave us to complete. While we have affirmed that the realities of hell do add force and clarity to our commission, this does not seem to be the primary emphasis in Scripture. Urging people to all they can possibly do in the light of urgent need is somewhat compelling, but does not take advantage of the powerful confidence of hope that God will complete His work through His people. Taylor does rely on this stronger framework when he tells his readers to ask God how their lives align with His purpose: "Lord, what wilt Thou have me to do, that Thy name may be hallowed, Thy kingdom come and Thy will be done in China?"

Read Taylor, "China's Spiritual Need and Claims," pp. 323-326 (all)

VIII. A Symphony of Effort

Examine this chart to get a sense of how many different approaches are underway to fulfill the task of seeing church planting movements in every people. In many ways, this chart updates the facts of the need in similar ways to earlier generations, but it also includes encouraging news about how much is already happening.

Examine Koch and Markarian, "God's Symphony of Effort," p. 558

9 The Task Remaining

Studying this lesson will help you:

- Differentiate between regular and frontier mission efforts using the E-Scale and the P-Scale.
- Define and use the terms people bloc, people group, unimax people group, sociopeople and unreached people group.
- Memorize the definition of a people group in reference to evangelization.
- Explain the essential missionary task using and defining the term missiological breakthrough.
- Describe the rough percentages of the world's population who live in unreached peoples and in reached peoples.
- Recall how many unimax groups are in the four major cultural blocs of unreached peoples.
- Describe the imbalance of missionary allocation in today's world.
- Describe the importance of "mother-tongue ministry" and "mother-tongue Scriptures" for establishing churches that multiply and endure.
- Describe the value of having culturally distinct churches.
- Explain the biblical grounds for and strategic value of urban ministry.

Just as mountains can be seen more clearly from a distance, the awesome strategic possibilities of our day can be seen with better clarity by stepping back to get a "big picture" viewpoint. Throughout this course we have stepped back, as it were, from the present day by tracing the progress of God's purposes from the time of Abraham until now.

We've seen the blessing of Abraham extended to the nations. The blessing spread at an uneven pace through history but, nevertheless, God has propelled His purpose forward with unrelenting passion. As we come to the present day we have to be stunned by the magnitude of the movement to Christ. Never before have so many people followed Christ. Never before has Christ been named in so many languages and obeyed faithfully in such a myriad of cultural styles. Never before has Christ been so viciously hated or His servants so widely persecuted. Yet never before has Christ been so openly worshiped. Could we now be seeing close-up what Abraham saw from a distance? Jesus said, "Abraham rejoiced to see My day, and he saw it and was glad" (John 8:56).

As we consider the realities of our day, we will understand even more clearly what it meant for God to promise blessing through Abraham to "all the families of the earth." This lesson focuses attention on the distinctive people groups of the earth. Once we master a few concepts and definitions regarding people groups, we can assess the remaining task.

Christ has given us a very narrowly defined task to finish. We are mandated to bring about a breakthrough of kingdom communities of obedient faith in every people group. From that powerful beginning in every people group, God intends to bring forth some magnificent surprises that are samples of the fullness of His kingdom to come. God is waging His war against evil in many different ways. He is marshaling His people to fight with Him against evil of every kind in order to bring forth the abundant blessing promised through Abraham. We'll explore some of the wider vistas of spiritual war and God's mission to bring society-wide blessing in Christ's name.

strategic People pursuing a God-given vision live with strategic intent. The vision virtually captures them. They no longer dream about what *could* happen. They become convinced that certain things *must* happen. They make choices as if each day held abiding value. They are not driven by obligation. They live in the dignity and liberty of knowing that they give their utmost for God's purposes.

I. Finishing the Task

Ralph Winter and Bruce Koch describe the amazing threshold upon which we stand at this hour in history. The phenomenal progress in some parts of the world highlights the remaining task. It is crucial to comprehend the nature of the remaining task before we try to quantify it.

A. Amazing Progress. Amazing progress has been made in the fulfillment of God's promise to bless all the nations through descendants of Abraham. The sheer numerical increase is astounding. Biblical faith is growing and spreading as never before in history. There is at least one active Christian out of every ten people in the world.

B. Tragic Reality. Social and cultural realities greatly inhibit the progress of the gospel. The gospel readily "spreads" within peoples where it has been established, but it does not easily "jump" from one group to another because of prejudicial barriers between peoples. The result is that billions are left isolated from the gospel. They might be able to hear and understand the gospel but may view Christian practices as alien or hostile to their culture. From their perspective, it is virtually impossible for them to openly follow Christ without abandoning their cultural identity and significant relationships.

C. Two Viewpoints on Evangelism Define Two Categories of Mission. The reason many do not follow Christ is not that evangelists can't get to them but that people can't find ways to belong to a church fellowship without losing their cultural identity.

1. **E-Scale and P-Scale: Two Viewpoints On the Process of Evangelization.** We are reviewing these scales which were introduced in Lesson 7 to help us grasp the nature of the task before us. They represent two ways of looking at evangelism: from the evangelist's viewpoint and from the potential convert's viewpoint.

    - **E-Scale—Evangelist Distance:** the cultural distance between evangelists and potential hearers of the gospel.
    - **P-Scale—People Distance:** the cultural distance between potential converts and churches that may welcome them into fellowship.

Read Winter and Koch, "Finishing the Task: The Unreached Peoples Challenge," pp. 531-533b. See the E-Scale and P-Scale diagrams, p. 532

2. **What is a Missionary?** There is a tendency to define "missions" as any Christian work that takes place at a significant geographical distance. A missionary is then understood to be one who is on a foreign or distant "field." For clarity, it is better to understand a missionary to be a worker laboring to reach people of a significantly different culture (E2 or E3). By contrast, an evangelist is one who labors to reach others of their own culture (E0 or E1). The work of evangelism may have a great deal of missionary intent. However, to distinguish the different roles of evangelists and missionaries, it is best to reserve the term "missionary" for those doing, mobilizing for or laboring in direct support of those doing cross-cultural work.

3. **Regular and Frontier Mission.** Almost every mission effort can be classified under one of two categories:

   - **Regular Mission:** Cross-cultural Christian work that spreads the gospel within people groups where churches have already been established (P0-P1).
   - **Frontier Mission:** Cross-cultural Christian work that seeks to establish churches within people groups where it does not yet exist (P2-P3).

   The kind of mission effort required in the latter category is different enough to warrant different strategies, methods and workers. That's why the special category of "frontier mission" is needed to describe church planting efforts among unreached people groups. There is no value judgment implied in drawing the distinction between regular and frontier missions. Both are necessary. Frontier mission efforts, however, have a strategic priority in completing the overall task.

   Example: An American missionary in Papua New Guinea teaches people who are already Christians from a jungle tribe to read the Bible in their own language. Their tribal church is thriving. Literacy will help them train pastors and lay leaders. The tribal culture is a very different culture (E3), but the missionary is working with Christians in their own culturally-relevant church (P0). This vital mission endeavor would come under the category of "regular mission."

   On the other hand, people from the same American church as the above missionary might only have to cross the street from the American church to be categorized as missionaries. If they were to work with displaced Kurdish refugees from Iraq, where there is presently no thriving Kurdish church, their work (even though it takes place in an American city) would be cross-cultural work (E2 or E3), and therefore be considered missions. Furthermore, their work would be among a people group lacking a church movement of their own, and therefore be categorized also as "frontier mission" (P2 or P3).

See "Regular Missions and Frontier Missions" chart, p. 538

D. **A Witness to All the Nations.** Matthew 24:14 helps us to understand what Christ expects us to have accomplished before He returns. Jesus states the mission goal of the Church in terms of the "gospel of the kingdom" being proclaimed globally. There are two important qualifying expressions that have everything to do with the completion of the task: "as a witness" and "to every people." We can't be precisely sure what Jesus meant by either phrase, but they raise the right questions to envision the total task before us.

   - **What is "a Witness?"** Is there some kind of demonstration and declaration of the gospel of the kingdom that is a minimal achievement towards which we should aim? The rest of Scripture and God's work in history provide some powerful ways of understanding how the gospel of the kingdom is declared and displayed.
   - **Who are "the Peoples?"** Some translations render the Greek phrase *panta ta ethne* as "all nations," which brings to mind politically defined countries. As we've already explored in Lesson 4, this same phrase occurs in Matthew 28:19. It actually refers specifically to ethnic groups or people groups. Who are these people groups? How are they defined? How many are there?

Read Winter and Koch, "Finishing the Task: The Unreached Peoples Challenge," pp. 533b-534a

II. The Unreached Peoples Challenge

There are four main ways that the term "people group" is being used today. We need to become acquainted with each one and use them appropriately. When our thinking about people groups is fine-tuned, it will help us work together with strategic clarity.

A. **Blocs.** *Blocs of peoples are a limited number of summary categories into which we can place peoples in order to analyze them.* These blocs can help us talk about all the unreached people groups on earth. There are two commonly used sets of blocs:

1. **Major Cultural Blocs.** Muslim, Hindu, Buddhist, Ethno-Religious, Non-Religious and Others. The majority of unreached peoples can be found within these blocs. Because religion significantly affects culture and worldview, these cultural blocs are identified by the predominant religion within the groups that make up each bloc. This does not mean that every person in those groups is an adherent of that religion.

2. **Affinity Blocs.** Patrick Johnstone and others have presented another way of grouping the peoples according to shared elements of language, history, culture, etc.

B. **Ethnolinguistic Peoples.** *An ethnolinguistic people is an ethnic or racial group distinguished by its self-identity with traditions of common descent, history, customs and language.* The value of the ethnolinguistic people approach is that it provides an easy way to identify peoples so as to mobilize prayer and stimulate initial planning. Since features of race and language are easily counted, lists of ethnolinguistic peoples tend to be stable. Ethnolinguistic peoples do not correspond to countries. A single country can have thousands of ethnolinguistic peoples. By the same token, a single ethnolinguistic people can be spread over a dozen different countries. Examine the Nigeria example on page 533.

C. **Sociopeoples.** *A sociopeople is a relatively small association of peers who have an affinity for one another based upon a shared interest, activity or occupation.* Sociopeoples are not necessarily groups which require a special church planting effort. They may require special evangelistic tactics, but not a full-blown church movement. On the other hand, they are very significant sets of people for preliminary evangelism as an intermediate bridge to long-range church planting goals. We can only estimate the number of sociopeoples since the different networks and social sets are virtually endless.

D. **Unimax Peoples.** *A unimax people is the* ***max****imum sized group sufficiently* ***uni****fied to be the focus of a single people movement to Christ.* The unimax approach helps identify the boundaries which hinder the flow of the gospel. At the same time, a unimax understanding helps indicate where dedicated Christians need to begin yet another effort of evangelization beyond boundaries of cultural prejudice. If widely applied, it will mean that no smaller group will be "hidden" from the view of missionaries in the midst of a larger ethnolinguistic group.

1. **An Affirmed Definition.** See "Mission Leaders Agree on Strategic Definitions" at the bottom of page 536. Memorize the definition of a people group: *For evangelistic purposes a people group is the largest group within which the gospel can spread as a church planting movement without encountering barriers of understanding or acceptance.* There have been others who have suggested different definitions of peoples. This important 1982 definition carries the weight of broad affirmation at the time of its formation and has proven useful for both field practitioners and sending churches to envision what should be the focus and the outcome of their work.

2. **Why Are There Different Counts of Unreached Peoples?** Different researchers use different criteria for defining peoples and for assessing their access to the gospel. Some mission leaders base their numbers on lists of ethnolinguistic peoples, others use estimates of the number of unimax peoples.

3. **More Unimax Peoples Than Ethnolinguistic Peoples.** The gospel "spreads" but does not easily "jump" over the barriers of hatred and fear that fragment the world's peoples. Even within a group with a shared ethnicity and language (an ethnolinguistic people), the social distinctions can prove to be daunting barriers for would-be converts. Instead of requiring such eager-to-believe people to divorce themselves from their own people group in order to follow Christ, we should make every attempt to establish a movement of people following Christ within every group.

4. **Can They Be Counted?** The unimax peoples definition was never intended to precisely quantify the total task. Instead, it helps us recognize where the frontier mission task is finished and identify where that task has not yet begun.

E. **Using All Four Definitions.** Each of the four understandings of people groups is helpful:

- **To summarize** the total task, use the idea of *blocs* of unreached peoples, whether major cultural blocs or affinity blocs.
- **To mobilize** prayer and awareness, or to initiate field action and partnerships, use *ethnolinguistic* distinctions.
- **To begin work evangelizing** an unreached people, start by identifying the *sociopeoples* which may serve as bridges to convey the gospel to the entire people group.
- **To plant churches** among an unreached people, use the *unimax* approach to identify the extent of the people you are reaching. New unimax peoples are discovered as we become aware of groups that will be bypassed by current efforts.

F. **A Note of Caution.** We need to avoid the notion of viewing the world's population as sets of distinct, non-overlapping, bounded sets of people with clear boundaries. The prejudicial barriers are often hard to discern. Powerful forces of urbanization, migration, assimilation and globalization are constantly working to change the composition and corporate identity of people groups everywhere.

Read Winter and Koch, "Finishing the Task: The Unreached Peoples Challenge," pp. 534a-537, and review chart on p. 534

III. The Essential Missionary Task

God has given us a mandate to accomplish. As we complete that mandate, it sets in motion all kinds of opportunities for God's people to co-work with Him in bringing healing and hope to the nations. The blessing of Abraham only begins with the message of salvation. Entire societies need to be transformed by God's work through the gospel, but it can only happen after a missiological breakthrough has occurred.

A. **Missiological Breakthrough.** The missionary task must never be understood as missionaries proclaiming the gospel to every person. Christ indeed wants every person to hear, but not from missionaries! The missionary task is to bring about the beginning of a gospel movement in every people, so that the people of that given culture will eventually hear the gospel communicated by someone from their own people group.

1. **The Essential Missionary Task** is to establish a *viable, indigenous church planting movement* within every people that carries the potential to renew whole extended families and transform whole societies.
   - **Viable**—growing on its own.
   - **Indigenous**—not seen as foreign.
   - **Church Planting Movement**—continuing to reproduce intergenerational fellowships capable of evangelizing the rest of the people group.
2. **Closure** is a term usually referring to establishing a breakthrough in every people group on earth. Closure was expressed powerfully by the watchword for the frontier mission movement, "A Church For Every People by the Year 2000."
   - **A Church**—not "the" Church, but rather an indigenous, locally-relevant church; not just one congregation, but a multiplying movement.
   - **For Every People**—every one of the unimax people groups of earth.
   - **By the Year 2000**—some overemphasized the importance of the year 2000. The watchword, coined in 1979, used the millennial milestone to draw attention to the exciting possibility of bringing about closure in a relatively short period of time if the vast resources of the Church were mobilized. The year 2000 passed without establishing a church within every people, yet thousands of groups were reached. But possibly of greater significance is the fact that the watchword succeeded in convincing believers around the world that the goal of "A Church For Every People" must, can and will be completed.
3. **Verifiable Progress.** Reaching peoples and establishing a breakthrough is a process. We may not be able to precisely *quantify* the progress toward closure, but it is important that we attempt to *verify* progress. Several commonly used progress scales are helpful. Patrick Johnstone has utilized a scale called the Church Planting Indicator.

   By our definition, a group would only be "reached" once they have a verifiable church planting movement capable of evangelizing their own people (level four on the CPI scale). Since some recently engaged groups now have churches but do not yet have a full blown church planting movement, some people prefer to speak of them as "least-reached peoples."

B. Beyond Breakthrough. We use the language of breakthrough because, for the first time, churches are established which express Christ's operative Lordship in the people group.

- **A "Testimony" of His Kingdom.** These churches become communities of glad-hearted obedience and submission to His Lordship. The new church, with or without the participation of missionaries, becomes the primary agent of God's blessing, another manifestation of the seed of Abraham. The blessing of His kingship becomes observable and accessible to the community, and the new churches provide a persuasive sign, we might even say a "testimony," of God's kingdom.
- **Closure Opens the Way for More.** Planting churches will not end our mission. In many ways, such closure will actually open the way for many great things. Many mission endeavors aim at fighting evil and manifest the kingdom through relief and community development efforts. While this is right and helpful, an important strategic priority is the planting of a viable church, which is the beginning of all that will bear lasting fruit.

Read Winter and Koch, "Finishing the Task: The Unreached Peoples Challenge," pp. 538-542d

This gospel of the kingdom shall be preached
in the whole world as a testimony to all the nations,
and then the end will come.
— Matthew 24:14

If the phrase "whole world" has to do with geography, and the phrase "all the nations" has to do with the groups of humanity, what kind of situation is Jesus saying will take place? What does He mean by "and then"? What kind of communication of the gospel will prove to be an adequate "testimony" to the nations?

IV. Looking at the Task Graphically

The concepts we've learned will help us make sense of the status of the World Christian Movement and the crucial need of the hour.

A. The Status. The "All Humanity in Mission Perspective" chart on page 541 summarizes the status of world evangelization in terms of the major cultural blocs, adherence to Christian faith and access to the church within one's own culture. The remaining graphics in this lesson are derived from this chart.

- **The Globe at a Glance.** The pie chart on page 540 displays the "All Humanity in Mission Perspective" data in an accessible visual fashion. The white areas represent all of the non-Christians living within unreached peoples. To better understand this chart, imagine a Hindu group that has an indigenous church planting movement but is still predominantly comprised of adherents to Hinduism. Thus you can have "practicing Christians" within the Hindu wedge.

- **How Many Unreached People Groups?** Using the unimax definition, the best estimate is 8,000. Most are found in just four major cultural blocs: Muslim (3,300 groups), Hindu (2,400 groups), Ethno-Religious (1,200 groups), and Buddhist (700). Remember that there are unreached people groups in the Non-Religious and Other Religions blocs as well. See "The Globe at a Glance" pie chart.

B. The Great Imbalance. The same basic data is arrayed in different ways on the "The Great Imbalance" chart on page 543 and the "Distribution of Missionaries in Proportion to World Population" chart on page 545. A key comparison is the number of missionaries allocated to reached peoples and unreached peoples. Only 10% of the global evangelical mission force is presently focusing on the 40% of the world's population that are currently beyond the reach of the Church. This means that the majority of non-Christians have never even met someone who follows Christ from their own culture. Two qualifying facts make this even more striking:

- **Consider the Even Greater Imbalance of Full-Time Workers.** The imbalance would be more apparent if we included all full-time Christian laborers such as music pastors and youth workers. The point is not that we need fewer pastors but that we need more missionaries.
- **Consider the Relative Difficulty.** Evangelizing unreached peoples is far more difficult than working with unbelievers who live in cultures already saturated with the gospel.

What kind of allocation would we like to see? Wouldn't it seem more appropriate to see at least 40% of the evangelical mission force working among the unreached peoples since they make up 40% of the world's population? How would we move toward this goal? Rather than pulling effective missionaries away from reached people groups, why not mobilize many new missionaries from the rapidly expanding global Church? The bottom chart on page 545 shows that there are more than enough resources in the world for the task—approximately 1,000 churches for every unreached people!

Read Winter and Koch, "Finishing the Task: The Unreached Peoples Challenge," pp. 542d-545

V. The Missiological Breakthrough: Mother-Tongue Churches

Barbara Grimes highlights the value of pursuing "mother-tongue ministry" in order to bring about "mother-tongue disciples" and churches that impact their entire society. Her key concern is the decision over which language to use in mission work. Too often the choice of language is based on what is expedient for the communicators instead of what is valuable for the hearers. Grimes stretches our vision beyond the question of which language will be adequate as a medium of exposure toward which language will be best for facilitating a people movement. The vision should always be more than merely bringing the message to every language. Instead, our vision needs to focus on what can happen *from* every language: worship toward God and witness to the society.

A. The Best Outcome: "Mother-Tongue" Churches. The prime value of using the local vernacular is seen in terms of enduring, fruitful churches.

B. The Expedient Distractions. Grimes points out two ways that appear to offer short-cuts through the difficulties of language-learning and translation.

- **Multilingual Populations.** Beware of attempting to use a trade language that only some members of a society may understand. Consider the perceptions and attitudes about what is foreign and what is credible. Realistically consider the number of people in that society who may lack fluency in the second language.
- **Bilingual Brokers.** Another temptation is to work through an interpreter. Leadership development is severely diminished with this method.

Read Grimes, "From Every Language," pp. 565-567 (all)

Conclusion of Key Readings for this lesson. 

VI. Globalization and Ethnicity

The dynamics of globalization affect how we understand the peoples of the world and our mission. Miriam Adeney gives a biblical and practical perspective on the idea of ethnicity in a rapidly changing, interconnected world. The boundaries and distinctives of ethnolinguistic peoples are blurring. Is a "people-specific" approach to mission still valid?

A. **Globalization Tramples Ethnicity.** The "creative destruction" of globalization tends to homogenize and devalue the particularities of cultures. How shall we respond? Ethnicity counters the dehumanizing bent of globalization. The gospel can affirm and redeem ethnicity in our world.

Read Adeney, "Is God Colorblind or Colorful?" pp. 415-416a

B. **God's View of Ethnicity.** We have already read this section in Lesson 2. Adeney argues that the value of ethnicity is found in God's creation of humanity. Ethnic identity can become idolatrous. Cultures are tainted by sin, but ethnic pride is not automatically sin.

- **God-Given Creativity** ordained that humans would create culture.
- **God-Affirmed Community** formed shared identities and (in a good sense) family pride.

C. **Ethnicity and Mission in a Globalized World.** Adeney offers four recommendations:

1. **Affirm the Local.** While we must judge patterns of idolatry and exploitation, those who pursue mission should love local culture, language, arts, industry and all that is distinctive. Avoid a one-size-fits-all approach.
2. **Be Pilgrims.** In a globalized world we should expect that cultures will increasingly overlap and change. The identity of peoples will blur and blend. Many balance multiple ethnic identities and a variety of heritages. "It is important to respect the way people identify themselves at any particular time, however much doing so may scramble our categories or lists of people groups."

3. **Build Bridges.** Forces of globalization push people to be satisfied with superficial relationships and fragmented connections. Mission efforts should aim to step into the margins and bring about profound and meaningful connections between ethnicities.

4. **Nurture Ethnic Churches.** "Ethnic churches are not only justified because they work, they are rooted in the doctrine of creation." Every church must welcome people of every race and culture. Some flourish in multicultural churches. Others treasure ethnic traditions. "Separate congregations are not bad. What is bad is a lack of love." Diverse ethnic churches have great value as they constitute a mosaic of cultures, enriching God's world.

Read Adeney, "Is God Colorblind or Colorful?" pp. 416b-422

VII. The Challenge of Cities

Cities are growing as never before in history. How does this affect our mission?

A. **The Challenge and Opportunity of Reaching Cities.** Roger Greenway surveys the explosive growth of cities and then describes why they are growing, and why poverty and great needs are concentrated there. He says that some growth, while increasing need, also increases receptivity and opportunity.

B. **Practical Issues.** Greenway lists five practical matters: poverty, racial and ethnic diversity, religious pluralism, anti-urban attitude and high cost. Much of the mission work among unreached peoples takes place in urban centers. A focus on people groups is not at odds with an emphasis on cities. To reach any city well requires that mission efforts find ways to focus on each of the diverse sociopeoples and ethnolinguistic peoples.

C. **A Theology of Ministry in the City.** The seven points that Greenway mentions add weight to his plea for mission efforts to focus on the city.

Read Greenway, "The Challenge of the Cities," pp. 559-564 (all)

VIII. Attempt Great Things

Vishal and Ruth Mangalwadi present an astounding review of the activities of William Carey. Since you have read about William Carey in Lesson 8, you understand his determination to fulfill the mandate of Matthew 28 as the primary focus of his ministry. But while attempting that "great thing," look what other great things God was accomplishing through his efforts!

Read Mangalwadi, "Who (Really) Was William Carey?" pp. 568-571 (all)

Conclusion of Certificate Readings for this lesson. 

After studying this section you should be able to:

- Explain the importance of recognizing subtle social boundaries in order to plant churches among every people group.
- Explain how good mission strategy express both faith and faithfulness while allowing for the Lordship of the Holy Spirit in mission decisions.

IX. The Mission of the Kingdom

Ralph Winter comments on the breadth of Carey's mission outreach. While the Bible never assigns the Church the task of engineering the arrival of the kingdom of God on earth, the Bible does enjoin the Church to fight evil *with* God. Is there any evil that is out of the range of Christ's cross and God's promise? While we labor to finish the Great Commission, God may give us assignments to join Him in resisting and overcoming social, spiritual and even biological evil. It's easy to agree that it would be good for diseases to be eradicated. Winter poses the provocative idea that it might be God's will in overcoming evil to eradicate diseases. Could such triumphs over evil become part of the witness to every people of the gospel of the kingdom? Winter does not move from his conviction that the mission of the kingdom centers on and begins with planting churches among every people. He calls us to consider further frontiers beyond the beginnings that church-planting breakthroughs represent in every people.

Read Winter, "The Mission of the Kingdom," pp. 572-573 (all)

X. The Challenge Before Us

Patrick Johnstone points out that Isaiah 54:1-3 promises that the gospel will not only extend to every *people*, but that it will expand to every point of *geography* and to the *cities*. He then gives detail to these three challenges.

A. The Geographic Challenge. Johnstone identifies what he calls a "Resistant Belt" and describes how this is equivalent to the "The 10/40 Window." Be sure you are aware of some of the stunning facts about this region of the world.

Read Johnstone, "Covering the Globe," pp. 547-549a

B. The Ethnic Challenge. Johnstone first describes the task of world evangelization in terms of people groups, detailing the useful ideas of affinity blocs and people clusters. Then he mentions church planting as the single most important way to reach the peoples. Johnstone lists different approaches to gospel communication that are examined for how they support church planting among unreached people groups.

1. **Scripture Translation.** Bible translation, as Barbara Grimes points out, is not merely a matter of exposing people to the gospel. The indigenous church movements we are hoping to see as a response to the gospel will usually need a mother-tongue translation and an effective literacy to use it.

2. **Literature.** Every Home for Christ (EHC) is an example of how literature ministry can be done well with a focus on new churches being planted among unevangelized people groups. EHC aims to plant "Christ Groups" in areas where there are no churches.

3. **Recording and Video Media.** Gospel Recordings works to produce evangelistic materials in every language. In doing so, they have often identified several unimax people groups that distinguish themselves by their accent, but can still use the same Bible translation. Once again, there are more unimax people groups than there are ethnolinguistic peoples. The medium of taped messages includes the phenomenal *Jesus Film* and videos.

Read Johnstone, "Covering the Globe," pp. 549a-556a, and Koch and Markarian, "God's Symphony of Effort," p. 558

4. **Broadcast Media.** Some of the most powerful radio broadcasting mechanisms on earth are missionary radio broadcasts. One of the best cooperative partnerships in world evangelization is the collaboration of missionary radio networks. Fantastic opportunities are opening up with satellite communications.

   As an example of how media is being used to support church planting among unreached peoples, read this fascinating story of how God is using radio in India to help launch gospel movements.

Read Mial, "The Impact of Missionary Radio on Church Planting," pp. 710-711 (all)

C. **The Urban Challenge.** Johnstone states that "pioneer missions" in the coming century will be focused on "the great cities of the world—a more complex and multi-layered kaleidoscope of needs." Listen to the challenge and hope brought by Johnstone and Viv Grigg, two leaders with a track record in urban ministry and a passion for the kingdom of God to break through in every city.

Read Johnstone, "Covering the Globe," pp. 556a-557

XI. The Place of Strategy

The idea of strategy strikes many in a negative way, as though strategists might displace the Holy Spirit in initiating and guiding mission efforts to true fruitfulness. C. Peter Wagner describes how most mission strategists actually understand strategy as an expression of both faith and faithfulness.

Take note of Wagner's understanding of faithfulness in light of the biblical truth of stewardship. Faithfulness, in this understanding, involves planning and working together toward success with a consecrated pragmatism. By consecrated pragmatism, Wagner means that while we should never change our doctrine or our ethical principles in order to do something that "works," we should remain flexible regarding methods.

Strategy does not eliminate the Holy Spirit. Good strategies present the Holy Spirit with plans that He can change. Good strategies also provide human co-workers a common vision around which they can unite.

Read Wagner, "On the Cutting Edge of Mission Strategy," pp. 577b-578a

10 How Shall They Hear?

Studying this lesson will help you:

- Define culture using Kwast's four layer model.
- Explain why understanding worldview is essential to effective cross-cultural communication.
- Describe what missionaries can do to communicate the gospel with sensitivity in cross-cultural settings.
- Explain how ethnocentrism shapes our perceptions and interactions with other cultures.
- Explain what it means to contextualize the gospel.
- Describe how a redemptive analogy works to help people hear the gospel.
- Explain what can go wrong when surface-level behavior is not accompanied by conviction about deep-level meaning.
- Describe the kinds of encounters that are needed to fully communicate the gospel.
- Explore the need to develop and utilize strategies for cultures that primarily consist of oral learners.

We have already seen that the gospel cannot be *discovered* by people, it must be *disclosed* to people. If the gospel were merely information, then perhaps God's plan would have been to let sincere seekers ransack the created order and piece together ideas about Him. But the gospel is not just *information*. It is essentially an *invitation* to relationship. That's why God wants everyone to get a chance to hear His invitation. He sends messengers to convey that message.

If the messengers are not sensitive as they convey the message across cultural barriers, then the message becomes only so much intercultural noise. One stereotype of a missionary is that of an arrogant, imperious bigot who imposes Western beliefs on innocent cultures. No one wants to be involved in this kind of religious propaganda. Happily, this stereotype is largely false. Most missionaries work at great length to adapt their message to the heart of another culture. In this lesson, we'll explore what missionaries have learned from Scripture and experience about how to communicate so that all may hear.

The complexity of culture explains why the gospel "spreads" powerfully within a culture, but does not "jump" easily across cultural boundaries. In this lesson we'll explore what culture is and how we can better make the jump across the cultural boundaries that have long obstructed the advance of the gospel among the least evangelized.

We'll also explore how to communicate within a culture at a deep level, and why it's important to look for keys God may have provided to communicate His truth in unique ways. Then we'll consider the cultural dimensions of the response to the gospel. What is true conversion? How does God change people without tearing them out of their culture? God wants more than a message conveyed. He wants a movement of obedience to Christ to flourish. How can new churches redeem instead of reject their home culture?

hearing We make ourselves heard everyday. To make God Himself heard is not a feat of speaking, but an act of assisted hearing. It is a marvel of heaven's power.

I. Understanding Culture

Lloyd Kwast presents a simple model of culture by taking a "man from Mars" approach, attempting to see features of culture from an outsider's point of view. He identifies four different related "layers" of culture. The deeper layers affect and give shape to the outer layers.

A. Behavior. Behavior includes customs, products, languages—just about any patterned way of doing things. This level of culture answers the question, "What is done?" or, in a more detailed way of asking, "What is the normal or appropriate way that things are done?"

B. Values. Much of behavior is dictated by a system of values: standards of conduct and judgment which guide what is good, best or beautiful. The value system often overlaps with a given culture's felt needs. "What is good or best?" is related to the question, "What is needed?" The "ought" comes from the "sought."

C. Beliefs. This level of culture answers the question "What is true?" A belief system, consisting of an array of ideas and cognitive patterns, shapes the decisions that turn values into actions. Sometimes theoretical beliefs can be held at the same time as the operative belief system. Theoretical beliefs do not usually affect values or behavior.

D. Worldview. At the heart of any culture is its worldview, answering the most basic question: "What is real?" The fundamental assumptions about reality often deal with questions about the core story, "Who are we?" "Where did we come from?" and "What is happening, or what will be happening?" Often the worldview assumptions are reflected in epic myths. Kwast says that in gospel communication, "sometimes a new...system of beliefs is introduced, but the worldview remains unchallenged and unchanged, so values and behavior reflect the old belief system."

Read Kwast, "Understanding Culture," pp. 397-399 (all)

II. Cultural Differences

Gospel communicators need to achieve more than a surface-level understanding of the cultures they enter. Awareness of these four layers of culture is essential for the gospel to be effective in a cross-cultural setting. Paul Hiebert observes:

> When we enter new cultures, we become keenly aware of the fact that other people live differently. At first we see the differences in dress, food, language and behavior. Then we learn that there are profound differences in beliefs, feelings and values. Finally, we begin to realize that there are fundamental differences in worldviews. People in different cultures do not live in the same world with different labels attached to it, but in radically different worlds.

A. Misunderstandings: Differences of Beliefs. If our impression of another culture is that it "makes no sense," then we can be sure that we are not making sense to them either. The solution is to become a learner.

B. Ethnocentrism: Differences of Feelings. Early in life we grow up as the center of our world. We are egocentric. We also grow up in a culture and assume that its ways are the right ways to do things. Ethnocentrism is based on our natural tendency to judge the behavior of people in other cultures by the values and assumptions of our own. Hiebert states, "When we are confronted by another culture, our own is called into question. Our defense is to avoid the issue by concluding that our culture is better and the other people are less civilized.... But ethnocentrism is a two-way street."

C. Premature Judgments: Differences of Values. Early reaction to the difference of other cultures can result in a negative assessment. Is cultural relativism the best alternative? Is every culture as good as any other? Every culture can be recognized for its value and integrity. But convictions about the nature of truth and righteousness require us to hold all cultures, including our own, under the judgment of biblical norms, affirming the good of human creativity, but condemning the evil.

D. Cultures Clash When Worldviews Clash. Paul Hiebert describes how two cultures clash as they meet one another. He uses this illustration as a template to advise those seeking to serve in cross-cultural settings to take care to learn the culture at deep levels of belief and worldview. "Indian culture is based on deep beliefs in purity and pollution, which touch every area of life." He says that Americans must take care to "understand how Indians see purity and pollution, and to reexamine our own beliefs of 'clean' and 'dirty.'"

Read Hiebert, "Clean and Dirty," pp. 423-424 (all)

III. Cross-Cultural Communication

The Willowbank Report urges us to contextualize the gospel with faithfulness to the original biblical presentation and with relevance to the new cultural situation. This usually means finding a unique way to present the gospel in every setting. There is no standard, universal way to express the gospel that is equally sensitive to every culture. God entrusts us with the responsibility to find the best ways to communicate His message. The Willowbank Report identifies two basic barriers that hinder cross-cultural communication of the gospel:

- The message is presented in alien cultural forms.
- Responding to the message is perceived as a threat to the culture and society.

We'll see these two barriers repeatedly in later parts of the course, usually using different vocabulary. In a sense, the gospel is truly alien. No one could have figured out this plan of salvation; it is a supracultural message from God. The gospel does challenge and change aspects of every culture and society that it touches. But both barriers can be minimized. It is our responsibility to see that the gospel is understood and to see that obstacles are not needlessly thrown before peoples responding to the gospel.

A. Understanding: The Gospel in Alien Cultural Forms. If the gospel is presented in foreign ways of thinking, it may be comprehended in some way, but it often fails to reveal the message of Christ clearly.

B. Acceptance: Threatening Social and Cultural Consequences. If the gospel is perceived as wreaking havoc on the social structure or violating the cultural values of the recipient people, it is usually rejected by all but a few.

Read the Lausanne Committee, "The Willowbank Report," pp. 512b-513b

IV. Cultural Sensitivity in Gospel Communication: Contextualizing the Message

"Contextualization" refers to efforts to present the gospel within the context of cultural and social forms that are recognized by the respondent community. We can speak of contextualization in three different ways. It can refer to communicating the *message* itself in a local context. We can sometimes use the term "contextualize" to refer to *messengers* of the gospel identifying with the people to enhance their effectiveness. We can also speak of contextualizing the *movements* of those who believe. We will discuss the contextualization of movements in Lesson 14. At this point let's focus on the idea of contextualizing the message of the gospel.

A short section of the Willowbank Report beautifully describes the work of contextualizing the gospel "with an equal degree of faithfulness and relevance." Such wisdom and sensitivity requires an "active, loving engagement with the local people, thinking in their thought patterns, understanding their worldview, listening to their questions, and feeling their burdens." Clear and faithful gospel communication is not something missionaries do on their own. Instead they work with local believers, so that "by common prayer, thought and heart-searching, in dependence on the Holy Spirit," they "may learn together how to present Christ and contextualize the gospel."

Read the Lausanne Committee, "The Willowbank Report," p. 513a-513b ("Cultural Sensitivity in Communicating the Gospel")

V. Non-Foreign Forms: Finding a Redemptive Analogy

Don Richardson asks the question that deals with the first barrier of alien forms. "Often the gospel is labeled as foreign...How can it be explained so that it seems culturally right?" Richardson calls for cross-cultural messengers to work carefully to learn the culture and history of the people in order to find ways that the message can be understood and received. He calls such a search a "culture probe." He describes some points of contact which he calls "redemptive analogies." He gives examples that show how God often prepares particular peoples to hear and understand the gospel. Later on in this lesson we will call this kind of clear communication a "truth encounter."

Read Richardson, "Redemptive Analogy," pp. 430-433a

VI. Conveying the Message Clearly: Local Forms and Messengers

We turn now to two examples of how the gospel was imparted clearly and wisely so that movements were encouraged to flourish. Watch how missionaries work with local people to encourage relevant, powerful movements by dealing with both of the barriers mentioned above: understanding and acceptance. Notice in both stories:

- teams of missionaries were involved in training and support
- the primary communicators were local people instead of missionaries
- the art forms and communication settings were culturally familiar
- the content of the message focused on Jesus as Lord
- the missionaries aimed to form multiplying churches

A. A Key Leader. Dean Hubbard tells the story of Bhimrao, an Indian believer who found sensitive ways to present the gospel that were understandable and relevant. He framed the message around their frustration with socio-economic oppression. He focused on Jesus as their rightful Lord who longed to bring them blessing. He chose forms which made sense, speaking their language and gathering them to make decisions all together. If he had urged one-by-one conversion, it may have seemed threatening. But when many were gathered, choosing Christ was seen as good for their entire people.

Read Hubbard, "A Key Leader," pp. 703a-704b

B. For "Jesus to Come Alive." Jim Gustafson reports how Thai villagers presented the gospel with sensitivity to Thai culture. Their approach was designed to "create a way for Jesus to come alive to the Northeast Thai." As you read the story, take note of the way that the message was framed as something other than a competing religion, but instead, all about Jesus who is above all religions. The expatriate missionary team helped locals gifted in "holy gab" to spread the message in many villages. The missionary team had people specializing in the arts present the message and celebrate in worship forms familiar to their culture.

Read Gustafson, "Pigs, Ponds and the Gospel," pp. 694d-695b (starting with "The ministry has one primary..." and ending with "...to be understood by them.")

VII. Transforming Worldviews Through the Biblical Story

To communicate the gospel effectively, cross-cultural workers need more than a point of contact to begin conversation or some clever way to hold interest. It is essential to connect on a worldview level. For the biblical story to be received and believed by a people, it must find place and connection within their worldview. The most powerful and simple way for this to take place is to help people see how the biblical story of the gospel fulfills the longings and hopes of their people. This requires local story-tellers who are familiar with the stories of the people and the great gospel story of the Bible. Bruce Graham sums up the importance of seeing that the nature of both worldview and the gospel is essentially a matter of story. He tells of his experience in learning how to encourage local story-tellers who were bringing about truth encounters in profound ways.

Read Graham, "Transforming Worldviews through the Biblical Story," sidebar, pp. 442-443 (all)

VIII. Communicating at a Worldview Level

Phillip Elkins tells how a team of missionaries found a way to communicate the gospel in keeping with the worldview of the Tonga people. Take special notice of two aspects of their efforts to grasp the Tonga worldview:

A. Understand Different Elements of Worldview. The missionaries worked to discover elements of the Tonga worldview that were foreign to their own. They did not immediately try to *correct* the worldview, but instead sought to *connect* with the worldview at a point of felt need.

B. Understand Their Story. A common feature of the worldview of most cultures is an underlying, defining story or collection of stories. The story can be a mythical drama or a portion of a historical saga. The story often recounts how the people group came to its present experience. For the Tonga, their defining story organized their belief that a Creator God had lived with them at one time but had left them. Gospel communication is effective when the biblical story is linked to the worldview story of the people.

Read Elkins, "A Pioneer Team in Zambia, Africa," pp. 677-681 (all)

IX. The Name and the Story of God

When a locally recognized name for God is used, instead of importing a foreign word to designate God, it is more likely that the epic stories that reflect their worldview can be connected and corrected by the biblical story. God, of course, reveals Himself in the Bible. As we found in Lesson 2, God's "fame name" is connected to the biblical story.

A. Using Indigenous Names For God. Don Richardson explores the important matter of what name is used to refer to God. Richardson suggests that using indigenous names for God can help people make sense of the biblical story in which God reveals Himself.

Read Richardson, "Redemptive Analogy," pp. 433a-436

B. A Breakthough of Understanding. Brian Hogan tells about the crucial importance of using a culturally relevant name for God.

Read Hogan, "Distant Thunder," pp. 683d-684b (the section called "Breakthrough of Understanding")

Conclusion of Key Readings for this lesson. 

X. Communicating the Gospel in Culture

Charles Kraft delves into the crucial matter of worldview to communicate the gospel in context, or to "contextualize" the gospel message. He regards worldview as a structured set of underlying assumptions. It is the deepest level of presuppositions upon which people base their lives.

A. Contextualization. To "contextualize" means to present something with regard to the cultural context. It means adapting ourselves and our presentation of God's message to the culture of the receiving people.

B. Worldview. Worldview works like a river: Surface behavior is fairly easy to observe, but it is dynamically affected by the unseen undercurrent of the assumptions by which people govern their behavior. The term "deep-level culture" refers to worldview. We need to communicate the gospel with a biblical critique of people's culture and worldview, but with profound respect for the only way of life that they have known.

C. Subsystems of Culture. There are subsystems of culture which are greatly affected by the worldview. It's tempting to present the gospel so that the religious parts of our home culture replace the religious parts of the local culture. This approach can only lead to a superficial expression of Christianity. Instead, the message must be directed so that the worldview is affected by the truth of the gospel. When the gospel affects the worldview level, then it can powerfully influence every part of that society.

Read Kraft, "Culture, Worldview and Contextualization," pp. 400-403a

I am sending you, to open their eyes
so that they may turn from darkness to light
and from the dominion of Satan to God,
in order that they may receive forgiveness of sins
and an inheritance among those
who have been sanctified by faith in Me.
— *Acts 26:17–18*

What is effective communication of the gospel? Read Acts 26:18 to find three ideas about the outcome of gospel communication: opening, turning and receiving.

Is this sequence significant? How are people's eyes opened by the gospel? Or by prayer? How do the phrases about "turning" compare with evangelism as you have seen it practiced?

XI. Worldview Change and Conversion

The gospel can be likened to a seed which must be planted and grow in the soil of local culture. Unfortunately, missionaries sometimes bring the gospel as if it were a potted plant to be transported and transplanted as a foreign life form. Kraft extends this illustration to help us understand how the churches that result from effective gospel communication almost always seem different from the churches of the missionaries' home culture. He says indigenous churches can be likened to trees that bear similar fruit yet appear much different from the "trees" of the missionaries' home culture. What is the responsibility of missionaries in the process of God transforming cultures by the power of the gospel?

A. **Worldview Change.** God intends to bring about good changes in cultures by the power of the gospel. One common mistake occurs when missionaries bring a surface-level change and fail to recognize that an alternate deep-level meaning has been applied to the change. The message of the gospel can be significantly warped. The better way to communicate the gospel is to bring understanding at the level of worldview assumptions. Missionaries can then work with local believers to find how God may be changing their surface-level culture of behavior.

Give particular attention to the analogy of the gospel sprouting and growing as a tree which on the surface may look different than the home church of the missionary, but can be a beautiful expression of the same spiritual life. The term "dynamic equivalent church" refers to a church movement that has different surface-level characteristics but expresses the meaning of the biblical message.

Read Kraft, "Culture, Worldview and Contextualization," pp. 403b-404a

B. **Allegiance Change: Conversion.** Communicating the gospel is not merely a task of getting the message across. The gospel is not simply *information to know about God*. It is an *invitation to follow God*. In our pluralistic age the vocabulary of conversion is being used less. But we need to be clear about how God wants people and their cultures to change as they follow Christ.

1. **A Radical Turning.** Conversion is essentially a change of allegiance, bringing people and their culture under the lordship of Christ.
2. **Lordship Brings Transformation.** Conversion should bring revolutionary change in three ways: worldview, behavior and relationships. (These three areas correspond to the three areas of encounter explored by Kraft next). Conversion should never "de-culturize" a follower of Christ.

Read the Lausanne Committee, "The Willowbank Report," pp. 517d-518c (from "The Lordship of Jesus Christ" to "...culture's joys, hopes, pains and struggles.")

XII. Full Encounter

Charles Kraft outlines three encounters necessary to communicate the gospel. Most Christians recognize the need for "truth encounter" in gospel communication at the cognitive level. But there are other dimensions of encounter by which the gospel brings about change throughout an entire people. Kraft identifies these three encounters. He first indicates how Jesus was involved in all three types and then describes how they can be balanced and work together.

A. **Truth Encounter Deals With Understanding.** The vehicle of action concerning this encounter is teaching.

B. **Allegiance Encounter Deals With Relationships**. The vehicle of action here is witness.

C. **Power Encounter Deals With Freedom.** The vehicle is spiritual warfare.

Each of these encounters is progressive and may unfold in different sequences. Kraft suggests these three stages to illustrate the almost endless possibilities of the way God works to bring forth the transformation of mind, loyalty and liberty that He intends. Usually all three are a part of evangelization efforts that bear fruit. Encounters of all three types should be viewed as part of the process of conversion.

Read Kraft, "Three Encounters in Christian Witness," pp. 445-450 (all)

XIII. Classic Power Encounter

Read the short but thrilling account of a classic power encounter, told by John Robb. Would you have dared to pray as they did? What other options were there for the missionary team besides the course of action they took?

Read Robb, "Strategic Prayer," pp. 163 (ending at "The Spiritual Nature of Social Problems")

XIV. Discipling Oral Learners

It is estimated that two-thirds of people on earth today are primarily "oral learners." This means that they learn best and their lives are most likely to change when communication comes to them in oral forms. The difference between oral and literate learning is much more than superficial forms or styles. Oral learners actually process information differently.

Completing world evangelization requires careful attention to be sure that the gospel is communicated and churches are multiplying in ways that oral learners can receive and achieve. Many mission organizations today are focusing on how to adjust their approaches to deal well with orality. An adaptation of a report prepared by the International Orality Network identifies five priorities to effectively disciple oral learning cultures.

A. **The Word of God Made Available Using Oral Strategies.** Certainly recordings help, but translators are finding ways of linking translations with oral forms of the Bible.

B. **Conveying the Gospel Using Oral Strategies.** Chronological Bible "storying" has been effective to communicate the gospel in ways that the hearers can immediately use to tell the gospel to many others.

C. **Discipling and Church Multiplying.** Oral strategies are being used to multiply churches.

D. **Oral Strategies Help Avoid Syncretism.** Because people are more profoundly affected on the worldview level, there is much less risk of syncretism. When the gospel or doctrinal material is conveyed in ways only used in literate cultures, there is much higher risk of a superficial grasp of the faith.

E. **Using Oral Strategies to Reach "Secondary Oral Learners."** There are millions of people who may be part of a literate culture but prefer to receive and process information in an oral learning way.

Read the International Orality Network, "Making Disciples of Oral Learners," pp. 437-439 (all)

Conclusion of Certificate Readings for this lesson. 

After studying this section you should be able to:

- Describe the value of decoding the gospel message from its original cultural setting and encoding it in a respondent culture.
- Explain the value of communicating the gospel through storytelling.

XV. Communicating Faithfully Between Cultures

Cultural barriers are not insurmountable. The message can get through. The proof is your own faith! You have come to understand the message of Christ and His kingdom in such a way that you, and many of those from your own people group, have entrusted your lives to Him. You have entered an eternal relationship with God. Do you have a perfect grasp of the truth? No. What you do understand is adequate though not perfectly accurate. Do you have a sufficient grasp of the truth to pass on the gospel to people of another culture? You likely have much more to learn—and not just about abstract theological ideas. We can be more confident of passing on the gospel in an effective and faithful way if we work to understand three worldviews: our own worldview, the worldview of the culture of Bible times and the worldview of our hearers.

David Hesselgrave describes the exciting process of communicating the gospel in a faithful and fruitful way. He presents the three-culture model popularized by Eugene Nida. The main idea is to communicate as much as possible of the biblical message with as little intrusion from influences of our own culture as possible. Because worldview operates at such a deep level of assumptions, we are usually blind to our own worldview assumptions. We can safely presume that our own grasp of the gospel is adequate but cluttered and flawed by our own cultural assumptions.

To minimize the distortion in our presentation of God's truth, we need to "decode" the message from the "Bible culture" and "encode" the message to people of the respondent culture. Be sure to understand the "Three-Culture Model" diagram on the next page (from page 426).

A Three-Culture Model of Missionary Communication

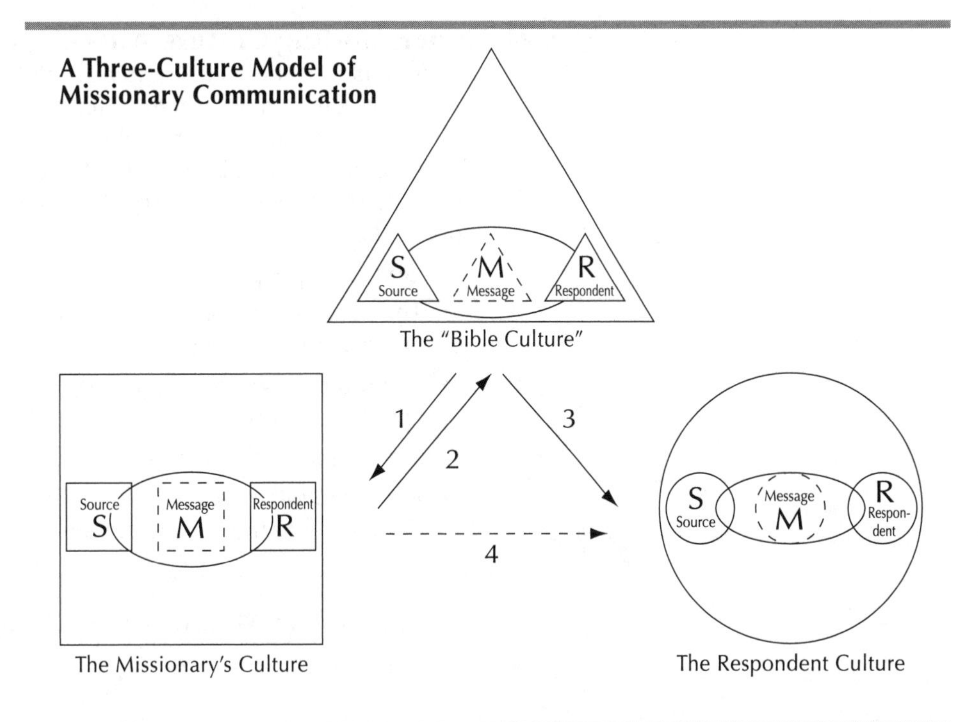

A. Back to the Bible. The first challenge of the missionary is to *decode* the truth in accordance with the most likely intended meaning of the authors. The human authors of Scripture always conveyed the truth in the dress of their culture. There are actually several different cultures and worldview elements represented in the books of the Bible. Basic humility requires us to delve into the cultural background of the stories and statements of Scripture. Then we can more accurately grasp and give the message to others. This process of Bible study is called "exegesis" (after the Greek word *exegeomai*, which means "to explain fully"). The process of interpretation is called "hermeneutics" (after the Greek word *hermenia*, which means "interpretation").

B. Finding the Best Expression. The second challenge of the missionary is to *encode* the truth in the respondent culture. The goal is to strip away as much as possible the extraneous ideas and distortions which may have come from the missionary's culture. Take note of the real purpose: to equip communicators in the respondent culture. As much as possible, missionaries should equip church leaders from the respondent culture to go directly to the "Bible Culture" and go through the same process of finding the best expression.

Read Hesselgrave, "The Role of Culture in Communication," pp. 425-429 (all)

XVI. Understanding Culture Aids Contextualization

Kraft summarizes some clear and powerful ideas about how a robust biblical theology of culture helps contextualization. The Bible is very positive about culture. It proclaims truth that transcends all cultures and is therefore relevant to all cultures. Each of these five ideas either points to biblical truth about culture or commends using the Bible itself in the ongoing process of contextualization:

- God loves people as they are culturally.
- The cultures and languages of the Bible are not special, God-made cultures and languages.
- The Bible shows that God worked with His people in culturally appropriate ways.
- God's work within a culture never leaves that culture unchanged.
- We are to follow scripture and risk the use of receptor-culture forms. We'll explore the term "syncretism" in Lesson 14.

Read Kraft, "Culture, Worldview and Contextualization," pp. 405d-406

XVII. Communicating Through Stories

Tom Steffen relates how he integrated stories into his evangelistic efforts. Storytelling can be one of the most effective ways to communicate the gospel on a worldview level. The story of what Christ has finished and will yet finish can be connected to the unfinished story of the hearers. Storytelling can become a practiced skill of gospel communicators. It's powerful and practical for everyone. Once again, notice the emphasis on the ongoing communication of the gospel beyond what missionaries themselves might convey. Storytelling not only conveys the message in a profound way, it makes it memorable and repeatable.

Read Steffen, "Why Communicate the Gospel through Stories?" pp. 440-444 (all)

11 Building Bridges of Love

Studying this lesson will help you:

- Explain how the incarnation of Christ, both His renunciation and identification, serves as a primary model for communicating the gospel.
- Describe some different aspects of humility that are crucial to missionary work.
- Describe how a missionary can begin to establish a sense of belonging in a new culture.
- Contrast the way the gospel flows in the different social structures found in urban, peasant and tribal societies.
- Explain the necessity of "bi-cultural" bridges for gospel communication.
- Describe how a missionary can maintain a single core identity as they communicate with widely different audiences of the church, the unreached and the secular world.

Missionaries can only make their message clear if they are recognized as credible messengers. How can missionaries from foreign cultures be received as trustworthy?

Ever since Paul's day, missionaries have been learning about effective relationships that span the gap between cultures. Forming relationships is essential to conveying the message in other cultures. This lesson explores how to form and extend those important relationships within different social structures.

Christ is our model. His incarnation is a tremendous pattern of identifying with the human condition and culture. Foreigners may be tolerated, but not trusted, unless they are accepted in some way as "belongers" with some understandable role in the society. How much of a "belonger" can outsiders become? Is it possible to so thoroughly identify with a new culture that people perceive the missionary as one of them? We'll find that identification has its limits. With Christ-like attitudes, however, missionaries have been learning how to humble themselves as "learners" before they assert themselves as communicators.

We'll see that the most effective communicators in any society are not missionaries, but local people who were born in that culture. Not every person communicates with equal power to others of their own society. We'll examine the fascinating possibilities of initiating gospel communication with the people who have the highest potential to lead many of their people to believe and obey Christ.

Ultimately, missionaries are not successful because they recognize intricate sociological structures or because they have mastered the local language. It is their love that opens the way for their speech. That love becomes the authentication of Christ's love. The heart of mission work is building bridges of love.

received Jesus framed the first mission very simply: "The one who receives you receives Me." It was more critical that His messengers were received than believed. The gospel has always been more than a message; it is an introduction to life under Christ's lordship. When His messengers have connected with others in significant relationships, Christ can be introduced in powerful ways.

I. A Biblical Model: Incarnation

The writers of the Willowbank Report have summarized the core issues of missionary humility and identity around the life and ongoing ministry of Jesus. When Jesus said, "As the Father has sent Me, I also send you" (John 20:21), He was not only expressing that we would be sent with the same purpose or that the ways of God mandating and guiding us would be similar, He was also saying that we should look to fulfill our ministry in the same way that Jesus accomplished His. How can we follow Jesus in His marvelous humility?

A. **An Analysis of Missionary Humility.** When considering cross-cultural communication, there are five aspects of humility worth considering:

1. **Challenged by the Importance and Difficulty.** The task of cross-cultural communication requires special effort to see beyond the limits of our own culture.
2. **Need to Understand.** Take the trouble to understand, appreciate and enter into dialogue with the cultures to which we go.
3. **Start Where People Are.** Humility seeks to begin with the needs and issues that the recipient people feel are important.
4. **Recognize Locals.** Humility recognizes the superior potential of local Christians to communicate in their culture.
5. **Trust the Spirit**. Humility relies on the Holy Spirit to do what we can never do: open the eyes of the blind and reveal Jesus.

B. **Incarnation as a Model.** With the source and model of humility found in Christ Himself, we are open to considering two large areas: sacrifice and service. Or, to use different words, renunciation and identification. Meditate on these crucial matters. How important is it to emulate our Lord in these ways to advance the gospel?

1. **Renunciation.** Jesus renounced status, independence and immunity.
2. **Identification.** Jesus took on our full situation. His example challenges our lifestyles and attitudes. The incarnation teaches identification without loss of identity.

Read the Lausanne Committee, "The Willowbank Report," pp. 514c-517a

II. Finding a Place: Building the Bi-Cultural Bridge

Communication across cultures requires relationships that span the gap between cultures. Paul Hiebert uses the term "bi-cultural bridge" to describe the critically important relationships between missionaries and their counterparts in the recipient culture.

A. **Forming Special Bridging Relationships.** A bi-cultural bridge is formed when members of two different cultures learn to understand and adapt to each others' culture, thus enabling meaningful two-way communication between the cultures. This actually results in a third culture with newly defined rules and shared assumptions. This illustrates why missionaries can never truly "go native" and become a member of the host culture.

B. Finding Effective Roles. Sometimes missionaries succeed in introducing themselves into a culture but discover later that the local people have ascribed to them unwanted roles and identities. Hiebert introduces the importance of roles and illustrates how missionaries must choose their roles carefully in order to develop effective relationships for cross-cultural communication. Before local people can consider the message, they must have an understanding of the messenger. Even before the question "Who are you?" comes the question, "What are you?"

1. **Roles in the Culture.** If missionaries fail to present themselves in appropriate roles, the people of the local culture will place them in a role that is intelligible to them. Sometimes those roles are not helpful for encouraging the kinds of friendships that enhance communication of the gospel.

2. **Roles in the Church.** Missionaries must be careful to examine the roles they are given in local culture since those same relationships are often carried over into relationships with fellow Christians. Instead of assuming a superior role or that of an authoritarian empire builder, missionaries should seek to relate to local Christians as siblings and servants, according to the biblical model.

Read Hiebert, "Finding a Place and Serving Movements Within Society," pp. 451-454b

---

Having thus a fond affection for you, we were well-pleased to impart to you
not only the gospel of God but also our own lives,
because you had become very dear to us.
For you recall, brethren, our labor and hardship, how working night and day
so as not to be a burden to any of you, we proclaimed to you the gospel of God.
You are witnesses, and so is God, how devoutly and uprightly and blamelessly
we behaved toward you believers;
just as you know how we were exhorting and encouraging and imploring
each one of you as a father would his own children,
so that you may walk in a manner worthy of the God
who calls you into His own kingdom and glory.

—1 Thessalonians 2:8–12

Read 1 Thessalonians 2:8-12. How do you see Paul expressing readiness to extend more than a message and to communicate the gospel in relationship with the people? What did Paul do to build trust? What kind of relationships were formed? Did Paul express superiority when he says that he addressed them as his own children? How does his vision of them walking after God's call make a difference in this apparent expression of paternalism?

III. Entry Roles: Becoming a Learner

A. Culture Shock: Starting Over. Hiebert says that the term "culture shock" describes the experience of people who realize that the new culture will be their life and their home. What most tourists experience is not true culture shock but what Hiebert calls "culture stress." With this distinction in mind, do most short-term missionaries experience genuine culture shock or do they experience a measure of culture stress? The cure is the same for either: Accept one's new role as a child still learning how to find one's way.

B. An Initial Role: Becoming a Learner. Donald Larson describes why the most important time of role definition that missionaries will face is when they initially enter into the culture. He says that the role of a learner serves well, because it demonstrates humility and offers dignity to the local people.

Read Hiebert, "Culture Shock: Starting Over," sidebar, p. 452, and Larson, "Closing the Gap," sidebar, p. 455

IV. Entry Relationships: Forming Effective Connection

When we consider how well the primary relationship will commend or sponsor the missionary to the rest of the community, the formation of roles and bridging relationships takes on extra complexity. Later in this lesson we'll look at how social structure affects communication throughout the community. Consider these two case studies from Wee Hian Chua, both of which recount stories involving teams consisting of two single women. Only one team was effective. Look for the concepts we've covered already in this lesson (humility, role definition and readiness to become learners).

Read Chua, "Evangelization of Whole Families," pp. 653-654b, and Kraft and Crossman, "Women in Mission," p. 294 (ending at "...Jesus as Lord of the Balangao.")

V. The Limits of Identification

William Reyburn explores the limits of missionary identification. An important part of the missionary task is to search for a point of connection or contact. Without establishing such a point of relational contact, missionaries have not assumed responsibility for communication. Deeply ingrained habits and attitudes can limit missionary identification.

A. Unknown Habits and Known Origins. Difficulties in identification can arise from our unconscious, habitual way of doing things—such as the way we walk. The greatest barriers of identification are the perceptions and categories of the new community. Most cultures have a distinctive category for those who have been born into the culture.

B. Attitudes. Deeply rooted attitudes, such as private ownership or what food we are willing to stomach, can be overcome by willing missionaries who are pursuing an authentic expression of love.

Read Reyburn, "Identification in the Missionary Task," pp. 470-475c

C. **False Identity Fails.** It may seem to go without mention, but since there have been attempts to identify with local people in ways that falsely represent religious identity, it's important to recognize that this approach brings about a setback rather than an advance for the gospel.

Read Parshall, "Going Too Far?" pp. 666d-667a (starting with "In my former country of ministry..." until it says "...leave that village immediately and never return.")

Conclusion of Key Readings for this lesson. 

VI. Bonding and Relationships

The idea of "bonding" adds dimension to the idea of building bridges. Tom and Betty Sue Brewster use the idea to show how missionaries can find themselves relationally connected and take the role of a learner.

A. **Bonding as Early Attachment.** The Brewsters introduce the concept of "bonding," an idea used to describe the initial attachment of newborn babies to their parents. The idea of bonding illustrates how missionaries can form deep attachments with local people and become "belongers" in a new culture. They suggest practical ways that missionaries can intentionally identify with a new culture by immersing themselves in their new social environment.

B. **Language and Culture Learning.** Pay special attention to the way the Brewsters refer to language learning. Many Americans consider themselves failures as language students. The Brewsters encourage us to consider language learning as a social, rather than an academic activity. As "learners" rather than "students," we most effectively learn language and culture in a rich social context of personal relationships.

Read Brewster, "The Difference Bonding Makes," pp. 465-469 (all)

VII. Identity with Integrity: Serving in a Terrorized, Globalized and Pluralized World

Do missionaries destroy culture? Are they harmful to society? We can assume that most people in a post 9/11 world would answer "Yes!" to these questions. We've already heard how the facts say otherwise (Woodberry, "The Social Impact of Christian Missions," pp. 286-290). We'll explore how Richardson answers this question in the next lesson (Richardson, "Do Missionaries Destroy Cultures?" pp. 489-492). In a world where holding dual identities is virtually impossible, how shall mission endeavors be conducted? How shall missionaries identify themselves among the nations?

A. **A World Made Wary of Missionaries.** Rick Love describes the three realities of the world after 9/11: anti-missionary attitudes complicated by the hostility of *terrorism*, the transparency of internet-exposed interaction because of *globalization,* and a false spectacle of Christians acting in bigoted intolerance increased by an environment of religious *pluralism*.

B. **A Triple Audience and a Three Dimensional Identity.** Rick Love sees three different audiences, each perceiving missionaries and what they say from a distinctive viewpoint:

1. **The unreached community,** to whom we aim to present the gospel.
2. **The onlooking secular world,** to whom we must at times work to defend the gospel.
3. **The church,** whom we seek to recruit and co-labor with for the gospel.

Love says, "It is increasingly proving impossible to communicate with any one of these particular audiences separately." Anything presented in one setting will eventually be made clear to the others. The only real solution is to find an identity which is the same from all three points of view.

C. **Aligning Our Identity.** Instead of adding more complicated, intricate security systems to protect multiple identities, Love suggests that we can simplify our identities by operating out of our core. He suggests that we will do well to align ourselves with three aspects of our "core."

1. **Clearly speak our core message,** the irreducible gospel message of Jesus Christ.
2. **Passionately pursue our core mandate,** which Love says may not have much to do with the words mission or missionary, but in fact may have more to do with the idea of blessing as seen in the Abrahamic promise.
3. **Truly represent our core identity,** which should have some kind of serving role in the community in which we live.

Read Love, "Identity with Integrity," pp. 477-481 (all)

D. Examples of Identity with Integrity:

1. **L. Mak** found himself rumored to be a much-despised missionary in a "closed" country. When he "googled" himself, he found out why. What preserved his relationships was the excellence of his professional work and the sincerity and love of his personal friendships.
2. **Bob Blincoe** found himself targeted by Saddam Hussein's regime in Northern Iraq. The community in which he lived surrounded him with their protection because they were convinced by his integrity and track record of service that his intentions were for the good of the local people.

Read Mak, "Google-Proof Transparency," sidebar, p. 478, and Blincoe, "As Unknown, Yet Well-Known," sidebar, p. 479

VIII. Communication in Social Settings

Communication across cultures involves multiple steps. We've seen how effective missionaries initially seek to learn language and culture in relationships with local people. We've seen how those relationships are enhanced when missionaries present themselves in socially recognized roles that are appropriate and acceptable. When missionaries fail to interact with respect for matters of social structure, such as roles and status, their words may be intelligible, but will not likely be received as credible.

Now we consider how gospel communication can flow in powerful ways throughout a society beyond the initial communication of the missionary. The focus of gospel communication should always be to enable local people to become effective, reproducing communicators of the life of following Jesus. Not every person within a society has the same potential for extending the gospel in effective ways. Some societies are structured in such a way that it becomes critically important that gospel communication be initiated by people with particular roles and status. Paul Hiebert explains how communication flows within three different kinds of social structure.

A. **Tribal Societies.** Tribal decisions are made by a limited number of elders. Most people movements have flourished in these kinds of social structures. Note how missionaries need to *evaluate* and *understand* the group decision-making process. According to the diagram of the society, to whom should the gospel be addressed? How will most people hear and decide to follow Jesus?

B. **Peasant Societies.** Leadership is exerted by a powerful elite. Caste groupings are common but not the only kind of societal group found in peasant societies. It is important to recognize that these kinds of societies abound in urban environments. Just because another category of social structure is called "urban" does not mean that peasant societies are not found in cities. People movements often take place in such social groupings. The question is raised, "To whom should we go first?" Should we go to the dominant elite? Or to the poor and powerless at the bottom of society? Hiebert describes how both approaches have been used with mixed success.

Read Hiebert, "Finding a Place and Serving Movements Within Society," pp. 454b-457a

C. **Urban or Metropolitan Societies.** Individual decision-making patterns are dominant. Organizations are voluntary. Cities are marked by diversity and complexity, so gospel communicators must learn well the specific urban context in order to communicate appropriately and to envision the kinds of churches that will flourish.

1. **Urban Social Organization.** Hiebert describes dynamics of roles (both simplex and multiplex) and families (both nuclear and extended). He describes why many of the diverse connections of kinship, informal associations and formal institutions all operate like a sub-cultural community.

2. **Churches in the City.** The diversity of urban settings means that there is need for many different kinds and structures of churches to reach the different peoples and sub-groups. Some of the tribal and peasant enclaves require intentional research in order to identify them and find appropriate ways to reach them. Take note of Hiebert's warning, "One of the greatest obstacles to effective church planting in the city is our own preconceptions of what constitutes church." We'll explore this more in Lesson 13.

Read Hiebert, "Finding a Place and Serving Movements Within Society," pp. 457b-459

D. **An Example of Why Social Structure Matters.** Brian Hogan describes how missionaries shared the gospel among the people most accessible to them: university students. It not surprising that the initial group to follow Christ consisted of teenage girls. These girls enjoyed growing in Christ, but they affected very few others. The movement the missionaries hoped to see was not going to happen in this way. But when the gospel encountered "older traditional Mongol men"—who were not in the urban centers, but living and leading as nomadic elders in rural areas—only then was it said that "real Mongols" were following Christ. Soon after, the gospel movement began to grow vigorously. Note how Hogan describes the urban social structure as being "overlaid...upon a nomadic tribal society."

Read Hogan, "Distant Thunder," pp. 682-683d

Conclusion of Certificate Readings for this lesson. 

After studying this section you should be able to:

- Describe four basic principles that will help missionaries communicate effectively in any society.
- Evaluate decisions regarding a missionary lifestyle in terms of effectiveness in influencing and identifying with people of the receiving culture.

IX. Communication and Social Structure

Effective missionaries aim to see most gospel communication accomplished by ordinary believers evangelizing through the normal dynamics of social interaction. Insights from the disciplines of cultural anthropology and sociology help missionaries find ways to instill movements that work with the dynamics of social structure instead of working against them. Eugene Nida analyzes social structure and its significance for gospel communication.

A. **Social Structure and Dynamics of Communication.** Nida presents a flexible diagram of society (p. 462) that helps compare how communication differs in different structures. The communication that flows horizontally is very powerful because it is reciprocal, which means there is trust. Horizontal communication carries the potential for a person who hears to become a person who passes on a message to many others. Outsiders find themselves restricted to vertical communication, which is never as powerful.

B. **Face-to-Face or Homogenous Societies.** Nida uses terms which overlap with the terms used by Hiebert. The term "face-to-face society" includes both "peasant" and "tribal" societies. The terms "folk" and "primitive" closely overlap with "peasant" and "tribal." Face-to-face societies are "homogenous," which means that most or all of the people participate in a common life.

1. **Folk or Peasant.** In these societal structures, there is a dependency on and interaction with other societies or urban centers.
2. **Primitive or Tribal.** In these societal structures, there is an independence from outside influences.

C. **Urban or Heterogenous Societies.** These complex societies contain minority groups in which there is communication that functions in very different ways. People are often living in transition between face-to-face communities and a larger mix of sub-cultures. Since they are living a "dual role," it is important for missionaries to recognize distinctions and connections between classes and subcultures.

D. **Communicative Approach in Any Society.** There are four principles of communication related to social structure which apply to any culture:

1. **Personal Friendship.** Relationships foster a connection with the entire communitys in what Nida describes as a sort of sponsorship dynamic. How much more meaningful would a message be if it was introduced by a trusted sponsor?
2. **Choose Effective Communicators for Your Initial Approach.** The most important of the four principles is to make the initial approach to those who are able to effectively pass on the communication.
3. **Allow Time.** Group decisions take time, often weeks and months. Individuals who are perceived to have made a decision which threatens group solidarity often bring about a larger negative response.
4. **Address Decision Makers.** If people are being challenged to make a decision which changes beliefs or social structure, it is imperative that such a message is conveyed to key people who are socially capable of making such a decision.

Read Nida, "Communication and Social Structure," pp. 460-464 (all)

X. An Example of Communication in Social Structure

Dean Hubbard tells the story of movements in India.

A. **Multiple Identities: Caste and Socio-Economic Condition.** The first leader mentioned, named Bhimrao, spent months traveling to scores of villages to communicate the gospel with Kowadi people. Eventually, the communication of the gospel culminated in a three-day festival. When opposition arose, the publicity brought the "Gathering of Christ-Worshipers" to the attention of other castes and communities. Without direct communication to them, these other groups became interested and began to follow Christ. Hubbard says that "it appeared that the gospel was leaping over traditional caste boundaries by virtue of a broader identity based on socio-economic condition."

B. **A Key Leader.** Two single women (yet another pair of single women!) found that they were perceived as the fulfillment of a vision seen by a Hindu priest. When the priest decided to entrust himself to Jesus, many others followed.

C. Well-Positioned Communicators. The movement among the Bansari got underway because of the influence of a "young, educated Bansari man" who approached an Indian Christian leader. He led 14 of his friends to Christ. The roles of three of the new followers "proved especially effective" to extend the gospel. Why? What were their roles?

Read Hubbard, "A Movement of Christ Worshipers," pp. 703-706 (all)

XI. Missions and Money

Regardless of how well missionaries may succeed in finding the best entry roles, they are eventually required to assume a long-term role in the society. These long-term roles are almost always complicated with financial expectations. This is true to some extent even when the missionaries are not from wealthy countries. Phil Parshall tells the fascinating story of how one missionary in a very poor country dealt with these complex issues.

A. Different Views. Joseph Cumming contrasts the different ideas about how money is expected to work in Muslim and Western societies. Many of these points of contrast can be found in societies other than Muslim.

B. Different Roles. Westerners are usually assigned roles by the receiving community, even if they are unaware of those roles and expectations. Parshall describes how he worked to live at the financial level of the people, earning the designation as a "brother" instead of a "VIP."

C. Righteous Rich? Some of the experiences of Jonathan Bonk are relayed in the introduction to his short sidebar article. He proposes that missionaries should closely examine the local society, seeking to identify a local role that corresponds in some way with what he calls, "the righteous rich."

D. Possible Solutions. Parshall says that there are no easy answers. Attempts must be made at adjusting lifestyles. Careful attention must be given to establish policies about the support of local Christian leaders. Decisions must be made about loaning money. Care should be given to recognize how money from Westerners compromises the testimony of local followers.

Read Parshall, "Missions and Money," pp. 482-485 (all), Cumming, "Different Views Concerning Relationships and Money," sidebar, p. 483, and Bonk, "The Role of the Righteous Rich," sidebar, p. 484

12 Christian Community Development

Studying this lesson will help you:

- Describe some of the most critical dimensions of global human need and comprehend the nature of poverty.
- List and evaluate four approaches to meeting global human need.
- Compare and contrast Christian relief ministry with transformational development.
- Describe the difference between absolute poverty and relative poverty.
- Explain how poverty results from broken relationships, misuse of power, and fear.
- Explain how efforts to encourage reconciliation between peoples are an important aspect of transformational development.
- Explain how church planting, when properly integrated with development efforts, can avoid the "rice Christian" problem.
- Explain why and how Christian community development offers greater hope when integrated with church planting.

It might seem from Jesus' words, "You always have the poor with you" (Mark 14:7), that God doesn't intend to change the plight of the poor. But the truth is that God has chosen to bring forth outposts of His coming kingdom in the poorest communities of the earth. Remember how John the Baptist was confused by the way Jesus conducted His mission? Jesus was expected to launch a campaign of God's judgment amidst the echelons of wealth and power. In Matthew 11:2-6 we read Jesus' response. He was healing broken lives and communicating the gospel amidst the poor. Christ's mission to the poor began the mission that He would later turn toward the people of all nations. The outcome is promised to be a triumph of God's justice in which the nations will hope (Matthew 12:18-21).

Such biblical hope frees us to be fully aware of the needs of the poor. We often turn our attention away from the evils of poverty because of despair. We cannot make ourselves gaze for long at what seems like an unceasing holocaust of harm throughout the earth. A closer inspection of what God is doing actually reveals that there is, in fact, no "God-forsaken" place on earth. God sees and anguishes with every moment of suffering. God is sending emissaries of His kingdom in significant numbers to bring healing and help in Christ's name. This lesson focuses on what those servants are doing. It's not really about needs and opportunities. Christian community development is all about hope.

Anticipating the progress of the gospel should rivet our attention even more upon the poor and broken of the world. Crowded into the "10/40 Window" region is the greatest concentration of unreached peoples as well as the largest concentration of physical and social needs. In this lesson, veterans of community development tell their stories and distill their experiences into valuable principles.

Hope is never without controversy. We'll examine the charge that missionaries destroy cultures as they try to serve them. We'll survey the nature of urban poverty and the potential for significant change. We'll see how missionaries are working to establish Christ's peace in the midst of ethnic hatred.

transformation One of the final statements in the Bible is, "Behold, I am making all things new!" That sums up what God has always been doing: making the entire world new. The gospel begins the re-creation by transforming people from the inside out. But the transformation doesn't stop until a sample of God's new kingdom is on display throughout whole communities. Transformation is God making people truly new and doing it now.

I. A World of Need

Jesus' words in Matthew 25 present six categories of suffering. There is good reason to see the identity of "these brothers of mine" in Matthew 25:40 as the apostolic people sent by the Messiah rather than suffering humanity in general. But regardless of how one interprets the parable of Matthew 25, the six categories of suffering help sort out the great needs that we find throughout the world. We dare not merely react to the needs in a superficial way. In order for us to respond to these needs in accordance with the purpose of God, we must grasp some of the complexity and extent of the suffering.

The next article by World Relief, one of the leading service agencies, warns that a sense of powerlessness to deal with the needs of the entire world can lull us into complete inactivity. We should refuse to view the world with a despair that assumes nothing can be done. The Bible makes it clear that God is not finished. He has always been pleased to multiply the seemingly small efforts of His servants into life-giving service that brings lasting change.

Hope means that we can strive to understand the problems of the world for what they really are. The suffering of the poor is rarely an unexplainable happenstance. Close examination of most human suffering reveals that societies are often mired in structural injustice. That injustice results in great devastation. Even worse, the poor lose hope that anything will ever change.

Take special note of the analysis of these problems. Hunger, for instance, is not really caused by a shortfall of food supplies. It is caused by a myriad of problems, the chief of which is distribution. The entire approach to illness has been primarily oriented around treatment of disease. We stand at a threshold of hope that many diseases can be eradicated. Many others are manageable by simple efforts of bringing primary health care and education to the fourth of the world's population that lacks any access to minimal health services.

Read World Relief, "State of World Need," pp. 592-597 (all)

II. Hope and Holism

Christian ministry to whole persons—body, mind and soul—as they live in whole communities, is called "holistic mission." The truth of the kingdom presents a comprehensive vision of God's purpose to redeem and to rule. No person and no portion of the communities of earth are beyond God's concern. This comprehensive vision enables Christians to seek God's ways and timing to touch the entire range of human need. The vision of God's kingdom motivates and integrates mission efforts.

A. **Fulfilled at the End, Furthered by the Church Until Then.** God's inbreaking kingdom is characterized by righteousness, justice and peace. The gospel of the kingdom declares that sin, disease and oppression are never the last word. Where Jesus is King, He brings forgiveness, healing and liberation. God alone will bring it to fulfillment at the end, when Christ comes again. But until then, God is always working to display tangible signs of the governing love of His kingdom. The primary agent of the kingdom is the Church, the redeemed community of the King.

B. **Hope Integrates and Motivates.** The hope of Christ's kingdom fuses together a double motivation of obedience and compassion.

1. **Jesus' commission** to disciple the nations holds before us a vision of Christ the King being followed by believers in all of the peoples of earth. Jesus Christ changes those who obey and serve Him, offering substantial hope that entire societies and communities will be transformed in observable ways.

2. **Jesus' compassion** to heal and serve demonstrated that there is no need which will not be touched in some way by the increase of His kingdom rule. Such hope can sustain the lasting compassion that stirred in the heart of Jesus. He did not pity the poor; He saw instead the worth of each person and each community. In that hope He exhibited a focused and sustained compassion. He saw God's destiny of blessing for the poor as well as the rich (Luke 18:35-19:10).

Read "The Lausanne Covenant," pp. 765c-766a

C. **Beyond Mere Balance.** Meeting basic human needs is inextricably linked with the gospel, just as it was in Jesus' ministry. Sometimes social concern is a consequence of evangelism; sometimes it is a bridge to evangelism. At other times social action accompanies evangelism and church planting as an integrated activity.

1. **Which Comes First?** A word of dynamic balance in holistic mission comes from missiologist Stephen Hoke:

> Asking, "Which is more important, evangelism or social action?" is a misleading question. Over the last generation it has led Westerners to spend fruitless years trying to analyze and rank which is more important. A more biblical approach, derived from studying the life of Jesus, would be to ask, "What comes first, evangelism or social action?" In Jesus day, the question would have been phrased, "What did Jesus do first, evangelize or minister to physical needs?"
>
> And the obvious answer is "Both" or "It depends." Sometimes Jesus healed the sick; sometimes He preached the gospel of the Kingdom. We usually see Him doing both. With the vision of complete personal and community transformation in view, Jesus did what the situation demanded. He always dealt directly with the presenting problem, be it physical or spiritual. When the sick asked for help, Jesus healed them. When people engaged Him in spiritual conversation, Jesus led them to make a decision about who He was. He never skirted the issue. He never changed the subject to move to more spiritual matters.
>
> So, in response to the question, "What did Jesus do first?" we can only respond, "It depends on the situation." Similarly today, in response to the question, "Which comes first, evangelism or social action?" we must respond with humility and honesty, "It depends on what the situation demands." When among unreached peoples a Christian is asked about Jesus, he or she may find it appropriate to share the gospel story in the context of their personal experience. There are many situations among unreached peoples where the only door open to Christians is to offer hope in the form of emergency relief or long-term community development. We can step eagerly and lovingly through these doors to establish a bridge for future relationship and hopefully effective evangelism.
>
> Because God is in control and engineers the opening and closing of cultural and political doors, we can feel free and confident to respond as Jesus would, without having to worry about which is more important. They both are. The real issue is timing and appropriate communication. So we follow Jesus' lead and respond as He would.

2. **The Leading Partner.** Veteran missionary and scholar Samuel Moffett helps reshape our understanding of what evangelism is and what it is not. In a kingdom context, he suggests that evangelism is not the only priority, but must be held in partnership with social action. Moffett says that confusing evangelism and social action in definition and separating them in practice hinders us from seeing churches planted among unreached peoples. They belong together—not just balanced, but in dynamic partnership. In Moffett's view, evangelism needs to be the leading partner. We must continue to be concerned with both hungers—the spiritual as well as the physical—as we seek to reach the two billion who live among unreached peoples. Though the numbers may change slightly from year to year, the idea of biblical balance remains unchanged.

The Spirit of the Lord GOD is upon me,
because the LORD has anointed me to bring good news
to the afflicted;
He has sent me to bind up the brokenhearted,
to proclaim liberty to captives and freedom to prisoners;
to proclaim the favorable year of the LORD
and the day of vengeance of our God...
So they will be called oaks of righteousness,
the planting of the LORD, that He may be glorified.
Then they will rebuild the ancient ruins.
They will raise up the former devastations.
And they will repair the ruined cities,
the desolations of many generations.
— Isaiah 61:1–2a, 3b–4

Jesus read this passage and announced that it was at least partially fulfilled in His day and in His person (Luke 4:16-30). But consider how these words may be relevant for those who follow Jesus today. Underline the phrases that express purpose (such as "to proclaim liberty...").

How is the presence of the Spirit of God related to the act of sending? The liberated captives and brokenhearted become "the planting of the Lord" for God's glory. They also become the ones who restore what was devastated. How can these verses encourage and guide those who are working among the urban poor?

Read Moffett, "Evangelism: The Leading Partner," pp. 598-600 (all)

III. Approaching a World of Need

When Christian missionaries encounter poverty and human needs, it isn't hard to see the problems. The difficult part is knowing just what approach to take in order to address the numerous needs and accomplish evangelism and church planting.

A. **Four Approaches to Human Need.** Four strategies have been used in recent history for meeting basic human needs. See the matrix below, from Samuel Voorhies' article. Identify what is valid about each strategy, as well as its strengths and weaknesses. Be sure to grasp the significance of the matrix. Two of the approaches look to *local resources and leadership*, expressed by the words, "Help From Within." The other approaches, seen under "Help From Without," may set up an increased reliance on *resources coming from outside*. Another helpful angle to consider when evaluating human needs is whether meeting the immediate needs outweighs dealing with underlying causes. To what extent should missionaries and/or local Christians be involved in any or all of these approaches?

Method / **Focus**	Help from without	Help from within
Structure	Strategy I Economic Growth	Strategy II Political Advocacy
Needs	Strategy III Relief	Strategy IV Transformational Development

1. **Economic Growth** often focuses upon macro-statistics and issues of a country instead of micro-economic factors such as adequate food, fuel and health for each family.
2. **Political Advocacy** often focuses upon oppressive regimes, violations of human rights and exploitative commercial structures which widen the gap between the "haves" and "have-nots."
3. **Relief** aims at providing basic survival necessities for victims of war, natural disaster and prolonged injustice.
4. **Community/Transformational Development** focuses on both adequate assessment and the use of personal and community abilities and resources. The goal is to meet basic needs with local leadership and resources. The term "Transformational Development" is synonymous with the term "Community Development."

B. **Limitations and Potential.** Each approach carries limitations and potential. While a lengthy consideration of Economic Growth and Political Advocacy is beyond the scope of this course, note the following evaluations:

1. **Economic Growth** has not proven to bring lasting help to the poor except when it is accomplished by means of what Voorhies calls "Transformational Development."
2. **Political Advocacy** is best done by and for insiders, rather than outsiders. It holds little promise without Transformational Development.
3. **Relief** aims at short-term survival. Unless a long-term plan is initiated from the start, relief efforts can produce the "rice Christian" syndrome. "Rice Christian" refers to the stereotype, almost never true, that people have converted to Christianity because a staple food, such as rice, was offered to them as an inducement.

4. **Transformational Development** aims at enabling a community to meet its own basic needs. Unfortunately, even Transformational Development efforts flounder without a foundational shift in values within the community. Therefore, there is a need for Christian Transformational Development which aims to bring about a new expression of church life that exhibits and multiplies the values of the kingdom of God.

Read Voorhies, "Transformational Development: God at Work Changing People and Their Communities," pp. 603b-605c

IV. Christian Community Development

Since relief efforts are crucial to preserve life, relief work and appeals for funding often get a higher profile. Meanwhile, many mission leaders have been focusing their efforts on development. Different leaders may use slightly different terminology to describe their work, but their work basically aims toward the same vision of bringing enduring transformation in Christ's name and by His power. Five different terms are commonly used to describe this approach:

- **Transformational Development.** Community developers aim to enable local people to mobilize local resources to meet basic needs in an enduring way throughout an entire community.
- **Christian.** Development workers seek to base the changes upon the values of the kingdom of God as revealed in Scripture. When people are changed and begin to emulate Christ's own character and concerns, many others throughout the community have examples and encouragement to participate in selfless service, trust and industrious hope. When Christian missionaries seek to do development work, they usually aim to plant new churches or renew existing churches as the basis for the crucial worldview and value shifts which are needed for lasting change.
- **Transformational.** The aim is for people and entire communities to be changed, not merely impacted in a passing way. Christian community developers do not view the sought-after changes as being accomplished by an exercise in social engineering. Christ Himself is seen as the source of significant transformation.
- **Holistic.** The entire range of human need is addressed.
- **Integrated.** All aspects of the ministry are tied together, linking diverse endeavors such as training in literacy, digging wells or enabling indigenous worship leaders.

With these ideas and terms in mind, examine three case studies, the first presented by Voorhies. Notice that all three development efforts involved the work of teams.

A. **God at Work Changing People and Their Communities.** Samuel Voorhies tells a story of fruitful development effort. Some aspects worth noting:

- **Problems and Resources.** Don't miss the first step, which is identifying the resources, after which the problems are considered. Would you have listed the problems or the resources first? As Voorhies describes the outcome, ask yourself how each of the different needs was met. Observe how much better it was to deal with the needs together on a community-wide basis.
- **How Was Worldview Changed?** What was the basis for the change in worldview? What was the place of the new church and its worship in the transformation? Consider the beautiful balance of God being recognized and people working together with hope: "We can do it ourselves with God's help, and to His glory we will become all that we can be."
- **Voorhies Lists Ten Principles.** Notice which principles emphasize the role of local people in bringing about change, and which principles emphasize the work of God. How can the role of outsiders work with both?

Read Voorhies, "Transformational Development: God at Work Changing People and Their Communities," pp. 601-603b, 605c-606

B. **Enabling Jesus Christ "to Be Born into Northeastern Thai Culture."** James Gustafson presents a case study that highlights the place of local churches in providing a foundation for "true transformation of society." The developers have gone to great lengths to plant churches that are remarkably in tune with the Northeastern Thai culture. Why does the cultural relevance of the new churches help them deal with other community needs? What does he mean when he says "development must serve, not lead?" How does this emphasis prevent the "rice Christian" syndrome as described previously? Gustafson describes an example of the "microcredit" system of offering small non-monetary loans to a "cooperative project." It is important to understand how this approach differs from relief efforts that give away resources. How does Gustafson's team operate in the reality of hope? Which principles on Gustafson's list match items on the list that Voorhies provided?

Read Gustafson, "Pigs, Ponds and the Gospel," pp. 693-697 (all)

C. **Christ's Love Demonstrated in a War-Torn City.** The Guzmans, both medical professionals from Latin America, worked with a team from other Latin American countries. Not all development work takes place in remote, rural agrarian settings. Their work took place in a Middle Eastern urban area ravaged by war and under constant threat of violence. Their team worked on different levels. They worked to rebuild the infrastructure with medical services and government agencies throughout the region. They also dealt with many specific needs in local communities. Some things to note in their story:

- **Incarnational Living.** They cultivated relationships with high government leaders as well as with nearby households and neighbors.
- **Scripture.** They worked to make the Bible available and understandable so that lasting changes would be framed upon the values of the kingdom of God and the example of Christ. Although their team highlighted medical services, they helped translate portions of the New Testament.
- **Avoiding Inducement.** They raise the important issue of how to integrate gospel communication with the provision of humanitarian services. They describe the problem of so-called "rice Christians" converting in order to obtain benefits. The Guzmans feel they avoided this problem by offering the same services to all and by motivating their work in Christ-like love.

Read Guzman, "Ourselves as Servants," pp. 700-702

Conclusion of Key Readings for this lesson. 

V. The Urban Frontier of Change and Hope

Pioneer urban missionary Viv Grigg describes the crying need for development efforts in the cities of the world.

A. **The Nature of poverty.** Grigg helps us understand the nature of urban poverty. There are key distinctions between first and third world poverty. Another way to understand this distinction is to see the difference between "absolute poverty" and "relative poverty."

1. **Absolute poverty** describes situations in which people have an absolute insufficiency to meet their basic needs.
2. **Relative poverty** describes situations in which people are on the margins of society. A person's standard of living is compared in relation to others in the community or nation. A family may be regarded as poor if they do not have a telephone or a car in North America. A family lacking a telephone or a car in India may not be considered impoverished at all. If neither family is suffering from an absolute lack of food, shelter or clothing, then their poverty is a relative poverty.

Compare some of the poorest communities of North America with the poorest parts of Calcutta. How would you categorize most of the poverty of North America? Is it absolute poverty or relative poverty? Why does the distinction matter?

B. Reachable Communities. Why is the distinction of "slums of hope" and "slums of despair" important when dealing with the huge complex of needs in cities? Is the city too large a community in which to accomplish development? Grigg says the challenge is "how to generate movements of disciples among the poor and subsequently among the rich." How does this statement display Grigg's hope-based approach to the city? Why does he propose the strategy of bringing the gospel to the city from the economic underside? From the small excerpt of Grigg's writing, what community development principles can you see Grigg applying in an urban context?

Read Grigg, "The Urban Poor: Who Are We?" pp. 611b-614

VI. Poverty and the Power of the Gospel

How we view the world's needs will shape our response. Bryant Myers challenges us to take another look at poverty.

A. The Standard View: Poverty as Deficit. While it is obvious that poverty is a lack of basic necessities, it may be misleading to view poverty as a problem that can be eradicated by economic solutions.

B. A Better View of Poverty: Poverty is More Than Deficit. Understanding the causes of the deficit helps us know how the gospel can bring about sustainable change. Watch for features of worldview that are being described.

1. **Broken Relationships.** The Bible suggests that broken relationships are at the root of the ills and grief of the poor. It leads us to understand the history of the impoverished and see the complexity of their predicament.
2. **Misused Power.** There has been controversy over the idea that people are poor because they have somehow suffered an abuse of power. Examining the plight of most poor communities often reveals some kind of exploitation.
3. **Fear.** Prolonged severance from blessing and safety sets in motion structures of fear which often invite a debilitating servitude to idolatry.

C. The Gospel as Truth and Power. Poverty is essentially a spiritual issue. Only the gospel—all of it—contains the hope that the poor will be enabled to live in communities where relationships are restored, abusive power is broken and fears are allayed.

Read Myers, "What is Poverty Anyway?" pp. 607-609 (all)

VII. The New Frontier of Hope

John Dawson describes how Christians are finding creative and powerful ways to pursue the reconciliation of peoples. We are mandated to establish a movement of discipleship under Christ's Lordship *within* every people. At this hour God is energizing hope that the wounds *between* the peoples can be healed in substantial ways.

A. **Business as Usual?** The human heart is bent toward envy, fear and contention. Racial strife is increasing. Many of these struggles are outgrowths of ancient conflicts. Reconciliation leaders have identified 14 general categories of deep-rooted, systematic alienation between peoples and elements of society. How shall we respond to such deep-seated hostility? Does God want us to respond?

B. **Seeing Jesus Beyond Church Walls.** Only Christians can act in the humility and the power of Christ's forgiveness to introduce the power of the Cross. As Christians lead the way in modeling humility and forgiveness, there is almost limitless potential for Christ to be glorified and for some of the wounds of the world to be significantly healed. Cross-cultural workers are finding creative ways to bring healing throughout communities long troubled by racial and economic discord.

Read Dawson, "Healing the Wounds of the World," pp. 622-626 (all)

Conclusion of Certificate Readings for this lesson.

After studying this section you should be able to:

- Answer the charge that Christian missionaries destroy tribal cultures.
- Describe how sustainable change comes about by the power of the gospel and empowered local leadership of new churches.

VIII. Transforming or Destroying?

Do the changes that missionaries bring sometimes destroy the culture? So goes the stereotype of missionaries as cultural imperialists. Is this perception based on historical fact or is it a myth perpetuated by critics and writers antagonistic to Christianity? Is the seemingly enlightened policy of "leave the innocents alone" a realistic option in today's world? As modernity and technology press global change at a breathtaking pace, negative change will take place if Christians do not intervene in positive ways. In these stories related by Don Richardson, look for principles of appropriate culture change that can guide missionary work in tribal cultures.

Read Richardson, "Do Missionaries Destroy Cultures?" pp. 486-492 (all)

IX. Transformation: The Missionary's Role

We earlier examined the four basic approaches to bringing about benefit for a community: Economic Growth, Political Advocacy, Relief and Transformational Development. As much as missionaries want to be of help, direct aid such as relief and economic growth programs can be debilitating if there is not a transformation at the grass-roots level. We've seen some of the basic approaches that missionaries have taken in community development. It's important to recognize that lasting change takes place only when local leaders act as the agents of change. And with a local church at the center of the changes, there is a life-giving continuity to the transformation.

We've already touched on the issue of missionaries bringing about unwanted change. Don Richardson asserts that missionaries are most often involved in what has been called "directed change," which helps tribal groups deal with inevitable transitions in the modern world. This kind of change rarely destroy cultures. At the center of lasting transformation are the beginnings of new Christ-following communities. In this approach to societal change, the missionary's role is to be a catalyst and a source of new ideas and information. This approach seems to take more time and leave more up to the Holy Spirit. But it is the only way to bring about changes which are not dependent on the presence or advocacy of outsiders.

Dale Kietzman and William Smalley explore the role of missionaries in bringing about cultural or societal change of any kind. Their comments pertain to the role of missionaries in changing the way communities work to meet basic human needs.

Read Kietzman and Smalley, "The Missionary's Role in Culture Change," pp. 503-505 (all)

13 Spontaneous Multiplication of Churches

Studying this lesson will help you:

- Describe organic churches in terms of the core reality of the presence of the living Jesus being served by His people.
- Explain why Jesus being obeyed as king means His kingdom can be at work through churches in their communities.
- Explain why and how churches can be fruitful by reproducing other churches.
- Explain why and how churches can be fruitful by bringing modest but substantial transformation in local culture and in global problems.
- Distinguish between New Testament commands, apostolic practices and human customs. Describe the value of this distinction for church planting.
- Explain why evangelizing whole families helps church planting movements multiply rapidly.
- Explain why dependency on outside funds frustrates rather than helps church movements to reproduce and influence their society.
- Describe how the images of salt and light illustrate the mission of churches to their own people group or city.
- Explain why churches need to be "cultivated," trained, renewed, or even re-planted in order to bear fruit in their peoples and communities.

We have seen the biblical mandate for reaching every people. We've examined the historical record to see the exciting story of how the gospel moved through huge geographic areas and ethnolinguistic basins. Most of us have not seen the kind of multiplying church movements that sweep through large areas or peoples. Of course, we've all seen churches, but perhaps few of us have experienced the kind of church movement that is crucially needed among unreached peoples.

Not just any church will do. We've borrowed words from botany to describe the kind of churches that are needed among unreached peoples: viable, indigenous churches. *Viable* refers to the capability of living things to survive and reproduce. Viable churches thrive and multiply. *Indigenous* describes living things that are native to or have originated from a particular environment. The term "indigenous church" refers to a church that arises from the soil of its own society. It is native to the culture, abidingly relevant and powerful, influencing entire communities with the life of the kingdom of God. We'll discover some surprising features of truly indigenous churches.

Following the botanical imagery further, what kind of *fruit* should we expect churches to bring forth in their societies? Most of us have never experienced churches bearing fruit in the transformation of their cities or societies. Since most of us haven't seen churches multiplying and blessing their communities with heaven-on-earth signs of the kingdom, it's easy to overlook the strategic value of planting and renewing such life-giving church movements.

Get ready to be surprised by what churches can be. In this lesson we will encounter living, organic, fruit-bearing churches that understand themselves to be an embodiment of the risen Lord Himself. These kinds of churches usually flourish as dynamic, multiplying movements. We'll explore and contrast different kinds of movements. It's precisely the presence of such movements that defines what it means for a people group to be "reached." We'll explore an example of how existing church movements can find fresh, fruit-bearing expressions amidst urban sub-groups and overlooked generations. Just knowing that churches can bring forth the power and beauty of Christ will give us confidence that He will not fail to fulfill His promise to bless all the peoples of the earth and to fill the earth with Christ's glory.

multiply Only living things multiply. God has formed the Church as a living thing, to represent His Son's character and to reproduce His Spirit's fruit in every part of the world. As God announced from the very beginning, the way to fill the earth is to multiply.

Lessons 12 through 15 are arranged in strategic reverse sequence. The outcome is portrayed first, followed in reverse order by the necessary stages to achieve that end. Lesson 12 described the fruit of the gospel's transforming power. Lesson 13 describes life-giving church movements which bear these fruits of social change and thriving evangelistic efforts. Lesson 14 addresses the challenge of how these movements are launched in entirely unreached peoples. Lesson 15 will conclude by considering the partnership and discipleship required to send, support and sustain the needed mission force.

We've defined the task of world evangelization as primarily a task of seeing that viable, indigenous churches are planted among every people group. Have we overstated the importance of churches in fulfilling God's mission? Many Christians, because of their disappointing experience with churches, would probably say yes. So it becomes crucial to understand that the vibrant church movements we are speaking of in this lesson are probably something that many Christians have never experienced. Many Christians have never even heard about such vital churches.

I. Church Planting Movements

David Garrison opens his report with a verse from Habakkuk that says God will do such amazing things that they will seem unbelievable. Then he tells how the leaders heard reports of churches exploding with such incredible numbers and spiritual vitality that they found it impossible to believe. After verifying many of the reports by visiting the movements, they gradually described the phenomena of rapid but sustained multiplication of churches as "church planting movements" (or CPM).

Reports haven't stopped coming. We have included a series of abbreviated reports. Try to envision each of them as you read.

A. **A Descriptive Definition.** After studying scores of these movements, mission leaders have found four common features:

1. **Rapid Multiplication.** Church planting movements do not simply add new churches. They multiply.
2. **Indigenous.** These churches emerge within their cultural setting, the vast majority of them not started by outsiders. If foreigners are involved, it is in the beginnings and in the background. The movements have a homegrown feel to those who are following Christ.
3. **Churches Planting Churches.** This may seem to be a restatement of the first feature of multiplication. But Garrison is identifying something distinctive by saying that churches can reach a critical moment when there is a surge of exponential multiplication. It is something like a "tipping point," like dominoes falling or a dam finally breaking. Many reproducing churches do not become movements. In a true church planting movement, the momentum of reproducing churches outstrips the ability of any of the planters to control it.
4. **Within People Groups.** Most movements see the most extensive multiplication flowing along family and ethnic connections where there is shared language and group affinity.

B. God's Work and Our Role. In every church planting movement there is a sense of God working in powerful ways. This sense of awe can be misleading because it could appear that Christians do little or nothing to stop or start the movements. But the truth is God has given Christians vital roles to play in serving these movements. This is why Garrison challenges us to be "students of the ways God is at work in these movements."

Read Garrison, "Church Planting Movements," pp. 646-648 (all)

II. What is Church?

Neil Cole dared to ask, "What is church?" He found that it was a dangerous question. While sorting out features and institutional descriptions of church, he realized that he was defining church according to his experience. This is to be expected, but what if his experience of church was something culture-bound or limited by traditions?

Cole's question led him to a broad but simple definition of church:

> "The presence of Jesus among His people
> called out as a spiritual family
> to pursue His mission on this planet."

By the "presence" of Jesus, Cole doesn't mean a vague theoretical notion of spiritual but invisible proximity. He means the living, risen Jesus Christ, operative and powerful in the midst of those who are committed to follow and serve Him together.

A. Organic Church. The core reality of the Church is Jesus Christ being followed, loved and obeyed. The Church is not essentially an organization, although churches always have some kind of institutional and cultural shape. In a very real way, the Church is an embodiment of the risen Jesus.

B. Christ First. When Christ is first, mission and the kingdom make sense. The primacy of the person of Jesus helps us derive our mission from Jesus Himself, not merely copy His example. We actually follow Him as He leads. By focusing on Jesus as King, it's easy to see that the kingdom of God is a reality whenever Jesus is served as King. The kingdom of God is not a campaign to get people active in particular agendas or projects.

C. Fruit! If Christ intends churches to be living, organic realities, then it becomes easy to see that He intends for them to bear fruit. The seed of the gospel of the kingdom brings forth changed lives, living out faith together. Cole says churches bear fruit in two ways:

1. **Organic Churches Reproduce.** The fruit of an apple tree is not really apples, but more apple trees. Within the seed is the next generation. This means that it is normal for churches to reproduce.
2. **Organic Churches Cultivate Fruit in Their Culture.** Our mission is to find and develop Christ followers, not merely gather more church members. The difference should be seen "in transformed lives that bring change to neighborhoods and nations." Cole goes on to say, "Churches don't always bear the fruit that they should without being challenged, so it's important to 'cultivate' them."

Read Cole, "Organic Church," pp. 643-645 (all)

III. The Spontaneous Multiplication of Churches

George Patterson has trained people to multiply churches in many parts of the world. His summary of key principles illustrates the kind of healthy, multiplying movements of churches that can bring the gospel throughout a region or people. Get used to Patterson addressing you as if you were a church planter. You will grasp his ideas easily if you imagine yourself as his apprentice learning how to plant churches.

A. Practical Principles Based on Biblical Assumptions. Patterson describes spontaneous multiplication of churches as the Holy Spirit moving churches to reproduce without the immediate presence of outsiders.

1. **A Basic Assumption and a Definition.** The final paragraphs reveal Patterson's fundamental assumption that the Church is a living creation of God, with a life from God that will reproduce. On page 635 Patterson defines a church as "a group of believers in Christ dedicated to obeying His commands." Compare this to Neil Cole's definition of church. Patterson and Cole's definitions are similar in these respects: It's all about Jesus being obeyed, and both see churches essentially as the living Christ at work among His people. That's why they both see churches as living entities that reproduce, bearing fruit by nature.

Read Patterson, "The Spontaneous Multiplication of Churches," p. 642 (the section named "Pray for Reproductive Power")

2. **Two Principles about Reproducing.** As you read Patterson, watch for two underlying principles at work when churches not only grow, but multiply. Churches multiply when two dynamics are taking place:

   - **Following Christ.** First, churches multiply if people are following Christ, not just hearing and circulating religious words. There is an emphasis on *obeying Christ.*
   - **Forming Leaders.** Second, churches multiply if leadership is encouraged and trained. There is an emphasis on *leadership development.*

B. Help Disciples Build Up Other Disciples. Because of limited space in this lesson, we will skip to the second of the four principles. Patterson sees the church planting missionary essentially as a trainer. Missionaries should never merely train a student; they should always train leaders on the job. For the missionary, the best focus is to aim at building up, or edifying, the new church through the leader being trained. The discipling relationship between missionary and leader becomes a model for new church leaders to follow.

The Lord's Supper should be the center of the church gatherings rather than the preaching of the missionary or even local leaders. When preaching and extensive public teaching is minimized, pastors-in-training learn to focus on nurturing their flock in relational ways instead of dominating them from a platform. New leaders are encouraged to disciple others more readily. When discipling ties are promoted among all members, the idea of multiplication has already begun.

Read Patterson, "The Spontaneous Multiplication of Churches," pp. 636c-638d

C. **Teach Obedience to Christ.** Probably the most important idea of multiplying churches is to promote the core reality of church: People obeying Jesus' commands in love. Do this above and before all else.

1. **Begin with Loving Obedience to Jesus' Basic Commands.** Whenever obedience becomes secondary, problems arise: institutional ideas begin to dominate; nominal Christians come to be tolerated; foreign traditions can be misunderstood as essential; and of course, the churches stop multiplying. Patterson uses a simple list of seven commands of Christ. Orientation to obedience is not legalism at all, since there is never a sense of meritorious righteousness earned by performance. Instead, a loving relationship with Jesus is encouraged that offers Him what the Bible calls the "obedience of faith" (Rom 1:5).

2. **Design Evangelism and Theological Training in Terms of Obedience.** Don't seek "decisions" for Christ; instead, seek to bring about repentance and faith throughout entire families. The emphasis needs to be the Lordship of Christ. Offers of going to heaven as a free gift are less likely to bring about this kind of relationship. Important doctrines need to be taught, but in connection with a point of obedience or with a problem that needs a solution in the church. Patterson suggests having a "training menu" of many important topics. When problems emerge, that particular item can be selected from the menu.

3. **Orient Teaching to Loving Obedience.** Teach every leader to help his or her people make important distinctions between:

   - **New Testament Commands.** These are primary, carrying the authority of heaven. They are at the heart of obeying Christ.
   - **Apostolic Practices.** These are not commanded. They may have value, but they are not expected to be part of every believer's practice.
   - **Human Customs.** These are practices not mentioned in the New Testament. They are often Christian traditions developed in Western countries and are foreign to the people. They may be valuable, but they are not necessarily looked to as an authoritative source for life and church practice. Distinguishing human customs from Christ's commands rescues young, maturing churches from most problems with legalism and syncretism.

Read Patterson, "The Spontaneous Multiplication of Churches," pp. 638d-640a

D. **Help Churches Build Up and Multiply Other Churches.**

1. **A Vision for "Great-Granddaughter" Churches.** Help churches reproduce by giving them a vision that they are intended to be a "grandmother" church. Encourage them to pray and plan for "great-granddaughter" churches. A "hub" strategy does not work. A "chain" approach will be flexible and endlessly reproducible.

2. **Train Believers to Evangelize.** Show believers how to evangelize neighbors and relatives. As they follow the natural connections of family and social ties, new churches will spring up in different locations.
3. **Train Church Leaders and Pastors to Train Other Pastors and Leaders.** Simple patterns of training are the most reproducible. If training in the "grandmother" church is kept simple, it will be reproducible for many generations to come.
4. **Keep Missionaries and Outside Funds Out of the Way.** Beware the missionary's greatest error: controlling national churches. Instead, keep missionaries out of the way. Insist that missionaries and others who are planting new churches seek to swiftly commend new churches to the Holy Spirit's power and care. Beware of stifling churches by providing outside funds. Mobilize local resources. Help the new believers to learn generosity and dependence on God. Outside funding almost always freezes church multiplication.

Read Patterson, "The Spontaneous Multiplication of Churches," pp. 640b-642b

IV. An Example of a Movement

Patterson has coached teams of people working far beyond Latin America and has found these patterns and principles to be effective. One of those who learned from Patterson was Brian Hogan. We've already started his story. Finish the story of the Mongolian movement. Try to identify how Hogan's team practiced what they learned from Patterson. Take note of how they combined meetings in homes with occasional larger gatherings as opposed to the attempts of others who struggled to conduct conventional Sunday services in appropriate facilities.

Best of all, consider the wisdom in the timing and mode of their departure. The presence of missionaries after a certain point in the process begins to suffocate the movement instead of serving it. Why does Hogan call this section, "The End of the Beginning"? The diagram on page 685 shows how part of the movement, which began among the Khalka Mongols has spread to other Mongolian peoples and to other countries.

Read Hogan, "Distant Thunder," pp. 684b-686

V. Evangelizing Whole Families

One of the features of growing churches is that they generally aim to evangelize whole families. We have already read the opening stories presented by Wee Hian Chua which contrast the approach of Western missionaries with the more family-oriented approach of the Chinese "Little Flock" movement. Scan through the stories again in order to note how the Western workers failed to present themselves as respectable members of any family. Thus, they had no appropriate role or status in the eyes of the Chinese village. Second, the Westerners did not aim to reach whole families, attempting instead to win individuals to the faith. As a result, the missionaries were considered to be "family-breakers." The individuals did not have as much power to make decisions as the missionaries had thought.

Their experience is contrasted with the evangelistic efforts of an indigenous movement of multiplying churches called the Little Flock Assembly. This movement not only sent out whole families as the evangelizing force, but they also aimed carefully to draw entire families to Christ.

A. **Different Social Assumptions.** Evangelizing whole families is appropriate in most cultures of the world. Chua mentions a few cultures as examples. He points out the philosophical roots of Western individualism in the statement "I think, therefore I am." Because of this, a Westerner usually assumes that he can think out and decide matters of faith for himself. Most non-Western social and family structures are built on the assumption that "I participate, therefore I am."

B. **The Biblical Data.** The Bible is filled with references to families who were recipients of God's blessing and salvation *as families.* Furthermore, there are many passages of Scripture that describe family units as the agents of mission and in many ways, the core of what constituted the Church.

Read Chua, "Evangelization of Whole Families," pp. 653-656 (all)

He fell down before Paul and Silas, and after he brought them out,
he said, "Sirs, what must I do to be saved?"
And they said,
"Believe in the Lord Jesus, and you shall be saved, you and your household."
And they spoke the word of the Lord to him
together with all who were in his house.
And he took them that very hour of the night and washed their wounds,
and immediately he was baptized, he and all his household.
And he brought them into his house and set food before them,
and rejoiced greatly, having believed in God with his whole household.
— Acts 16:29–34

In Acts 16:29-34, you'll notice that the jailer's household is mentioned four times. What people might have been part of this man's household? Did the different members believe for themselves or were they another captive audience of the jailer? What does this say about households being a primary focus of evangelization?

Conclusion of Key Readings for this lesson. 

VI. The Church Influencing Culture: Optimistic Realism

Churches are intended by God to bear fruit in two ways: by reproducing themselves and by bringing forth life-giving changes in the world. But in the opinion or experience of many, churches seldom bring transforming changes to their societies.

A. Pessimism and Defeatism. Some have disapproved of cultural engagement in the world. Others subscribe to a defeatism which says there is no point in trying to bring change.

B. Realistic Optimism. The history of the Church gives many examples in which churches have been a force for "purging, claiming and beautifying [its culture] for Christ." But the church's cultural and social responsibility is better based on Scripture. The Bible gives ample basis for culture change in creation, but even more in the truth of the kingdom of God. Jesus Christ has been given authority in all of heaven and earth. He has placed His Church in the world to be salt and light.

The report commends a "sober Christian realism" framed upon the truth of God's kingdom. We have known the present reality of Christ's life-giving power since He first came and yet we also find ourselves in an ongoing struggle against evil until He comes again. Although Jesus Christ now reigns, "He has not yet destroyed the forces of evil; they still rampage." Thus, in every culture, Christians find themselves in "conflict and often suffering." With Christ, we are called upon to fight against the powers of evil. Complete victory will come at the end of the age.

Read the Lausanne Committee, "The Willowbank Report," pp. 525b-526b ("The Church's Influence on Culture")

VII. Salt and Light

Tim Keller has been working for years encouraging urban churches to influence the culture and society of New York City.

A. The Kingdom Both Rich and Sharp. Keller describes a polarity of ideas about the kingdom:

- On the one hand, the gospel can be reduced to an individualistic message that helps people get to heaven—a "get out of jail free" card with no transformation.
- Against this, another idea of the kingdom has become very popular, in which Jesus' death doesn't so much assuage God's wrath for sin as it absorbs the world's evil and violence. Jesus' life is exemplary, showing the way of non-violence and service. Jesus now, according to this version of the kingdom, calls us to work for peace and justice in the world. Basically, the gospel is reduced to a call to "repent of living for yourself and join Jesus' kingdom program." This may be, as one author put it, "all call and no grace." Keller says that this can amount to just one more legalism.

According to Keller, both of these are extremes to avoid. We need to see that the gospel is sharp; that is, dealing with atonement for sin and justification by grace. But the gospel is also rich; that is, it equips us to pursue justice and cultural renewal.

Read Keller, "Cities and Salt: Counter-Cultures for the Common Good," pp. 615-616a

B. Light. Jesus tells the disciples that they are to be a "city on a hill." Keller takes this to mean that by Christ's power, the Church will somehow become an alternate city within the cities of earth. This does not mean the Church is to be a separated enclave. Instead, it is to seek the good of the cities and cultures that it inhabits.

C. Salt. The Church is to be a preserving force. This reveals that Christ has not designed the Church to take over by Christianizing society as a whole. There is a more modest expectation of rich cultural presence preserving as salt and illumining as light.

D. Word and Deed. Churches working to understand their mission in their community and culture should, of course, heed not only the biblical call to evangelize but also the call to do justice and care for the poor. Some fear that mercy and justice ministry could displace vigorous evangelism. Keller suggests that moving beyond such a dichotomy is helped by being sensitive to this distinction: A gathered, corporate, "institutional" church is different from a scattered, "organic" church consisting of Christians serving in their work settings and other dimensions of social influence.

According to this view, the institutional church exists primarily to evangelize and to disciple people. But the organic church, consisting of scattered Christians, is more broadly "called to resist and to seek to heal all the results of sin in the world—spiritual, psychological, social and physical." This means that discipleship should not be, as one author put it, an "after-hours" Christianity that fails to encourage believers to integrate their faith and work in order to bring renewal and reform to every part of society.

Read Keller, "Cities and Salt: Counter-Cultures for the Common Good," pp. 616a-618a

E. Urban. Keller says that it is critical for churches to influence cities in order to bring substantial change to cultures.

F. Movements. A church on its own is inadequate to bring about significant change. A gospel *movement* is required to reach an urban cultural center. Keller continues the biological imagery that we noted at the beginning of this lesson. He likens the necessary inter-connected network of multiplying churches and ministries to an *ecosystem*. "The core of this ecosystem is a multiplying body of new churches." Churches, however institutional or organic they may be, are not enough. Many inter-related ministries must be the expressions of Christ's kingdom in every area of life.

1. **New Churches Reach More.** Keller offers several reasons why new churches, of the dynamic sort that we have been describing, have the ability to reach the incredible diversity of peoples and subgroups in our urban world. Keller claims that planting new churches is the single most important strategy for reaching a city.

2. **New Churches Sustain and Revive.** What about existing churches? New churches and ministries are the best way to inspire and renew them. New churches bring grass-roots support for the necessary array of ministries.

Read Keller, "Cities and Salt: Counter-Cultures for the Common Good," pp. 618a-619

VIII. Taking on the Great Problems

Rick Warren issues a challenge to take on the five greatest problems of our day. He has called them in other literature the "five giants." They are: spiritual lostness, egocentric leadership, poverty, disease and ignorance. Consider what Warren is saying. He calls for more than churches effectively in evangelizing their community. He calls for more than churches to be salt and light in their own community. He sees the church as a global Christian movement, uniquely positioned and empowered by God to take on the major world challenges which have local manifestations but truly global solutions. He says that the church is "God's chosen instrument of blessing. It is the greatest force on the face of the Earth." If God has intended for the church to take on such things, then churches should rise up and make bold plans together in order to face the challenge.

Rick's wife, Kay Warren, tells of her journey recognizing that God was giving her and many others a critical role in taking on one of the greatest global challenges of our day, HIV.

Read Warren, "The Church—The Greatest Force on Earth" and "Wiping Out HIV," pp. 620-621 (all)

A. **Widening or Focusing Our Mission?** What do you think? Are these challenges part of the mission of the Church? If so, this focuses our mission on the strategic necessity of churches, instead of widening our mission so that every possible task and need becomes mission. Where there are no churches, it is critically important to plant them. Where there are churches, it is important to encourage and challenge them to pursue the fullness of God's purpose.

B. **The Need to Mobilize.** Of course, as Garrison pointed out, churches do not multiply on their own. They must be intentionally coached, equipped and trained to do so. If that is true, then it is also true that, left to themselves, churches do not automatically take on such major challenges like Warren calls for, or even the more localized salt and light dynamics that Keller calls for. Churches must be "cultivated"—mobilized, revived, prompted, renewed and revitalized to carry out all that God desires.

C. **The Outcomes of "Frontier Mission" and "Regular Mission."** At this point it may help to revisit the distinction between "frontier mission" and "regular mission" we set out in Lesson 9. By "frontier mission" we refer to the completion of the task of world evangelization. By "regular mission" we mean spreading the gospel cross-culturally in people groups where churches have already been established. Consider the value of frontier mission from these points of view:

- **Kingdom Outcomes.** This is an overarching reality that encompasses evangelism and transformation. In terms of the kingdom of God, the outcome of frontier mission is that Jesus will be truly served, obeyed and worshiped as Lord in every people.
- **Evangelism Outcomes.** In practical terms of evangelism, frontier mission aims to bring about a "missiological breakthrough," or the beginnings of a movement that can potentially evangelize the rest of the people.
- **Transformation Outcomes.** In practical terms of transformation, frontier mission aims to bring about the beginnings of a movement that can potentially bring about lasting change in the culture and society.

Much of what we are exploring in this lesson is not frontier mission even though it certainly is part of the regular mission of God's people. But the incredible value of what God wants His people to accomplish beyond the "missiological breakthrough" highlights the strategic priority of frontier mission.

IX. Bringing Forth the Blessing: Beyond Dependency

Glenn Schwartz gives some vivid examples of why unwise funding actually hurts more than it helps, building a case for wisdom and balance. He highlights the value of helping churches find God's provision in local resources instead of making them dependent on outside help. In many ways, what Schwartz describes is the opposite side of the dynamic movements that we have been exploring.

Many churches in the wealthy West unwisely splash surplus resources in misguided ways that may feel as if "compassion" is being expressed. But such funding often causes a dynamic of dependency in which multiplication is shut down. Instead of bearing fruit, dependent churches merely manage mild growth or survival. The alternative is to always seek churches that will reproduce using local resources.

Read Schwartz, "Dependency," pp. 657-659 (all)

X. Mission Comes Home

In this lesson, we have envisioned what peoples and cities look like when they are "reached." But do people groups stay "reached?" Is it possible for churches to become culturally distant from the ever-morphing and moving cultures of our day? How do churches keep relevant and culturally close to the peoples and cities in which they are growing? Andrew Jones recounts the journey which took him to foreign countries but then brought him back to the very cultural setting which was "home" to him.

Jones' journey brought him to engage with postmodern subcultures in the USA. He was part of the early emergence of the so-called "emerging church" movement. He offers some biblically informed views about these movements. Compare his description of these churches with the organic churches and simple house churches that we have seen in this lesson. Jones is now in Europe continuing ministry in what has been called a "post-Christian" culture. He organized some of what he is learning into three categories.

A. Obeying Jesus, Finding the Person of Peace. Jesus' instructions to begin in the home of a receptive person of influence mean that mission is not a matter of attracting people to programs. Instead, ministry takes place in their homes and in familiar settings.

B. Imitating Paul. Jones sums up how Paul pursued his work by first sowing the ground with *Prayer*, then working as a *Herald* or story-teller, then instigating new structures as an *Apostle*, and then conveying what is important as a *Teacher*. This rhythm of ministry spells out the acrostic PHAT.

C. Holistic Mission. Jones says that venturing into business can be an important aspect of ministry and identity. He mentions micro-business and "For-Benefit Businesses."

Read Jones, "Mission Comes Home," pp. 649-652 (all)

Conclusion of Certificate Readings for this lesson.

After studying this section you should be able to:

- Describe what makes a church truly indigenous.
- Recognize the similarities of people movements and reproducing chains of churches.
- Explain why training leaders is essential to sustaining church planting movements.
- Describe the features and values of theological education by extension (TEE).

XI. Truly Indigenous Churches

We continue to consider the kind of churches that will multiply. Everyone would agree with Charles Kraft that churches should be both "Christ-honoring and culture-affirming." But what is a truly indigenous church? William Smalley challenges the early formula of what constitutes indigeneity in churches. The early formula, "self-governing, self-supporting and self-propagating," seems to be an easy diagnostic tool for deciding if a church is indigenous, but that assumption deserves examination.

A. Three "Selfs" Reflect Institutional Features. Upon careful scrutiny, the three "selfs" each reflect an assumption that churches are essentially institutional realities. These aspects—government, funding and expansion—are the very areas foreign influence can most easily dominate. We still want to see these features of independence. But churches can often be thoroughly independent of direct foreign control and yet alien to the local culture.

1. **Misinterpretation of Self-Government.** Western patterns of government are borrowed as if they were biblically mandated. Many churches are structured with slavish imitation of Western governmental ideas, such as voting for leaders or organizing sub-committees.

2. **Misapplication of Self-Support.** The very indigenous church in Jerusalem accepted outside funding. What matters most is not the source of the income but how the funds are handled.

3. **Misunderstanding of Self-Propagation.** At times it is precisely the foreignness of a church that is the reason why it grows. Just because a church appears to be increasing without outside help does not mean that it is indigenous.

B. The Nature of an Indigenous Church. An indigenous church is *a group of believers who live out their life, including their socialized Christian activity, in the patterns of the local society, and for whom any transformation of that society comes out of their felt needs under the guidance of the Holy Spirit and Scripture*. Smalley points out that churches are social entities and, as such, borrow patterns of life and thinking from their society. He points out that the Holy Spirit brings changes in keeping with the culture.

C. Missionaries Often Do Not Like Them. Indigenous churches are usually sufficiently distant enough from the missionaries' culture that they often offend or bother missionaries. Missionaries have been the primary force thwarting the emergence of contextualized churches.

D. Missionaries Can Serve Them. The missionary task is to communicate the truth of Jesus Christ and help people follow Him in culturally appropriate ways that are faithful to the Scriptures as guided by the Holy Spirit. Technically, missionaries cannot "found" an indigenous church—it must be planted and emerge with a life of its own. Once again, we see the illustration of the gospel as a seed sprouting in the soil of the society. Because missionaries do not often enable local movements in this way, most indigenous churches get their start apart from missionaries. This does not have to remain true. It's time for missionaries to expect and desire that the Church will have different cultural manifestations in different settings.

Read Smalley, "Cultural Implications of an Indigenous Church," pp. 497-502 (all)

XII. Unvalued Pearls: The Value of People Movements

In his classic work, *The Bridges of God*, Donald McGavran surveys the growth of the Christian movement since Pentecost. He shows that throughout history most of the people who had ever followed Christ have done so as part of what he called "people movements." The term "people movement" is used here to describe a wave of group decisions to follow Christ by people who share culture and kinship, while retaining their identity and relationships within their people. These people movements, which McGavran often called "people movements to Christ" or "Christward movements," can and should be recognized, nurtured and sustained. One outstanding feature, which is almost always part of sustained people movements, is multiplying networks of simple and powerful churches. McGavran describes five advantages of people movements.

A. Enduring Churches. McGavran describes these churches as being "rooted in the soil of hundreds of thousands of villages." They are independent of Western dominance and tested by local persecution. If anything could have made them collapse, they would have been gone long ago.

B. Indigenous Churches. Earlier in his writing, McGavran distinguished the "mission station approach" churches from "people movement" churches. The mission station approach is the pattern of missionaries inviting converts to become part of highly Westernized congregations on mission stations. People movement churches, on the other hand, remain immersed in their own cultures.

C. **Spontaneously Expanding Churches.** McGavran refers to an important piece of mission strategy written by Roland Allen, called "The Spontaneous Expansion of the Church" (from which this lesson title is derived). Allen declared that if new churches were fully equipped and released by missionaries to multiply themselves, they would indeed do so without any direct help from missionaries. Such an idea, written in a colonial era, was disturbing to many, but nonetheless true. Even today, the tendency is to plant churches that are dependent on missionary care. Such churches rarely grow. In the midst of people movements there are usually too many converts for missionaries to care for. Independent churches, however, have a chance to multiply without missionary interference.

D. **Enormous Potential for Growth.** People movement churches have great potential for ingathering within the people group. "The group movements are fringed with exterior growing points among their own peoples." There are windows of opportunity to be recognized and, on rare occasions, there are bridges reaching beyond their own people group to another people group. Looking for and using these bridges is the primary activity of what we call pioneer church planting (to be discussed in greater depth in Lesson 14).

E. **Displaying Christ's Power.** The churches are so lightly institutionalized and so devoid of foreign influence that what is outwardly manifested is a "change in inner character made possible by the power of God." The churches do not lean on outside funding or base their success on buildings. Instead, the people themselves are the spectacle. They become known as "people with churches, who worship God."

Read McGavran, "The Bridges of God," pp. 343b-346 (beginning with "The Churches Born of People Movements")

XIII. An Example of a People Movement

Most people movements have swept through populations that are considered to be middle and lower classes. Clyde Taylor describes a "Christward movement" surging through an upper class population in Latin America. The movement features cell churches that meet in homes, professional settings or on university campuses. The training of leaders is simple. The multiplying of house churches or cells is intentional. What do you think about the practice of organizing separate churches for converts from other class brackets? Taylor says that the guiding principle behind this is to see "how best to win the most people to Jesus on *all* levels." The exciting thing to Taylor is not that government leaders or wealthy business elite are becoming something like "trophy converts." The abiding value is that a church-planting movement is spreading "through a segment of society that has been unreached until now."

Read Taylor, "An Upper Class People Movement," pp. 708-710 (all)

XIV. Theological Education by Extension

We return to the first portion of Patterson's article in which he describes how he was part of a theological training institution that shifted from focusing on conventional residential seminary institutions to what came to be called Theological Education by Extension, or TEE.

A. **A Different Way to Train Leaders.** The shift to TEE was widespread throughout the world. The shift did three things:

- First, instead of drawing people from a distance to be uprooted from family and employment for months or years at a residential seminary, TEE brought instructors or trainers directly to students in their communities.
- Second, this enabled training to be brought to those who were already recognized as worthy leaders instead of untested young people who were usually sent to institutions at great cost.
- Third, the focus became less upon mastering theology on an academic level. It became much more a matter of training leaders to actually serve and plant churches.

Read Patterson, "The Spontaneous Multiplication of Churches," pp. 633-634b

B. **Disciple-Making Movements Born in Love**. Patterson's approach is very intentional. Movements of reproducing churches may be spontaneous, but they are rarely accidental. As seriously as Patterson worked with strategic intent, he still considers serving such a movement to be essentially a work of love.

The preliminary steps invariably shape everything that follows. At the beachhead stage it's crucial to think through how the church will be of the people and led by the people. The most successful church planters avoid public preaching of the gospel. They work from the very earliest stage to train and to coach local leaders to communicate the gospel, primarily by way of family ties in small home settings rather than formal preaching venues. New churches are formed in the simplest of ways so that the people can see the church being born from the essence of their community.

Read Patterson, "The Spontaneous Multiplication of Churches," pp. 634c-636c

14 Pioneer Church Planting

Studying this lesson will help you:

- Describe why church planting among unreached peoples is difficult, feasible and crucially important.
- Describe conglomerate churches formed by extraction evangelism and evaluate their potential for multiplying.
- Explain how people-specific church planting efforts can lead toward reconciliation and unity.
- Use the C-Spectrum to compare contextualization of new movements.
- Define syncretism and describe why it is a necessary risk to plant culture-affirming, Christ-honoring churches.
- Distinguish three kinds of Christward movements: people movements, church planting movements and insider movements.
- Explain why a "person of peace" is so critical in beginning Christward movements.
- Explain the distinction between an identity as a Christ-follower and a socio-religious identity labeled as a "Christian."
- Explain the difference between implanting the gospel and planting churches when speaking of insider movements.

Now we come to the strategic heart of this course. The plight of unreached peoples is not just that they have not heard the gospel. The real tragedy is that they have never seen how Christ can be followed by their own people without committing what amounts to cultural suicide. There is no indigenous church. The salt and light of God's kingdom does not touch their communities. This lesson is about how to bring about the all-important beginning—the missiological breakthrough.

Recall the image of the gospel being brought as a seed to new soil and being allowed to bear fruit indigenous to the new culture. To push the analogy a step further, pioneer church planting aims to nurture entire groves of such living expressions of Christ's kingdom. The new churches bear the same fruit of Christ's character, but usually on stalks and branches of social customs which appear quite alien to the missionary's home culture.

We'll face two key issues about pioneer church planting. First, the issue of encouraging a church movement to express the cultural identity of a single people group. Some have looked on such people-specific churches as exclusive or even racist. Others point to the value of penetrating many different people groups with distinct, but not divided, church movements.

Second is the issue of the radically different cultural complexions of the churches that grow in frontier mission situations. Is it sound practice to encourage movements of believers to follow Christ without affiliating themselves with what we would recognize in the West as a church structure? Is it possible to be a follower of Christ without taking on the label "Christian"?

We must have God's wisdom about these complex matters. There are about 10,000 peoples in which there has yet to be a fruit-bearing implanting of the gospel. Every one of them will be different in some way. There is no standard plan or formula. To step right into the fray we'll dig into contemporary cases of pioneer church planting.

breakthrough To breakthrough is to begin the finish. From Satan's point of view, a missiological breakthrough permanently penetrates the darkness of his domain. From God's point of view, He is at long last welcomed, known and followed. From the people's point of view, breakthroughs introduce enduring hope. Breakthroughs are turning points in history. It's hard to imagine being part of anything of more enduring significance.

I. A Church in Every People

Donald McGavran makes the surprising statement that "It is usually easy to start one single congregation in a new unchurched people group." What is truly difficult, but essential, is planting not one church, but a cluster of growing churches which reflects the cultural soul of the society. This missiological breakthrough is so crucial that McGavran states that the goal for mission should be to plant a cluster of growing congregations "in every unchurched segment of mankind."

A. Conglomerate Churches and Extraction. Follow McGavran's description of how "conglomerate" churches are gathered. He calls it the "one-by-one out of the social group" method. "Extraction" is the practice of urging an individual or family to divorce themselves from their family and culture in order to follow Christ. The impetus for extraction can come from a combination of missionaries and local churches pulling the convert toward a foreign or Christianized sub-culture. Alternatively, extraction can take place when members of the local culture ostracize or "squeeze out" the follower of Christ from their society. Either way, it's extraction. It invariably slows down, and often entirely freezes, a movement to Christ. The churches that result from evangelism by extraction are "sealed off" from the culture instead of permeating the entire people group with the life and message of Christ.

B. Seven Principles for Beginning Christward Movements. Each one of the following principles could be expanded with libraries of research and illustration. You'll find that some of them review what you've covered in earlier parts of this course. Seek to grasp these principles well enough to identify when or how they are being implemented in the case studies that we will read later as part of this lesson.

1. **Aim for a Cluster of Growing Churches.** Always aim to plant a movement of multiple congregations. When there are several congregations, there is a rich web of friendships and supportive relationships which can withstand outbursts of hostility from those who oppose the movement. A cluster of congregations can more clearly display what it means to follow Christ in many different settings and sites.

2. **Concentrate on One People Group.** Missionaries should aim to draw converts from one segment of society, maybe a sociopeople, such as the taxi driver illustration. As the church forms, it will have a "built-in social cohesion" in which "everybody feels at home." The sense of belonging is far more crucial than most Americans realize in the societies of most unreached people groups.

3. **Encourage Converts to Remain With Their People.** Encourage every member of the new church to remain in close contact with his kin.

   - **Trophies of Extraction Evangelism?** Missionaries should be dismayed when converts are cast out from their families. Instead, some missionaries have actually commended the new believer for "paying the price" to follow Jesus. Social exclusion may take place, but severance from one's people should never be reckoned as a standard price for following Jesus.

   - **Patiently Bear Disfavor.** McGavran recommends coaching new converts to aspire to exemplify all of their society's ideals. To do this they must retain ties and identity with their people. This can be more costly than accepting the status of an outcast.

- **Retain Most Cultural Practices.** There are areas where new converts cannot remain one with their people, such as idolatry or obvious sin. But in most matters they can continue to embrace the values and practices of their people.

4. **Encourage Group Decisions for Christ.** Group decisions can bring about a "critical mass" of new believers who can stand together, resist mild or severe ostracism, and more likely present an effective invitation to the rest of their people to join them. McGavran suggests delaying baptism until there are large enough numbers to withstand ostracism.

5. **Aim for a Constant Stream of New Converts.** Why would missionaries ever fail to aim for a steady stream of new believers? It's quite common. There is a window of time during which new believers have great power to persuasively tell their story. Missionaries very often fail to maximize this optimum time by preoccupying these potential new messengers with teaching. Of the two "evils" of too little teaching or a sealed-off community, the missionary should always favor keeping new believers in life-giving contact with their community. The extremely brief period of instruction that Paul offered to churches shows that the Holy Spirit can be trusted to bring people out of darkness into light.

6. **Help Converts Exemplify the Highest Hopes.** Pioneer church planting is successful when the churches have "witnessed" (as defined in Lesson 5) in such a way that the value of following Christ can be observed. The church should aspire to surpass the ideals of their society. Every feature of noble character and wisdom that the people group has valued can probably be found in Christ. The new churches must realize that they exemplify the hope and destiny of their people.

7. **Emphasize Brotherhood.** God unfolds the process of transforming complex societies over many years. McGavran recommends celebrating brotherhood from the first moment, but looking forward to days when God will bring about truly transformed societies in which antagonism of class and race is overcome.

   - **Celebrate Equality Within Imperfect Social Institutions.** All persons are equal in Christ. However, the initial thrust of the gospel is not necessarily the challenging of evil social institutions.

   - **Obedience to Christ in Every Segment.** The best way to achieve reconciliation of the races and peoples of earth is to see many from every segment and race introduced to an obedient relationship with Christ. Under Christ's Lordship, genuine brotherhood, justice, goodness and righteousness can be increased.

Read McGavran, "A Church in Every People: Plain Talk About a Difficult Subject," pp. 627-632 (all)

II. Can Jesus Be Followed in a Muslim Way?

As the remaining unreached people groups are approached with the gospel, there is an urgent need to de-Westernize the gospel message. We must stand ready to welcome new movements toward Christ that are faithful to the biblical essentials. A Muslim convert from Asia called Shah Ali (not his real name) presents his story with the help of Dudley Woodberry. Ali points out two primary problems in Muslim evangelism.

- First, Christianity was perceived to be foreign.
- Second, relief efforts sponsored by Christians were perceived as manipulative.

Numbers are not mentioned in this article, but this movement of Muslims to faith in Christ is one of the largest ever in history. There are thousands following Jesus in this way. The success of movements such as this heightens the controversy about them. This is all the more reason for you to understand the issues. In the years ahead it will be important for many mission leaders and supporters to be well-acquainted with these issues.

A. **Christian Faith in Muslim Dress.** In addressing the problem of Christianity being perceived as foreign, Ali describes four different aspects of a strategy for radical contextualization:

1. **Presenting the Message in Contextualized Ways.** Ali used Qur'anic vocabulary and other terms which were thought of as specifically Islamic to present Jesus. Muslim theological terms were used such as "Allah" for God and "Injil" for the gospel.

2. **Messengers Retain Contact and Identity with Community.** In one experiment that failed, twenty-five national (not foreign) couples were sent into Muslim villages. Only one of them was from a Muslim background. Though the workers were accepted as helpers, they were not accepted as credible messengers. Subsequently, only workers from Muslim background were sent. They were all sincere converts from Islam who had chosen to retain features of their Muslim cultural heritage, even though they were committed to following Jesus. They continued to sincerely refer to themselves as Muslims (which means "submitters to God") and found ways to publicly pray to Jesus Christ with forms of ritual prayers which would be recognized as honorable. They filled their prayers with biblical meaning focused on Christ.

3. **Encouraging the Movement in Relevant Forms.** New converts were encouraged to follow Christ openly, but to continue to use the mosque (the Muslim place of community prayer and teaching). Islamic leaders were encouraged to follow Christ, but to continue their role of influence. The term "Messianic Mosque" refers to a mosque that is dedicated to following Christ even though some forms of Islamic faith and practice are retained by the believing community.

4. **Following Christ as a Completion.** Perhaps the most radical idea is that Muslims might find Jesus to be the one who fulfills their culture rather than the one who condemns it. Jewish believers have long embraced Christ as the fulfillment of their Jewishness and regard themselves as "completed" Jews. This idea is abundantly clear from Scripture. Can this same idea of completion be applied in any way to other religious traditions? Some think so. Others do not.

B. **Toward Responsible Self-Help.** The second major problem Ali encountered was the perception that when Christians offered humanitarian help, it was an inducement to follow a foreign religion. The standard approach to the charge that humanitarian efforts by Christians have been manipulative and coercive has been to divorce evangelism from development efforts in this largely Muslim country. Ali's co-workers chose not to follow this approach. Instead, they sought to integrate church planting, evangelism and development efforts. The main features of the integration are that workers are not foreign and all people in the communities are served, regardless of their interest in or willingness to convert to Christianity. The development strategies are renewable and are carefully designed to mobilize local resources with no handouts.

Read Ali and Woodberry, "South Asia: Vegetables, Fish and Messianic Mosques," pp. 715-717 (all)

For I will not presume to speak of anything except what Christ
has accomplished through me,
resulting in the obedience of the Gentiles (peoples) by word and deed,
in the power of signs and wonders, in the power of the Spirit;
so that from Jerusalem and round about as far as Illyricum
I have fully preached the gospel of Christ.
And thus I aspired to preach the gospel, not where Christ was already named,
that I might not build upon another man's foundation; but as it is written,
"They who had no news of Him shall see,
and they who have not heard shall understand."
— Romans 15:18–21

In Romans 15:18-21 we find Paul's reason for writing the book of Romans: to encourage fellow believers to align their lives with him in a specific dimension of God's mission purpose. Does Paul operate with a sense of priority? What rationale does he offer for that priority? How does Paul's communication of the gospel result in both the "naming" of Christ and the building of foundations? What kind of foundation was Paul building?

Consider how God-focused Paul was about his mission. How can you simplify your life so that what matters most is what Christ accomplishes through you among the nations and that your identity (or "boasting") is what takes place unto God from the nations? Or is this kind of life only for a few apostles?

III. Learning a Different Way: Two Case Studies

Helping a movement form where there has never been a following of Christ is a daunting task. Read and compare two stories of church planting among unreached people groups. Both of them began with failure. But the church planters were persistent and eager to learn, and God intervened to help them find a different approach. In both stories, significant movements are still growing today.

A. A Movement of God in a Graveyard. David Watson and his son, Paul Watson, tell the story of how David began working in an area rumored to be "the graveyard of missions and missionaries" in India. This movement is the same movement that David Garrison mentions on page 646. He and other leaders refused to believe the explosive multiplication of churches that had taken place so suddenly. But the story started with costly failure.

1. **Grievous Failure.** The reputation of that area of India being a graveyard for missions seemed ominously real. After working for more than year to plant one "beachhead" church, six national co-workers had been martyered. Watson was ousted from the country. In despair, he asked God to show him how to get the task done. Watson turned to God's word and God showed him some new ideas and patterns.

2. **New Ideas.** Our short case study doesn't list all that Watson learned, but you'll find three principles that he and his Indian co-workers discovered while working among the Bhojpuri people.

   - **Persistent Prayer.** The amount of prayer driving the movement surprised Watson.
   - **Obedience-Oriented Discipleship.** Watson found that the movements sustained the most remarkable growth when people were encouraged to read Scripture (or have it read to those who were illiterate), obey Christ in whatever they learned in Scripture and share what they were learning and obeying with others. The cycle of hearing, obeying and sharing developed mature believers rapidly.
   - **Person of Peace.** Watson found that following Jesus' instruction in Luke 10 about finding a person of peace enabled the gospel to multiply rapidly within existing family and community networks.

Read Watson and Watson, "A Movement of God Among the Bhojpuri of North India," pp. 697-700 (all)

B. Learning the Hard Way. Tim and Rebecca Lewis attempted to plant churches in Northern Africa by contextualizing the forms and styles of their gatherings made up of individual believers from different parts of the city.

1. **Early Success Turns to Failure.** Even though they had used forms that were familiar, those who gathered did not relate as a family. The believers had little in common. The initial gathering collapsed, as had just about every other gathering in that area. They attempted one other strategy: They tried to gather people of the same narrowly defined people group. This was an even more remarkable failure. What had seemed easy to do was actually very hard.

2. **God Showed a Different Way.** God overhauled their concept of church by surprise. Entirely unlooked-for, a letter from two brothers, who had recently come to faith in Christ by a Bible correspondence course, asked for someone to visit them in their home in a remote town. When the worker arrived, the house was packed. The entire network of family and friends eagerly received the gospel and pledged as a group to follow Jesus. Decades later, this movement continues to grow. Like David Watson, Tim and Rebecca turned to the Scriptures and found principles for what they were seeing.

   - **Believing Does Not Require Leaving.** From John 4 they observed how Jesus refused to allow the gospel to be rejected because the Samaritan woman thought that she had to join the Jewish religion. The Samaritans welcomed Jesus *within* their community. They called Jesus "The Savior of the World" in part because they found that they could become true worshipers without leaving their community.
   - **Person of Peace.** From Luke 10, Tim and Rebecca saw that Jesus instructed his disciples to work within the communal structures by looking and waiting for key people to invite them into their household.
   - **A Church Born within a Natural Community.** Instead of attempting to gather individual believers and form them into family-like fellowships, God showed them how to plant the gospel as a movement within existing households and communities.

Read Lewis, "Planting Churches: Learning the Hard Way," pp. 690-693 (all)

IV. One Insider Movement Starts Another

Rick Brown recounts the story of two movements to Christ that have been called "insider movements" by some of those who serve them. The story that follows contains some dramatic supernatural work of God. Note that missionaries did not play a part in this portion of the story. As you read, pay attention to two things: the community-oriented relationships of the followers and the identity of the followers.

A. **Community.** The followers remained in their family and community relationships. Respected key leaders helped many commit themselves to follow Christ. They did not form any new institutions or structures which could be considered anything like church gatherings, programs or buildings. They continue as simple "house church" movements, regularly reading the Bible in a language without foreign-sounding vocabulary and grammar.

B. **Identity.** They were baptized openly as followers of Jesus and made no secret that they had put their faith in Jesus Christ as Lord and Savior. But the followers of Christ felt no need to change their religious identity from Muslim to Christian.

Read Brown, "A Movement to Jesus Among Muslims," pp. 706-707 (all)

Conclusion of Key Readings for this lesson.

V. Contextualizing Christ-Centered Communities

Is it possible to go too far in making the gospel accessible to Muslims such that we end up with a diminished, or even sub-biblical, version of the gospel message? How can we evaluate the movements that result with respect to biblical requirements and the wide array of diverse denominational traditions? Read so that you can begin to evaluate mission efforts with a respect for the complexity of the issues and the boldness that we must find to apply the lessons of Acts 15 in our day.

A. A Spectrum of Options. John Travis (not his real name) presents a spectrum of options developed by field workers and Muslim converts for expressing identity as a Christ-following community in a Muslim situation. Keep in mind that Travis is referring to the identity of communities of faith, not the identity of missionaries who approach muslim communities.

Read Travis, "The C1 to C6 Spectrum," sidebar, pp. 664-665

B. A Critique of Over-Contextualizing Messengers or Movements? Phil Parshall presents a critique of efforts which allow or even encourage Muslims to remain in mosque worship patterns as a standard expression of following Christ. In reading this article carefully, keep in mind that the C-1 through C-6 spectrum does not refer to foreign Christians presenting themselves as muslims.

The issues are: How shall muslims who follow Jesus identify themselves? What kind of movement shall the new Christward movement portray itself to be? Carefully sort out the three distinct ideas of contextualizing the *message* itself, the identity of the *messengers*, and the *movement* which emerges in its context.

1. **Contextualization or Syncretism?** Parshall sees syncretism as an extreme form of contextualization. He considers C-4 efforts to be bold effort of contextualization, but he considers C-5 efforts to be syncretistic for the most part. In his view, "Messianic Mosques" go too far in attempting to present the gospel in a way that is accessible to Muslims.
   - **Contextualization** refers to presenting the gospel within the context of cultural and social forms which are recognized by the respondent community.
   - **Syncretism** refers to a blending of Christian faith and non-Christian beliefs and practices. This blending is so distant from orthodox faith and practice that it becomes doubtful that adherents are following the essentials of biblical faith.
2. **Mosques Redeemed?** Parshall presents his concerns in reference to a movement of "Messianic Mosques" in Asia which has recently been the subject of careful research. He reveals some aspects of that research and challenges the idea that mosques can be redeemed.
3. **Missionaries Deceptive?** Parshall tells the story of a worker who falsely presented himself as a Muslim.

Read Parshall, "Going Too Far?" pp. 663-667 (all)

VI. How Shall They Follow Jesus?

John Travis responds to Parshall's critique. Consider the way Travis poses the questions and deals with the issues. His approach is consistently from the viewpoint of the potential converts. He asks "What shall a Muslim do to follow Jesus?" In contrast, Parshall's questions and guidelines are usually framed from the viewpoint of what missionaries ought to do.

A. **Continuing in Community.** Travis describes how some C5 Muslim converts participate in mosque meetings in order to keep their relationships vital and their community leaders from being shamed. Without deception or secrecy, they continue to present the Bible (Torah = the Law, Zabur = the Prophets, Injil = the Gospels) to many throughout their community, resulting in a steady stream of new believers in Jesus.

B. **Concerns with Parshall's Critique.** The research regarding the movement in Asia is again considered.

1. **Recognizing the Long Process.** The new believers are part of a highly resistant group which has rebuffed the gospel for centuries. What is the place of the Holy Spirit to work over the years to come?
2. **Examine the Fruit.** An important criterion is transformed character, seen in lasting fruit of the Spirit.
3. **Was There Any Other Way?** There would be no movement to examine without this radical approach. What can we learn? How can we exploit this experiment in contextualization for the practical wisdom that we need for the thousands of other people groups?

C. **Difference Between C5 Believers and C5 Missionaries.** Although Travis is concerned as well with C5 missionaries, the primary issue is C5 believers. While allowing the possibility that God may lead a few specially-called people to be C5 missionaries, he points out that every Muslim convert is forced to find a place on the "C" scale. How shall they follow Jesus?

D. **Rejecting Divergent Beliefs.** What about the Qur'an and Muhammad? Though Travis does not state it this way, it's worth considering that denying the prophethood of Muhammad never saved anyone in God's sight. Correction of error is not a saving act of cross-cultural communication of the gospel. Travis reports that in his experience, it is possible to remain a part of the Islamic community and not affirm standard Muslim theology. New believers soon find that they cannot affirm all that is taught about the Qur'an and Muhammad.

E. **Guidelines Regarding Syncretism.** Travis offers a list of seven guidelines. They differ from Parshall's list of five guidelines in this important way: Parshall's list concerns what *missionaries* should do to avoid syncretism; Travis' list concerns what *new followers* should do to avoid syncretism. We need both lists. Compare them and consider how they may be applicable in religious settings other than Islam.

1. **Jesus Christ alone is Savior.**
2. **Follow Christ in community with other believers.**
3. **Study the Bible.**
4. **Renounce and be delivered from occultism.**
5. **Religious customs are not performed to earn merit.**

6. **Religious beliefs are examined in light of Scripture.** Beliefs are judged or reinterpreted so that they are either maintained, modified or rejected according to biblical standards.

7. **Show evidence of new birth and growth in grace.**

Read Travis, "Must All Muslims Leave 'Islam' to Follow Jesus?" pp. 668-672 (all)

VII. Contextualization and Syncretism

The gospel has already been likened to a seed that must be planted in the soil as opposed to a potted plant to be transported. Charles Kraft extends the illustration to help us understand how the churches that result from effective gospel communication almost always seem different from the churches of the home culture of the missionary. He says indigenous churches can be likened to trees that bear similar fruit, but appear much different from the "trees" of the missionaries' home culture.

A. **Contextualization.** Consider carefully how Kraft describes contextualization as an ongoing *process* instead of passing on or packaging a *product.* Contextualization may not be something that outsiders can somehow "do" to a church. Churches must emerge—and once again the botanical analogy helps—as a living entity with expressions that are appropriate and relevant to the local culture.

B. **Syncretism.** Syncretism refers to situations in which foreign religious practices have been adopted, but deep-level worldview has not changed. Syncretism is sometimes mistakenly thought to be an extreme form of contextualization. They are actually different dynamics. True contextualization is process of churches finding expressions that are biblically faithful and culturally appropriate. In true contextualization, there are deep-level worldview changes which relate in clear ways to the practices and articulations of belief. Missionaries can help in this process. But when outsiders attempt to impose local cultural forms, it often fails to be relevant (see Lewis, pp. 690b-691a). On the other hand, outsiders can successfully encourage local leaders to find ways to use their own cultural forms (see Gustafson p. 695a).

C. **Two Paths to Syncretism.** Outsiders may feel safer observing new converts acting and speaking in ways that are similar to Christian practice in their home culture. But in fact, this is the kind of situation in which syncretism is much more likely to result. Kraft describes the two most common paths to syncretism:

- **Too Careless?** One path is allowing the receiving people to attach their own worldview assumptions to Christian practices. External practices are imported. Internal belief structures are not changed.

- **Too Careful?** The other path is when sincere missionaries import both a worldview package as well as a recommended pattern of behavior. Their intent is to guard new converts from ever experiencing even a moment of theological error, and to bestow upon them the great blessing of living as Western Christians do. The result is usually an isolated, conglomerate church which is perceived by the larger society as a foreign religious intrusion.

D. Syncretism, the Necessary Risk of Contextualization. Kraft says that syncretism is a constant risk of working to help bring about culturally appropriate, Christ-honoring churches. He says that it is better to meet the risk than try to avoid it. He recommends that we operate with a "deep trust in the Holy Spirit," by turning the attention of new believers to the Scriptures, giving them encouragement and freedom to make biblically informed decisions. As believers learn to use the Scriptures themselves and learn to walk with the Holy Spirit, God brings about the changes He desires (see Hogan p. 684b as an example of how local believers find biblical ways to solve complex behavior issues).

Read Kraft, "Culture, Worldview and Contextualization," pp. 404a-405d

VIII. Insider Movements

Rebecca Lewis (the same Rebecca Lewis who told of her church planting experience in "Planting Churches: Learning the Hard Way") defines insider movements and presents some of the biblical grounds for affirming their validity.

A. Two Dynamics of Insider Movements:

1. **Continued Community.** The gospel takes root in pre-existing social networks. No new structures are needed. Rarely are believers gathered from diverse social networks. Lewis contrasts the conventional approach of planting churches with the insider approach. Since there are no resulting new organizations established, she does not use the term "planting churches" to describe insider movements. Instead, she introduces the term, "implanting the gospel."
2. **Retained Identity.** Believers retain their identity as members of their socio-religious community while living under the Lordship of Christ and the authority of the Bible.

B. Not Seen on the C-Spectrum. Defined in this way, insider movements cannot be recognized in terms of how contextualized they may or may not be. Many insider movements may seem to be found on the C-Spectrum as C-5 or C-6. But this designation misses the point about what is most distinctive about them.

C. Kingdom Circles: A Way of Seeing the Biblical Support. Lewis draws a simple diagram to differentiate between having a particular religious identity and being a part of the kingdom of God by relationship with Christ. This diagram helps illustrate why participating in the particular religious tradition of Christianity may not necessarily be essential to being part of the salvation and blessing of Christ. The circles help illustrate what Lewis means by the expression, "going through" Christianity or Judaism.

Read Lewis, "Insider Movements," pp. 673-675 (all), and "Kingdom Circles," sidebar, p. 675

IX. Three Types of Christward Movements

At several points in the course we've encountered the idea of "people movements," made widely known by Donald McGavran. In Lesson 13 we encountered the term "church planting movements," defined by David Garrison. There are obviously many similarities between these. But Garrison was careful in other writings to distinguish church planting movements from people movements.

And now we find yet another kind of movement: insider movements. How do these three movements compare? Rick Brown (the same author who wrote "A Movement to Jesus Among Muslims" assigned earlier in this lesson) and Steven Hawthorne help distinguish them.

The same two dynamics that Lewis used to define insider movements can help us to compare the kinds of movements and to appreciate how God is using each of them in tremendous ways. For the most part, in each of them, most people choose to follow Christ along with their natural communities. And in each of them, people embrace a new spiritual identity as Christ followers. But how they form or join church structures, or how they change or retain socio-religious identity does vary.

Read Brown and Hawthorne, "Three Types of Christward Movements," sidebar, p. 676

X. A Movement Begins

We turn to the thrilling story of how the gospel was implanted amidst an entire clan in a staunchly Muslim land, as told by Ken Harkin and Ted Moore.

Examine the story, particularly taking note of the two dynamics of continuing community and retaining identity. Seeing these rather theoretical concepts played out in the drama of recent events is helpful. Look for other themes from this course found in the story. How does this movement seek to glorify the name of Christ? How is suffering a part of advancing the gospel? Who could be seen as a "person of peace" in this story? What part did prayer play? How did God intervene with supernatural power?

Read Harkin and Moore, "The Zaraban Breakthrough," pp. 687-690 (all)

Conclusion of Certificate Readings for this lesson. 

After studying this section you should be able to:

- Describe some of the challenges and opportunities of seeing Christ-following movements among Hindu peoples.
- Describe the historic backdrop for questions about Christian identity and describe the potential for different ideas about Christian identity to emerge in the future.
- Evaluate the practicality of focusing on one people group in culturally distinctive churches which aim not to be exclusive or divisive.

XI. A New Movement with Ancient History

Gilbert Hovsepian and Krikor Markarian tell a small bit of the present-hour drama of how Persian people are following Christ.

A. Ancient Roots: From Persia to Armenia. In Lesson 6, we explored how the gospel moved eastward, gaining significant followings in the ancient Persian Empire. A missionary sent from Persia was largely responsible for the gospel coming to the Armenian people. You may want to refer to the map on page 242 of the Sunquist article (ancient Persia is where Iran is today). Consider the grievous blow to the gospel when enmity between the Roman and Persian Empires devastated the Persian Church. For many centuries the Persian people have formed their socio-political identity within and under Islam.

B. A New Move: Armenians in Persia. Armenian believers have played a huge role in declaring the gospel in the midst of a repressive regime. The reaction to harsh enforcement of Islamic law has brought a new receptivity. When Armenians were martyred, Iranians by the thousands began to follow Christ, meeting in networked underground movements of small house groups.

C. The Complexity of Identity. For centuries, if someone in Persia/Iran was Christian, it was assumed that they were of Armenian descent, since in their worldview, to be Persian was to be Muslim. But something unusual is taking place. Because of the antipathy toward the harsh Islamic regime, many thousands of people are hungry for an alternate identity. It is amazing to find that a new identity is becoming commonplace in some cities. Someone can be asked, "Are you a Persian-Christian?" This means that within the Persian ethnic identity, there is a new identity, acceptable to many, of being a Christ-follower. It is evidence of a truly indigenous, self-reproducing movement. There are well over a million Christ followers now, supported by fresh Farsi Bible translation and radio/television broadcasts.

Read Hovsepian and Markarian, "The Awakening of the Persian Church," pp. 712-715 (all)

XII. Movements in the Hindu World

H.L. Richard sums up the history, complexity and hope of Christward movements in the Hindu world.

A. A World of Diverse Teachings and Practice. Richard explains why the notion of monolithic Hinduism was more of a generalization invented by Western imperialists than it was a reality. In fact, what is regarded as Hinduism, as a teaching or as a religious practice, is incredibly diverse.

B. The Complexity of Indian Society. The incredibly intricate social infrastructure of Indian society means that it is fraught with obstacles and opportunities for movements toward Christ. The history of people movements could well be only the beginning. There are a few emerging movements of Christ worshipers. They signal that there is hope of significant future movements toward Christ which would retain family and community identities and relationships, but devote themselves to obey and worship Jesus Christ.

Read Richard, "Christ Movements in the Hindu World," pp. 589-591 (all)

XIII. Unity and Uniformity

We return to Ralph Winter's important address at Lausanne in 1974. He presented what he felt to be "the most important issue of evangelism today." It is still of vital importance decades later. He rightly turns to Scripture for wisdom on these matters. Winter points out a common presumption in American culture-Christianity that there ought to be just one national church in a country. The rest of his presentation challenges the parallel assumption that distinctive church planting movements are divisive.

A. **Unity and Liberty.** The key point is that Christian unity cannot be healthy if it infringes upon Christian liberty.

1. **Christian Unity** is not a matter of reversing denominationalism, but of celebrating a healthy diversity within the worldwide Christian Church. Winter likens the Church to an orchestra, with churches of different cultural backgrounds playing their very different cultural instruments to the same score of the Word of God.

2. **Christian Liberty** can be seen in the diverse congregations of Paul's day—practicing different lifestyles regarding diet, Sabbath-keeping and so on. Paul was determined to allow Christians to follow different Christian lifestyles. He was opposed to anyone who would try to preserve a single pattern as normative for all Christians. The gospel required diversity with regard to peripheral matters. In fact, this concern is what finally brought about his martyrdom. The gospel should not result in or preserve alienation between cultural traditions. Instead, by affirming the liberty of different segments of society to retain elements of their lifestyle that are not contrary to the gospel, these peoples are being welcomed into the World Christian family. They flourish under the Word of God which ultimately calls for the elimination of every kind of prejudice.

B. **Unity is Not Uniformity.** Winter discusses why we should aim to plant different churches for different people groups.

1. **The Power of Attraction.** The example of a "youth church" shows the potential for unified groups attracting many other people of the same type. Such an approach is encouraged if it is recognized that the "youth" church is a means to attracting many other young people. Should we use this strategy with an "ends justifies the means" pragmatism? Winter says that the powerful strategic idea that more people will follow Christ if they can join their own kind of people is grounded on the firm biblical truth of Christian liberty.

2. **Never Exclusion.** Winter responds to the critique that churches which focus on a particular social group are thereby excluding others. The diversity of churches does not imply forced segregation. Churches have become diverse because given freedom to choose, people consistently seek fellowship with others most like themselves. God is not threatened by diversity—He created it. Biblical unity does not require uniformity.

Read Winter, "The New Macedonia: A Revolutionary New Era in Mission Begins," pp. 356d-360

XIV. Reflections on the Identity and Future of the Christian Movement

In his provocative style, Ralph Winter challenges us to think carefully and broadly about what we consider to be "Christian." He used questions as titles for two different articles. The questions are intended to unsettle our assumptions about who may be in and who may be out of God's kingdom. The first article was written in response to the article by Phil Parshall called "Going Too Far?". Winter's article reflects on past centuries of Christian identity. By contrast, the second short article looks forward, asking similar questions about what the diverse Christian movement may become.

A. **Going Far Enough?** Winter challenges us to consider how the longstanding tensions between Muslim and Christian worlds almost certainly skew the way that the religious identities are held as categorical opposites. We seem to display a greater tolerance for beliefs and practices which are far more aberrant from orthodox Christianity than what Muslims practice.

Read Winter, "Going Far Enough?" sidebar, pp. 670-671 (all)

B. **Are We Ready for Tomorrow's Kingdom?** Winter provokes our thinking by exposing some elements of pagan culture that have been part of mainstream Christendom for centuries. Winter suggests that the only way to not sink into a blinded syncretistic culture-Christianity is to attempt to convey the gospel to other cultures. Engaging in cross-cultural mission may be the only way to maintain a biblical faith. Winter points out that the largest growing edge of biblical faith is comprised of those whom many would consider "outside and beyond" Christianity. Among the movements that might offend or disappoint most American evangelicals are: the huge waves of "African Initiated Churches," the almost unseen movement of unbaptized caste Hindus in India and the house church movement in China. Without endorsing these movements, some of which carry apparent aberrations from the faith that are quite significant, are we prepared to work or walk with these phenomena in some way? How shall we depend on the Holy Spirit? How shall we scrutinize our own traditions? How shall we delve more deeply into the Scriptures for a more profound grasp on the essentials of faith and obedience?

Read Winter, "Are We Ready for Tomorrow's Kingdom?" pp. 393-394 (all)

15 World Christian Discipleship

Studying this lesson will help you:

- Describe what it means to be a World Christian.
- Explain what is meant by a "wartime lifestyle" and why it is important for Christians to adjust their lifestyles for Christ's global cause.
- Describe specific disciplines and practices that help World Christians pursue a life of strategic significance in God's purpose.
- Describe a variety of ways that ordinary believers can take initiative to engage with God's greater purposes, beyond the traditional roles of the missionary and the sender who prays and gives.
- Describe the factors that contribute to short-term mission being done well. Describe the integration of business and mission and some of its unique challenges.
- Identify some of the most helpful ways to determine what might be your best contribution to God's global mission.
- Describe the strategic value of reaching international visitors.

The "perspectives" you have gained in this course give you a vantage point from which you can behold your God accomplishing His purposes. You can now see how swiftly God's hand is moving because you have observed the Ancient of Days unfolding His plans through all of history.

Hope helps you see what is not yet visible. You can pray on, even when you don't see immediate answers, because you can see His glory coming like the dawn on every benighted people and city. You may never be able to read your Bible again with a self-centric viewpoint. You are going to see Christ, and Him glorified everywhere you look. He may not be honored yet, or even named, but you can see His day as surely as Abraham saw Isaac coming. Now you know what the increase of His kingdom might look like in terms of new churches, transformed communities and reconciliation between peoples. You have traced the facts of the numerical increase of His kingdom. More people are being drawn under the blessing of His lordship than ever before. You can feel the spiritual war raging, but you can see His glory coming. Yes, you see things differently now.

This lesson is about how that vision can integrate your life for His global purpose. We'll learn about the crucial role of senders and the special work of mobilization. We'll mark out the pathway of becoming an effective missionary. We'll discover the value of strategic partnerships.

Now that you have perspective on the World Christian Movement, you can no longer be an onlooker. Step into the movement. God gives you a place and a role. When God calls people, He does not call them to go away from Him to distant places. God always calls His servants closer to Himself. He may call you to be closer to Him as He works among the poor of Cairo, or the Hindus of Delhi, or the Muslims of Jakarta. He may call you to be with Him as He renews His churches in America to risky faith and blazing hope. You may not know where you will go, or what He wants you to do years from now, but you do know the One who has promised to fill the earth with glory. You have embraced the purpose upon which He has set His own passion. You are free to follow Him with the same single-hearted hope.

teamwork The only heroes who operate alone are figures of fiction. The true stories of accomplishment and significance always unfold as stories of teamwork. In Christ, one's life is multiplied by others. The only way to exchange the illusions of fame and self-importance for God-granted greatness and blessing is by walking in partnership with others.

The title of this course has a double meaning. It is a *movement* of *World Christians*, who focus their lives on God's purpose. In a word, it's about discipleship in God's purpose. But the course is also an invitation to join a *Christian movement*, exploding throughout the *world* with diversity and increasing unity. This aspect means that it's about partnership in God's global family. Discipleship and partnership. Intentionality and community. God's purpose with God's people. Look for these themes throughout this lesson.

I. Into the Story

We've each been given a place in the grand story. David Bryant describes what it means to be a "World Christian." He does this by reversing the narrative that most of us live: While it's true that the Father loves the world so much that He gave His Son, the greater love is probably that the Father loves the Son so much that He gives Him the world. A comparison of John 3:16 and John 3:35 supports this idea. We have each been given a part in the story of the world coming back to God by His Son. And thus Bryant's title, "Beyond Loving the World: Serving the Son for His Surpassing Glory."

A. **The Story.** Bryant compares the Narnia fantasy tale to our day. Like the figures in that story, whether we know it or not, we have been caught up in a tremendous war, with an astounding leader bringing forth something of utmost worth. Best of all, He is with us—or rather, we are with Him.

B. **World Christians.** Although every Christian is summoned into this war, many are unaware or refuse the role offered to them. But many have determined to make Christ's global cause the unifying focus of all they are and do. One way to describe them is the term, "World Christian." World Christians are not better people or some kind of elite who achieve a higher echelon of discipleship. They are day-to-day disciples for whom Christ's global cause has become their integrating, overriding priority. Other ways of describing what it means to be a World Christian include:

1. **The Person-Driven Life.** The urgency of the task and the desperation of the needs has compelled many to be part of the work. The idea of a "purpose-driven life" is a powerful way to describe World Christian discipleship. But in the long run, World Christians are sustained in their commitment by quiet exhilaration that springs from the confidence that ultimately Jesus will be loved as Lord by all peoples. To live a truly purpose-driven life, we must live what Bryant calls a "Person-driven" life.

2. **Serving a Monarch Not a Mascot.** It's all too common to regard Jesus as an inspiring figure and call upon Him for help in times of crisis. He can become someone we admire and ignore at the same time. But World Christians, instead of looking to Christ as merely a helper, set their lives to be servants of Jesus.

C. **Volunteers in the Day of Power.** Bryant points to Psalm 110 as a biblical template for World Christians. Using this Psalm, early Christians celebrated that God had exalted the Risen Jesus above every power. There are two time frames mentioned in the Psalm. The day of wrath speaks of the final coming of Christ. But before that, in the present time, verse 3 speaks of "the day of battle" (sometimes translated "day of power"). During this time frame of the day of battle, the Messiah is given the mandate to extend His rule. He accomplishes this even in the midst of great enemies.

Psalm 110 predicts that in this day of battle, His people will "volunteer freely" to serve Him (v. 3). Bryant says that World Christians "rise to serve Him every day, willing and ready…to volunteer freely to be with Him wherever He is engaged…to serve Him and to fulfill His global purpose."

Read Bryant, "Beyond Loving the World," pp. 718-721 (all)

II. Life on Purpose

Claude Hickman, Steven Hawthorne and Todd Ahrend blend their ideas and mobilization experience in an article showing how World Christians can pursue a life of strategic significance in God's purpose. World Christian discipleship is best likened to a journey which is pursued with intent and purpose.

A. **Not a Map but a Compass.** To find one's way on a journey, there are innumerable patterned routines to follow. Almost any culture offers standardized scripts or schemes for a successful, respectable life. Such pre-set life-plans are likened to maps. As much as we may want God to give us a detailed map of our life, this is not His way. Instead of giving step-by-step instructions, God reveals His purpose in the great story of the Bible. This revealed purpose is like a compass, which always helps believers move toward the "True North" of the fulfillment of His global purpose. This means that there is a wideness to God's will. Instead of assigning a narrow set of steps, God entrusts us to find the best way to pursue His purpose.

B. **Practices of the World Christian Journey.** In earlier editions of this course, World Christian discipleship has been a matter of either serving as a missionary (as a "Go-er") or helping to support or recruit missionaries (as a "Sender" or "Mobilizer"). It was thought that multiple roles opened the mission enterprise for everyone. But instead, people often felt sorted out and slotted into one of these roles. It may be best to speak of *practices* instead of *roles*. Every World Christian should expect to major in one practice, minor in the others, and plan on practicing them all. As World Christians move through different seasons and connections, they will find themselves emphasizing one practice over the others.

Read Hickman, Hawthorne and Ahrend "Life on Purpose," pp. 725-728c

1. **The Practice of Going: Immersing Ourselves Cross-Culturally.** Not everyone will or should gain the training and experience needed to pursue dedicated, decades-long cross-cultural mission work. But we are seeing almost everyone involved in short-term mission or finding business-as-mission opportunities.

2. **The Practice of Welcoming: Connecting with Those Who Come to Us.** Every World Christian should be ready and eager to befriend, serve and disciple visitors and contacts from the nations. Some make this strategic approach the primary focus of their lives.

3. **The Practice of Sending: Supporting Those Who Go.** Every World Christian, even those who are missionaries, should be involved in supporting, encouraging and praying for cross-cultural missionaries. Some specialize in sending as their primary contribution to world evangelization.

4. **The Practice of Mobilizing: Empowering Others in His Purpose.** Every World Christian will find seasons in their life when they help cast the vision for the Great Commission, renew conviction, recruit new laborers or train others to be cross-cultural disciple-makers. Many will find God giving them a strategic role in mobilizing which becomes their life-work for God's purpose.

C. **Essential Disciplines: Turning Grand Intentions into Real Life Decisions.** Aiming your life toward God's great purpose is fine, but to get anywhere, you need to make decisions daily. To fight the drift of mainstream culture, there are basic disciplines that have proved practical and valuable. Four of them are essential for World Christians:

1. **The Discipline of Community: Walking with Others.** Resist the temptation to go it alone. Link your life with committed communities of others pursing the same vision.
2. **The Discipline of Prayer: Co-Working with God.** The best praying is never happenstance. World Christian conviction dies without intentional, well-informed praying. Coordinate your life with others to pray regularly for world evangelization.
3. **The Discipline of Simplicity: Living to Give.** Every believer, even those sent as frontier missionaries, should order their lifestyles in ways that liberate them to give generously and regularly to advance world evangelization.
4. **The Discipline of Learning: Grow What You Know.** Increase and update your vision of God's work in the world, or it will fade. Structure your life ways that help you take in what is currently unfolding. Grow in your understanding of God's great story working out in history.

Read Hickman, Hawthorne and Ahrend "Life on Purpose," pp. 728c-730

III. Live with Intentionality

Caroline Bower and Lynne Ellis suggest that the issue is not so much "*What* will it take to finish the job?" but rather, "*Who* will it take?" The short answer to their question is all of us working together in all the diverse ways that God has equipped and endowed us with gifts, skills and opportunities.

A. **A Different World.** Caroline's story illustrates how many important opportunities can be seized by Christians who might not qualify as conventional missionaries. At the same time, in our globalized world, some standard approaches to serving as a missionary may have limited fruitfulness.

B. **The Whole Church From the Whole World.** It is not just wealthy or Western countries. Every believer, every church and all ethnic, age and expertise groups—each of them has a contribution to the mission of God.

C. **No Compartmentalized Lives.** World Christians need to lead the way in calling upon all believers to integrate their skills, gifts, passions, relationships and professions toward fulfilling the mission of God.

D. **Initiative.** Bower and Ellis challenge us to take initiative to fully engage in God's mission.

Read Bower and Ellis, "Live with Intentionality," pp. 737-739 (all)

IV. World Christian Lifestyle is a "Wartime" Lifestyle.

Unless you deliberately press your values to be in alignment with your vision, you will end up losing your vision. Lesser values and cultural habits of heart will prevail so that your vision will eventually fade. Ralph Winter proposes a bold, decisive reconsecration to live for God's purpose. Winter challenges the assumptions underlying traditional American lifestyles. Winter does not subscribe to the idea that if we make do with less, then poor people somewhere else in the world will have more. Be sure to understand that Winter's appeal is not based on the commonplace idea that it might be noble to redistribute wealth so that everyone has enough.

Instead, Winter says that strategic simplicity releases wealth to be allocated where it is most effective in Christ's redemptive war to overcome evil and bring blessing upon the nations. Ultimately, worthy lifestyles are not built around deprivation in order to bring equality. Worthy lifestyles are instead focused on better allocation of resources for God's kingdom victory. The bonus is living free from the self-inflicted damage of traditional American lifestyles. Winter is enough of a realist to urge Americans to find creative ways to break into such liberating lifestyles with others of like mind.

Read Winter, "Reconsecration: To a Wartime, Not a Peacetime, Lifestyle," pp. 722-724 (all)

Conclusion of Key Readings for this lesson. 

Since every World Christian should seek to be involved in each one of the practices of Going, Welcoming, Sending and Mobilizing, we now explore some aspects of how to pursue each of them effectively. The rest of this lesson is not ordered according to the four practices. Instead, it exposes us to practical wisdom in each of the practices as they intersect with local church life, short-term mission, international visitors, business as mission and tentmaking. We'll explore how and why to pursue life-long cross-cultural work and partnership with mission efforts from other countries.

V. The Awesome Potential of Local Churches

George Miley expresses the high hopes of many—that their church will become a sending base for ministry to unreached peoples. Miley points out that churches are incredibly varied. Each church is laden with God-given potential and resources that can powerfully advance world evangelization. Some churches will express that life through traditional channels. Some churches are owning their part in the total task of world evangelization. And some churches are aspiring to focus their energy on one of the remaining unreached peoples as a way of making a strategic contribution. They take on a particular people with "whatever-it-takes" zeal. Miley calls this approach "people-group focused mission." Miley has observed hundreds of churches attempting this kind of mission. He points out that it can be done poorly or it can be done well.

A. People Group Focus Pursued Poorly. Miley lists five things to avoid. Study them carefully. In years to come, you may be in a position to advise a church at some of these critical points.

B. People Group Focus Done Well. Many churches are doing a fantastic job. Their effectiveness has much to do with attitudes of humility and patience. One key feature of churches which are effective in evangelizing unreached people groups: They either form a partnership with an established mission agency, or they end up forming a new mission agency. Miley describes again the distinction between modality and sodality, using the terms "apostolic structures" and "pastoral structures."

Read Miley, "The Awesome Potential for Mission Found in Local Churches," pp. 746-749 (all)

C. Mobilizing Your Church. Many people are part of churches which do not pursue God's purpose. How can a World Christian help influence his/her church in fruitful ways? Larry Walker offers counsel, warning against being critical. Instead, he suggests taking the time to understand the unique nature of one's church and to patiently work within it to help bring forth the unique purpose God has for it.

Read Walker, "Be a Church Whisperer," sidebar, p. 749

VI. Maximizing Short-Term Mission

Short-term mission (STM) ventures have received some justifiable criticism, but the number of STMs is increasing rapidly. In order to help leaders and participants pursue STM in a valuable way, Roger Peterson surveyed the growing STM phenomenon and offers important ideas about how these ventures can be done well.

A. Short-Term Mission Described. STMs are on the rise, moving from and to almost every part of the world. There are three different roles in any STM: senders, goer-guests and host-receivers. Three features distinguish STMs from conventional mission efforts: STMs are swift, temporary and voluntary.

B. The Critical Criterion: Connection to God's Mission. STM, as with any kind of Christian mission, is best defined and evaluated by how closely we align ourselves with God Himself as He pursues the fulfillment of His mission.

> God's purpose, sometimes summed up with the Latin expression *missio Dei* or "mission of God," has been unfolding...for thousands of years. The degree to which we honestly attempt to understand and to contribute to what God has already been doing will be the degree to which our short-termers will work in sync with the *missio Dei* rather than mutating to the "missio me" of STMs done poorly.

This long-term view leads to the challenging question: "How can short-term ventures make long-term contributions to God's ancient, ongoing global purpose?" By asking this question, Peterson finds three factors contributing to STMs done poorly and three factors contributing to STMs done well. Connecting well with the global missionary task means that STMs should also seek to have vital connection with the seasoned, time-tested mission agencies and national churches.

Read Peterson, "Missio Dei or 'Missio Me'?" pp. 752-756 (all)

VII. The World At Your Door

One of the practices mentioned by Hickman, Hawthorne and Ahrend is "Welcoming." Every World Christian will have opportunity to help befriend, serve and convey the gospel to international visitors. Every year in the USA, there are hundreds of thousands of international students and scholars living in American cities. Doug Shaw and Bob Norsworthy highlight the incredibly strategic value of reaching international visitors while they are residing in the homeland of Christians.

Read Shaw and Norsworthy, "Welcoming the World at Your Door," pp. 750-751 (all)

VIII. Restoring the Role of Business in Mission

Steve Rundle says that a conceptual barrier is falling, one that has kept many people from thinking of themselves as having a part in mission. He calls it a "spiritual-vocational hierarchy" that governs the way some people think of roles in Christian ministry. This hierarchy treats some vocations, such as full-time Christian workers, as more God-pleasing and honorable than others. This has relegated many people, business people and others, to the sideline of missions as those who can just "pay or pray." Now business leaders want to be on the "playing field." Not only is the full engagement of business people a welcome development, it is necessary to meet the challenge of mission in our day.

A. **Back to Normal.** Using business as a vehicle for missions and ministry is not new. Throughout mission history, beginning in biblical times, working in business has been blended with laboring to fulfill Christian mission.

B. **Four Variations.** Rundle helpfully clarifies the integration of business with mission by listing four variations:

1. **Tentmaking.** Christians finding employment in cross-cultural contexts.
2. **Marketplace Ministry.** Christian business professionals becoming effective witnesses in the workplace.
3. **Business as Mission (BAM).** Business ventures created and managed specifically for the purpose of advancing the cause of Christ in less-reached parts of the world.
4. **Christian Microenterprise Development.** Microenterprise development seeks to help the world's poorest people start successful, God-honoring businesses with the help of small loans.

C. Challenges and Opportunities. Take note of the challenges that Rundle mentions. Modifying the model of mission opens up challenges about accountability. Complexities abound regarding identity, security and funding. There is also a clear need for training. We have exciting times ahead, Rundle says, because "God is using the forces of globalization to bring the entire church, and all its resources, back into mission."

Read Rundle, "Restoring the Role of Business in Mission," pp. 757-763 (all)

He who loves his life loses it;
and he who hates his life in this world shall keep it to life eternal.
If anyone serves Me, let him follow Me;
and where I am, there shall My servant also be;
if anyone serves Me, the Father will honor him.
Now My soul has become troubled; and what shall I say,
"Father, save Me from this hour?"
But for this purpose I came to this hour.
Father, glorify Your name.
There came therefore a voice out of heaven:
"I have both glorified it, and will glorify it again."
— John 12:25–28

In John 12:25-28, Jesus revealed the inner workings of His soul while He was making the most important decision of His life. He revealed His choice in the same breath as He extends an invitation for His friends to follow Him. The implication was that they would soon be facing the same life-shaping decision that He was facing. He was making the public appearance that would result in His death on the cross days later.

He mentioned two different options for the decision before Him. The two options were expressed in two different prayers. What were the prayers? How would the Father have answered either prayer? Jesus chose a course of suffering by which He would glorify God. The single criterion which helped him make that decision was this: "But for this purpose I came to this hour."

Do you know the purpose for which you have come to this hour? What might unfold in your life if you were to ask God to glorify His name with your life? In what way would you be following Jesus by praying and living for this purpose?

IX. Considering Your Role

A. **Willing.** Casey Morgan tells how he and his wife decided to go as missionaries to China. They didn't experience a powerful call. They certainly didn't consider themselves to be part of God's specially qualified elite. They discovered that they were just willing. The best summons into mission is not a call of obligation to go, but instead an invitation to come along with those who are already on their way. How is Morgan's experience different or similar to yours? How can you live so that you are making the greatest contribution you can to situations where, as Morgan says, "the strategic need is the greatest"?

Read Morgan, "Just Willing," pp. 740-741 (all)

B. **All or Nothing?** Greg Livingstone reflects on the time when involvement in missions was an all-or-nothing, all-your-life decision. Now, because of the ease of short-term mission, many can explore the idea of working as a cross-cultural missionary by actually experiencing the rigors and challenges first hand. In light of this article, consider what God has entrusted to you for His purpose.

1. **What Do You Have to Offer?** Livingstone cautions against asking if you have what it takes. Instead, ask what you might be able to contribute to a church planting team. Instead of assessing what you lack, consider what you have to offer.

2. **Honesty About Your Weakness AND the Strength of God.** If you are going to be honest about your weaknesses, be just as honest about the empowering strength of God.

Read Livingstone, "All or Nothing?" sidebar, p. 741

Conclusion of Certificate Readings for this lesson. 

After studying this section you should be able to:

- Describe the practical steps a person can take on a journey to becoming engaged in cross-cultural mission.
- Describe what makes strategic evangelism and church-planting partnerships work best.
- Describe some specific ways of getting connected to on-going ministries of mission outreach, mobilization and training.

X. Charting a Path to the Nations

Stephen Hoke and Bill Taylor point out the importance of stepping boldly into what you have been learning. They highlight two categories that correspond to the two practices of going and sending. The distinction between those who go and those who send takes on a nurturing, life-giving flavor with the terms "goer" and "grower." Read through the approach that Hoke and Taylor present as if God were calling you to be a "grower" who will coach other aspiring missionaries to reach their highest effectiveness. If you are considering whether God wants you to go as a cross-cultural missionary, then the value of each step will be obvious. There's no need to work through these steps in the precise sequence listed.

A. **Phase One: Getting Ready—Stretching.** Each of the four steps mentioned in this section are the beginnings of life-long growth and learning.

B. **Phase Two: Getting There—Linking.** Relationships with mission agencies and hands-on learning with missionaries are the primary features. It's not so much a search for what you would like to do. It becomes a process of discovering what would be best for you to do.

C. **Phase Three: Getting Established—Bonding.** Learning goes on, either as an apprentice to a seasoned missionary or as an able mentor to others.

Read Hoke and Taylor, "Your Journey to the Nations: Ten Steps to Help Get You There," pp. 742-745 (all)

XI. Challenges and Opportunities

Consider the stories and statements of Nicole Forcier and Ruth Siemens. Both of them describe pathways to mission involvement that have been overlooked or misunderstood. Thinking through these issues may not only help you to become involved in these ways yourself—it will also enable you to become someone who can help others find themselves serving as a tentmaker or a business person in mission.

A. **Conflicting Models of Mission.** Nicole Forcier's story illustrates the tensions and challenges that many are facing as the models for mission engagement widen. What parts of this story may be pertinent to you, either as one who goes or as one who is involved in sending?

Read Forcier, "Blessing Berabistan," sidebar, pp. 758-759

B. **Tentmaking Realities.** Ruth Siemens dispels the idea that tentmaking only has biblical grounds from one verse, in the book of Acts (18:3). There are many examples of tentmaking in Scripture. Siemens explains that tentmaking compares well to the conventional approach of sending "full-time" missionaries. But there are many "hybrids" of the models. She corrects some of the misimpressions about tentmaking.

Read Siemens, "Tentmakers," sidebar, pp. 760-761

XII. Join the World Christian Movement

Throughout this course we have been tracing the development of the most significant movement in history—the World Christian Movement. It is certainly the longest-running movement, if we trace its beginnings to Abraham. There is good reason to believe that it is the most influential stream of human activity the world has ever known. Find your part in this movement.

A. **Become a Student of the Mission Industry.** To move beyond a spectator status, it's crucial to become acquainted with the heart of the movement: the professionals and organizations that sustain work so significant that it takes several generations to fulfill. This highly developed mission enterprise can properly be called the "mission industry."

1. **Mission Agencies.** Place great value on these incredible institutions. You've already traced the heritage of these organizations throughout history. They are not add-on or stop-gap structures making up for a temporary lapse in local church obedience. Mission agencies express the life of the Church in powerful ways and enable the obedience of many churches. Get acquainted with the different types and the accomplishments of the amazingly diverse world of mission agencies.

2. **Training Institutions.** Do more than just learn about schools and training opportunities or regard them as something for young people to work through. Enroll yourself in a course of learning beyond *Perspectives*. Perhaps of even greater importance than continuing as a learner is to mature in your role as a mentor to others. Collaborate with training institutions and your local church to maximize the effectiveness of others.

3. **Associations and Societies.** The mission industry is filled with serious professionals. Why not gain the professional skills that you will need as a mobilizer or a missionary by linking with the larger World Christian Movement through publications and conferences?

4. **Local Churches.** Understanding the role of your local church is important. Don't expect too much or too little. Local churches gain wisdom and vision from a dynamic partnership with organized mission structures. Mission agencies need the support and prayer that local churches can offer.

B. **The Essential Role of Those Who Mobilize.** If the total task is held in view, then it becomes obvious that those who mobilize are as essential to the World Christian Movement as missionaries. Mobilizing is so strategically necessary that full-time mobilizers should be considered equally worthy of mission budgets. In the following reading, how does Ralph Winter encourage you to mobilize?

C. **Knowing God's Will.** Winter challenges many of the frustrating myths that believers have about knowing God's will. Be sure to comprehend the value of placing His cause above your career. Understand the ways of God with regard to how much He lets us know about His will before we do it.

Read Winter, "Join the World Christian Movement," pp. 731-736 (all)

XIII. World Christian Partnership

We are part of a global mission force. Completing world evangelization is a task to be shared by churches from all over the world. Western Christians continue to have a valuable role in the task, but increasingly, the most viable role for Americans will be found in dynamic partnerships with churches and agencies from all over the globe. We are enjoying a day of maturity in partnerships as never before. Why are these partnerships important to you? In a matter of months or years you may have the opportunity to be part of forming a strategic partnership or you might be approached by a mission agency with an appeal for funds. Bill Taylor and David Ruiz sketch out some of the most important principles to observe.

A. **What's Working Now.** Bill Taylor mentions four reasons that global partnerships are proving to be fruitful.

1. **Initiative with Relationship.** Partnerships work when they form in an environment of sustained trust and relationship-building.
2. **Cross-Cultural Wisdom.** Understanding cultural differences avoids needless risk of relating as senior and junior partners instead of equals.
3. **Common Goals.** Committing to common objectives helps to focus on fruitfulness.
4. **Accountability and Evaluation.** Constantly monitoring and evaluating cultivates the partnership to highest fruitfulness.

B. **Ancient Principles for Today.** David Ruiz points out four principles from 2 Corinthians 8.

1. **To God First.** By giving ourselves to God first, He is part of the partnership (v. 5).
2. **As Those Who Serve.** We see that we can forego issuing orders, and position ourselves side-by-side to serve the cause (v. 8).
3. **As Those Who Give.** We follow Christ's example to give up control in order to give the most (v. 9).
4. **Mutual Benefit and Equal Worth.** We see that each partner has something to provide and to complement what the other partners bring (v. 24).

Read Taylor, "Now is the Time," and Ruiz, "Old Ways for a New Day," p. 376

Name: ______________________________ Date: ______________ ____ / 20pts

QUESTIONS	IN-CLASS REVIEW
1. How does God's promise to Abraham in Genesis 12:1-3 reveal God's purpose? How does this change or enhance your view of God? (3 pts)	
2. We are blessed to be _______________ . Explain why this is a statement of responsibility but also of hope and significance. (2 pts)	
3. How does the fact that God's purpose for his people was given as a promise provide a more compelling mandate for mission than if it were given as direct command? (2 pts)	
4. What does Stott mean by a "triple fulfillment" of God's promise to Abraham? Identify the "seed of Abraham" in each fulfillment. (3 pts)	
5. Give an example of the fulfillment of God's promise of blessing to Abraham resulting in tangible blessings in the lives of Abraham or his descendents in the book of Genesis. (1 pt)	

QUESTIONS	IN-CLASS REVIEW

6. ___What gives us the strongest mandate for global mission? (1 pt)

   a. The many verses that refer to "all nations."
   b. The Great Commission and the Great Commandment.
   c. The example of Jesus.
   d. The entire story of the Bible.
   e. Biblical stories that show how God's people acted with compassion.

7. God's promise of blessing upon all peoples will be fulfilled by ________ (a, b, c, d, e) because ________ (f, g, h, i, j). (2 pts)
   a. those joined with Christ by faith
   b. Jewish people and the 144,000
   c. Christ alone, without human help
   d. angels with signs and wonders
   e. the Lamb and the Lion

   f. the bilateral covenant obligates them
   g. God will not share His glory
   h. they will conquer the counter-kingdom
   i. they inherit the hope and the promise of the blessing
   j. they will open the way for the gospel

8. Describe the three directions of God's mission purpose. (3 pts)

   Toward God:

   For people:

   Against evil:

9. Identify the directions of God's mission purpose which are most strongly reflected in each of the following phrases. (3 pts, ¼ pt for each correct answer)

   a. toward God
   b. for people
   c. against evil

Exodus 9:13
___ Let my people go
___ that they may serve Me

Acts 26:17-18
___ turn…from the dominion of Satan
___ to God
___ that they may receive forgiveness of sins

Psalm 67
___ You will judge
___ Let the peoples praise You
___ That your way may be known on earth

Psalm 110:1-3
___ Rule in the midst of Your enemies
___ Your people will volunteer freely
(be freewill offerings)

2 Corinthians 4:15
___ grace which is spreading to more and more people
___ may cause the giving of thanks to abound to the glory of God

Name: ______________________________ Date: ____________ ___ / 20pts

QUESTIONS **IN-CLASS REVIEW**

1. Explain what Piper means by "Missions exists because worship doesn't." (2 pts)

2. While both motivations are valid, Hawthorne and Dearborn express that hope for God's glory and God's kingdom is a more compelling and sustainable motivation for mission than compassion for people. Do you agree? Why or why not? (2 pts)

3. How does Verkuyl compare Jonah and the Church today? Do you agree with this comparison? Why or why not? (3 pts)

4. In traditional translations of the Lord's prayer we find the phrase, "Hallowed be Thy name" (Matt 6:9). What does this mean? Why is it significant? (3 pts)

5. ___ True or False. God exclusively used the "attractional" approach in the Old Testament, calling the nations to come to the temple. But in the New Testament because of Christ, God began to use the "expansive" mechanism of mission, sending His people out to the nations. (1 pt)

QUESTIONS	IN-CLASS REVIEW

6. What was God's mission purpose for the temple? Mention both Solomon and Jesus in your answer. (3 pts)

7. Reflecting on what Hawthorne and Adeney present, how does God-given creativity relate to the ultimate worship of the peoples bringing the "glory and honor" of every people into the heavenly city (Rev 21:26)? What is the significance for today? (2 pts)

8. ___ Based on Psalm 96, what does Hawthorne say is the purpose of salvation? (1 pt)

   a. to bring blessing upon all nations
   b. to see people set free from personal sin
   c. to bring transformation to entire communities
   d. for the earth to "rejoice" (Psalm 96:11)
   e. for people to serve God in worship

9. Match the following: (1½ pts)

   ___ Name-tag name — a. a revelation of God's character
   ___ Window name — b. God's public renown among the nations
   ___ Fame name — c. words used to refer to God

10. In Exodus 33:18-34:8, God told Moses He would proclaim His "name" before him. List at least three phrases or ideas from Exodus 34:6-7 which reveal that for which God wants to be "famous." These phrases also appear in Numbers 14:15-19, in which Moses prayed with respect for how God wanted to be known among the nations. (1½ pts)

Name: ______________________ Date: ____________ ___ / 20pts

QUESTIONS	IN-CLASS REVIEW

1. John the Baptist's question in Matthew 11:1–3, "Are You the Expected One, or shall we look for someone else?" shows that he did not fully understand Jesus' mission. What was John looking for in a Messiah? How is this similar to or different from the expectations that people have regarding Jesus today? (3 pts)

2. Explain how prayer can be understood as rebellion against the status quo. Why is this emphasis significant for mission? (2 pts)

3. What does Matthew 24:14 state must happen before the end of the age? In your opinion, how does this give hope and focus to the Church for completing world evangelization? (3 pts)

4. Explain the "mystery of the Kingdom" in terms of Christ's two comings and God's desire for a time of mercy for the nations. (3 pts)

QUESTIONS	IN-CLASS REVIEW

5. Choose **one** of the three directions of God's purpose (against evil, for people, toward God) and describe in one or two sentences how the kingdom of God helps us understand that part of God's purpose. [This is a reflection question. Do not search for specific answers from the readings.] (1 pt)

6. ___ What does Ladd mean by the phrase the "gospel of the Kingdom"? (1 pt)

   a. That God gives eternal life in His eternal kingdom.
   b. That God has defeated the enemies of death, sin and Satan.
   c. That Jesus entrusts His followers with the task of putting a final end to injustice and suffering.
   d. That one day God will destroy all evil and establish His righteous rule on earth.
   e. a and c
   f. a, b and d

7. Identify the correct point on the diagram below for each of the following. (4 pts, ½ pt each)

   ___ the present evil age

   ___ God's enemies disempowered by Christ's death

   ___ purging of all sin and evil from the earth

   ___ the age to come

   ___ V-E Day comparison

   ___ D-Day comparison

   ___ winning allegiance to Jesus as King

   ___ a time of mercy for the nations

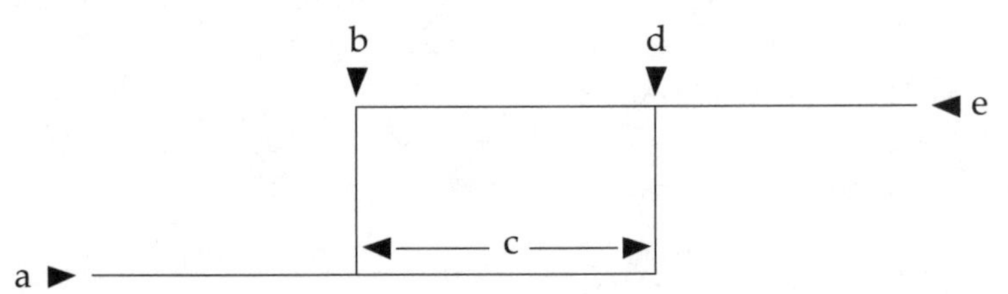

8. Robb says two complexes, idolatry and strongholds, often dominate in least evangelized settings. Match the complexes with the phrases below by marking "I" for idolatry and "S" for strongholds. (3 pts, ½ pt each)

   ___ entangled with false gods

   ___ perpetuates despair and fatalism

   ___ locked allegiance

   ___ broken by God showing Himself greater

   ___ denies that Christ can be obeyed

   ___ thought patterns

Name: ______________________________ Date: ____________ ___ / 20pts

QUESTIONS	IN-CLASS REVIEW

1. Describe why Matthew 28:18-20 should be seen as a mandate that Christ expects the Church to finish. What will be present within all the world's peoples when Christ's followers finish this task? (3 pts)

2. Give two examples of how Jesus modeled God's heart for all nations by deliberate outreach to Gentiles, who were despised by most Jewish people. How do you think the disciples felt when confronted with Jesus' teaching about the Gentiles? Why? (3 pts)

3. Respond to the questions of a sincere pluralist by presenting at least three features of the uniqueness of Jesus Christ. (3 pts)

4. ___ What is the best way to understand the phrase "all nations" (*panta ta ethne*) in Matthew 28:19? (1 pt)

   a. Gentiles in general
   b. ethnicities defined by language and culture
   c. political nation-states
   d. the 70 nations in Genesis 10

QUESTIONS	IN-CLASS REVIEW

5. If Jesus was eventually aiming to reach all nations, why did He concentrate on the Jewish people? And what was the strategic significance of Jesus focusing on a few disciples? (3 pts)

6. According to Hawthorne, what is the similarity between the Great Commission and the Great Commandment? What is the one crucial difference? Why do we need both? (3 pts)

7. List and describe the four times that the word "all" is used in Matthew 28:18–20. (2 pts)

8. How does "teaching them to obey all that I commanded you" (Matt 28:20) extend the reality of Christ's kingdom? (2 pts)

Name: ______________________ Date: ____________ ____ / 20pts

QUESTIONS	IN-CLASS REVIEW

1. Why does M.R. Thomas say that the Acts 15 council was the "greatest crisis" of the Church? How would it have been possible for the movement of Christ-followers to become one of many now-defunct "splinter-sects" of Judaism? (2 pts)

2. Describe the two key principles found in 1 Corinthians 7 and 9 used by Paul in his ministry to Gentiles, as mentioned by both Talman and Anthony. What are some reasons that applying these two principles might make some Christians uncomfortable? (2 pts)

3. The apostles were confident that the Holy Spirit had been given to the Gentile believers. Why was this crucial for their decision in Acts 15? According to Dye, why is this same confidence crucial for missionaries today? (2 pts)

4. How did Jesus' disciples fulfill His promise that they would be His witnesses? How does this kind of witnessing differ from some common ideas about witnessing in our day? (2 pts)

QUESTIONS	IN-CLASS REVIEW

5. What does McClung mean by "apostolic passion"? (2 pts)

6. In the analogy of "The Wall and the Canyon," which barrier keeps more people from following Christ within peoples without churches and why? (2 pts)

7. Match these phrases with either the wall (W) or the canyon (C). (4 pts)

___ singing foreign Christian songs in a foreign musical style

___ two years of language study on the field

___ changing one's name to a "Christian name"

___ learning to live within a new culture far from home

___ becoming fluent enough to preach

___ being rejected from your family for being baptized

___ being told honoring your ancestors is idolatry

___ developing a "Hindu friendly" translation of the Bible

8. ___ Which was **not true** of Paul's apostolic bands? (1 pt)

a. operated independently of the church that released them
b. based on Jewish forms of missionary work
c. economically self-sufficient
d. worked in cross-cultural settings at times
e. supervised by the Jerusalem council (Acts 11 and 15)

9. ___ True or False. According Dye, the Holy Spirit can be trusted to deal with sins in the same sequence in every people group. (1 pt)

10. ___ True or False. According to Tson, defeating Satan and destabilizing his kingdom is part of God's strategy to alleviate suffering. (1 pt)

11. ___ True or False. According to Tson, is this paradox true or false? The shame of martyrdom brings about God's glory. (1 pt)

Name: ______________________________ Date: ____________ ____ / 20pts

QUESTIONS	IN-CLASS REVIEW

1. "If local churches would just do their job, we wouldn't need all these missionaries." What misunderstanding about the history of church structure does this statement reflect? How does Winter use the delayed birth of the Protestant missions movement as an example of the need for both structures in the body of Christ? (3 pts)

2. What motivated some missionaries to stand up against colonial rulers? Cite one type of injustice that missionaries successfully campaigned against mentioned by Woodberry. (3 pts)

3. List the five advances of the gospel into Asia. What was different about the first and the last advances that made them most effective? (2 pts)

4. Classify the following groups as a "modality" or a "sodality" by **circling** either "M" or "S." (4 pts, ½ pt each)

   M S Campus Crusade for Christ
   M S The synagogue of Nazareth
   M S A church planting team
   M S A relief agency
   M S Paul's missionary band
   M S The Episcopal Church
   M S A monastic order
   M S A private business

QUESTIONS	IN-CLASS REVIEW

5. Give an example after the biblical period when God advanced His purpose even though His people showed themselves unwilling to be sent as missionaries. (1 pt)

6. Using the example of Robert de Nobili in India or that of Matteo Ricci in China, describe the strategy employed to communicate the Christian message in the 17th century. Were people responsive to their methods? Why? (2 pts)

7. For each of the following situations listed below, determine whether the following person(s) were acting voluntarily (V) or involuntarily (I), and also whether they were coming (C) or going (G) as part of God's mission purposes. Write V or I and C or G in the spaces provided. (4 pts, ½ pt each)

V/I	C/G	
___	___	Daniel (Babylon)
___	___	Ruth (Israel)
___	___	Goths (Romans)
___	___	Boniface (Germanic tribes)
___	___	Ramon Lull (Muslims)
___	___	Nestorian traders (China, India)
___	___	African Slaves (North America)
___	___	International Students (North America)

8. Where missionaries have had the liberty to work over periods of time, measures of human flourishing (literacy, economic development, life-expectancy, etc.) tend to______________ . (1 pt)

   a. disappear when missionaries leave.
   b. correspond to climate conditions and government stability.
   c. remain greater in those areas.
   d. be sustained only for Christians.
   e. improve in the countries sending the missionaries.

Name: ______________________________ Date: ____________ ___ / 20pts

QUESTIONS	IN-CLASS REVIEW

1. Briefly describe the difference between E-1, E-2 and E-3 evangelism. Which one does Winter say is the most powerful? Which is considered the highest priority from a strategic viewpoint? Why? (3 pts)

2. Describe what Winter means by the polarization of mission that took place during the second era? What caused some Americans to be less optimistic during this time? Do you agree with Winter's assessment that Americans have become more optimistic during the 3rd Era? (3 pts)

3. What caused confusion and tension during the two transitions between the three Protestant mission eras? (2 pts)

4. Match the stage on the left with the phrase that describes it. Which stage do you think would be the most difficult for a cross-cultural worker? Why? (2 pts)

___ Pioneer Stage	a. missionary works by invitation
___ Parent Stage	b. participating as equals
___ Partner Stage	c. initial contact
___ Participant Stage	d. expatriates train national leadership

5. ___ True or False. There are now fewer cross-cultural missionaries from the West than cross-cultural missionaries from non-Western or Majority World countries. (1 pt)

QUESTIONS **IN-CLASS REVIEW**

6. ___ Which of the following is **not true** about Christianity in the "Global South" according to Jenkins? (1 pt)

   a. In the future even more diverse forms and styles will be practiced.
   b. The "center of gravity" shifted sometime in the last century.
   c. The largest Christian communities are in Africa and Latin America.
   d. The number of Christians became greater in the Global South around 2005.
   e. In the near future the vast majority of believers will be neither white or Euro-American.

7. Non-Western missionaries __________ North American and European missionaries. (1 pt)

   a. usually need special training before they can be released by
   b. are shifting to unreached peoples, leaving urban and inland areas to
   c. strategically avoid countries where there is work already being done by
   d. are growing numerically faster than
   e. are cheaper to send and therefore more strategically valuable than

8. "People blindness" is ________ . (1 pt)

   a. a failure to notice the sub-groups within a country.
   b. when non-western missionaries ignore opportunities beyond their own country.
   c. when an entire people group is held in spiritual darkness.
   d. sometimes used to describe situations which are both P-3 and E-3.

9. For each of the following situations, decide whether it should be evaluated on the "P-Scale" or the "E-Scale." Use "P" or "E" to answer. (3 pts, ½ pt each)

   ___ An Anglo-American shares the gospel with a Mexican migrant farm worker.

   ___ While in the airport in Johannesburg, a South Korean missionary shares the gospel with a Japanese businessman.

   ___ A church in India invites a high-caste Hindu woman to a social gathering. She leaves when they serve beef.

   ___ An Iranian Muslim cleric remains a secret believer for fear of being seen as a traitor.

   ___ A Norwegian missionary goes to Siberia and witnesses to atheistic Russians in Siberia.

   ___ An unchurched couple has marriage struggles so they check the Yellow Pages for a church with free counseling.

10. Identify the strategic focus, leaders and primary sending geographical region associated with each of the Three Eras of Protestant mission history. (3 pts maximum, 1 pt each correct Era)

	1st Era	2nd Era	3rd Era
Focus			
Key Leader(s)			
Primary Sending Region			

Name: ______________________ Date: ____________ ____ / 20pts

QUESTIONS	IN-CLASS REVIEW

1. Why do you think assessments of the progress of world evangelization, such as Mandryk's "State of the Gospel" are important? Describe the impact William Carey's similar assessment had during an earlier time. (3 pts)

2. What was William Carey's motto? Why do you think both parts are essential? In your opinion, does the senquence make a difference? (3 pts)

3. What new realities does Mandryk want us to comprehend when he speaks of "mission from everywhere to everywhere"? (2 pts)

4. Explain how the phrase "May the Lamb that was slain receive the reward of His suffering" motivated the Moravian movement. Do you think this kind of motivation has a place in the lives of today's missionaries? Why or why not? (3 pts)

5. ___ True or False. Moravians exemplified what individual heroes can accomplish if they are radically devoted to Christ. (1 pt)

QUESTIONS	IN-CLASS REVIEW

6. ___ What were Moravians known for? (1 pt)

   a. willingness to suffer
   b. community
   c. "tentmaking" in their trades
   d. prayer
   e. all the above
   f. a and d

7. Which of the following could be seen in the mobilization efforts of each of the four main figures of the Three Eras (Carey, Taylor, Townsend, McGavran)? Check all that apply. (1 pt for getting all that are correct)

   ___ appealed to the Bible as the grounds for action

   ___ showed confidence that world evangelization will be completed

   ___ called for united prayer related to the task

   ___ called for others to be involved in specific and strategic ways to complete the entire task

   ___ used demographic and population figures to make their case

8. ___ What example does William Carey use as inspiration for the commitment needed? (1 pt)

   a. Catholic mission orders establishing churches in colonies.
   b. Secular trading companies and their efforts to make money.
   c. The Irish *peregini* and how far they traveled with the gospel.
   d. Paul and his missionary band going where Christ was not known.
   e. The great explorers and the risks they took.

9. ___ What proposal does William Carey make for the "the use of means for the conversion of the heathens"? (1 pt)

   a. The British should use their power to Christianize the world.
   b. Protestant churches should send missionaries directly rather than form sodalities like the Catholics.
   c. Mission stations should be established to extract the heathen from their non-Christian surroundings.
   d. Mission societies should be formed to send and support missionaries.

10. Describe at least 4 ways that women have been an important part of mission efforts throughout history. (4 pts.)

Name: ______________________ Date: __________ ____ / 20pts

QUESTIONS	IN-CLASS REVIEW

1. The attainment of "closure" will not mean the end of mission. It will be the end of the beginning. Explain. (2 pts)

2. Some would say that ethnic or "people specific" churches are a form of segregation within the Body of Christ. What does Adeney say are some of the positive values of having ethnic churches? (2 pts)

3. Why are "mother-tongue" Bible translations especially important for establishing mature and enduring church movements among unreached peoples? (2 pts)

4. According to Winter and Koch, what is the "essential missionary task?" Why is it essential? (2 pts)

5. Match these major cultural blocs with the estimate of the unreached unimax groups that reside within each. (1 pt)

___ Hindus	a. 1200
___ Ethno-Religionists	b. 700
___ Buddhists	c. 3300
___ Muslims	d. 2400

QUESTIONS	IN-CLASS REVIEW

6. ___ Which best defines an unreached people group? (1 pt)

   a. No missionaries work among them.
   b. The people have never heard of Jesus.
   c. Less than 2.5% are evangelical Christians.
   d. Lacks an evangelizing movement of churches.
   e. Resides within the 10/40 Window.

7. Write the definition of a people group for evangelistic purposes that was affirmed in 1982. (Can you quote it from memory?) (1 pt)

8. Define these terms as they are used in the phrase "viable indigenous church planting movement." (2 pts)

   viable:

   indigenous:

9. What is the difference between "regular mission" and "frontier mission?" In your own opinion, why are both important? (3 pts)

Choose the best answer for questions 10, 11 and 12 from these choices:

a. About 40% of
b. Less than 1000
c. Half of
d. One out of five
e. About 10% of
f. Slightly more than 70% of
g. Nine out of ten of

10. ___ the world's population lives within unreached people groups. (1 pt)

11. ___ evangelical missionaries are working among unreached people groups. (1 pt)

12. ___ evangelical missionaries work within groups that are predominantly Christian. (1 pt)

13. Why is the distribution of missionaries described in questions 10-11 considered to be a "great imbalance?" (1 pt)

Name: ________________________ Date: ____________ ___ / 20pts

QUESTIONS	IN-CLASS REVIEW

1. What is "worldview" and why is it important for missionaries to try to understand the worldview of the people they are reaching? (2 pts)

2. Give an example of "redemptive analogy" from the reading and explain how it helped communicate the gospel. (2 pts)

3. How does learning and communication take place among oral learners? How is this a challenge to the way that Western missionaries have typically done ministry? (2 pts)

4. Circle one adjective on each line which best describes oral learning according to the International Orality Network. (2 pts, ½ pt each)

Individualist	or	Relational
Sequential	or	Random
Abstract	or	Concrete
Story	or	Television

5. ___ Why can oral learning strategies help world evangelization? (1 pt)
   a. Oral learners hear the gospel in a way they can easily use to pass on to others.
   b. As many as two thirds of the world are oral learners.
   c. Oral strategies affect oral learners on a worldview level.
   d. Bibles cannot be distributed in many closed countries.
   e. Radio is proving to be the most effective way of "storying" the Bible.
   f. all of the above
   g. a, b and c

QUESTIONS	IN-CLASS REVIEW

6. Kraft describes three encounters. Indicate which kind of encounter corresponds to each description and story. (5 pts, ½ pt each)

   a. Truth encounter
   b. Allegiance encounter
   c. Power encounter

   ___ understanding ___ Robb's story on p. 163

   ___ relationships ___ Elkins' story on pp. 680d-681b

   ___ freedom ___ Graham's story on p. 442

   ___ vehicle of teaching ___ Tippett's story on p. 445

   ___ vehicle of witness

   ___ vehicle of spiritual warfare

7. Demonstrate your knowledge of Kwast's model of culture, showing how the four levels work together in cross-cultural communication of the gospel. Complete the sentences in the best way. (6 pts, ½ pt each)

   a. worldview c. values
   b. beliefs d. behavior

   - ____ is the underlying framework for ____ , which inform ____ which in turn shapes patterns of ____ .
   - According to Graham, the heart of a people's _____ is epic story.
   - Ethnocentrism takes place when we judge the _____ of another culture by the _____ of our own.
   - The people of India have much different _______ regarding purity than Americans, which shapes their ______ regarding what is kept clean.
   - Missionaries have sometimes imposed changes of ______ in accordance with their traditions but without a change of ________ and _______, the changes are superficial.

Name: ______________________ Date: __________ ____ / 20pts

QUESTIONS	IN-CLASS REVIEW

1. Suppose a business-as-mission professional involved in church planting in Pakistan is being prayed for by his home church. Considering the article by Love about identity, should his home church leaders introduce him at the prayer meeting as one of their "missionaries?" Why or why not? (2 pts)

2. The Willowbank Report mentions two main characteristics of the incarnation of Jesus (Renunciation and Identification). Choose one characteristic and describe how Christ's example helps us understand and carry out effective cross-cultural ministry. (2 pts)

3. Below are three of the five aspects of missionary humility presented by the Willowbank Report. Choose one and describe how you see that particular aspect demonstrated in one of the stories told by Reyburn. (2 pts)

   a. recognizing the challenge to see beyond one's own culture
   b. willing to learn and understand and engage in another culture
   c. starting with the needs the people feel are important

4. According to Hiebert, what is a "bi-cultural bridge" and why is it necessary for communicating the gospel cross-culturally? (2 pts)

5. ___ True or False. According to Hiebert most short-term missionaries and tourists who dare to interact with the local culture experience culture shock. (1 pt)

6. ___ True or False. Urbanization is creating a globalized urban culture, therefore cultural research is not as necessary for church planting in cities. (1 pt)

QUESTIONS	IN-CLASS REVIEW

7. Love says that missionaries in today's globalized world need to forge a single "core" message and identity that will be understandable to what three audiences? (1 pt)

8. Hogan describes a movement that began in one subset of urban Mongolia (pp. 682–683d). Why did it begin to grow rapidly only when a certain kind of leader became part of the movement? What does this story say about social structure and the move of the gospel? (3 pts)

9. Complete this sentence in the best way. The gospel moves differently in urban settings because the relationships are generally _____ (a, b, c, d) which means people know each other _______ (e, f) intimately. (1 pt)

   a. multiplex
   b. simplex
   c. metroplex
   d. complex
   e. less
   f. more

10. According to Hiebert, one of the _________ (a, b, c) to church planting in the city is _______ (d, e, f, g). (1 pt)

    a. gateways
    b. obstacles
    c. opportunities
    d. spiritual warfare
    e. social networks
    f. our preconceptions about churches
    g. reluctance to live among the poor

11. According to Reyburn, difficulties can arise in identifying with a different culture because of __________ . (1 pt)

    a. deeply rooted attitudes about ownership or food
    b. unconscious, habitual ways of doing things
    c. the categories and perceptions of the host community
    d. all the above

12. True or False. According to the Brewsters: (3 pts, ½ pt each)

___ A few times a week is usually enough time for a missionary to spend out in the local community.

___ The first few weeks of a newcomer's stay in a new culture are of crucial importance.

___ New missionaries are better able to cope with a new culture when they first arrive than a year later.

___ It is generally best for missionaries to enter a new culture gradually.

___ Language learning is essentially an academic activity.

___ When a missionary bonds with the local people, it's basically the same as "going native."

Name: ______________________________ Date: ____________ ____ / 20pts

QUESTIONS	IN-CLASS REVIEW

1. Evangelism and social action have been described as the "two hands of the gospel." Comment on which "hand" should be extended first. Give your rationale. (2 pts)

2. According to Voorhies, why does **Christian** community development offer hope for lasting change? (2 pts)

3. What is the difference between relative poverty and absolute poverty? (2 pts)

4. Poverty can be understood best, according to Bryant Meyers, in terms of three problems. Explain how each produces poverty and then explain how the gospel addresses each of them. (4 pts)

   broken relationships:

   misuse of power:

   fear:

QUESTIONS	IN-CLASS REVIEW

5. What is "Transformational Development?" What distinguishes this approach from other approaches to human need? (3 pts)

6. Describe how "microcredit" works. Give at least one example. Explain how it can bring lasting benefit to local economy. (2 pt)

7. ___ Which of the following is the least significant cause of hunger? (1 pt)

   a. poverty
   b. political power struggles and war
   c. inadequate distribution infrastructures
   d. there simply isn't enough food

8. ___ Which of the above is the leading reason for the hunger problem? (1 pt)

9. ___ True or False. Poverty takes different forms but it is basically a lack of resources to meet essential needs. (1 pt)

10. Complete the sentence in the best way. The term "rice Christian" refers to situations in which it appears that food was ________ (a, b, c, d,) in order to __________ (e, f, g, h). (2 pts)

    a. provided in Jesus' name
    b. distributed to secret believers
    c. offered as inducement
    d. sold on the black market by believers

    e. avoid absolute poverty
    f. pressure people to become Christians
    g. begin a microcredit enterprise
    h. bring glory to God

Name: ______________________ Date: __________ ____ / 20pts

QUESTIONS	IN-CLASS REVIEW

1. Describe the two main ways that healthy church movements can bear fruit. (3 pts)

2. Explain the importance of viewing churches as living organisms instead of defining them by their institutional features. (3 pts)

3. How does the emphasis on obedience to Jesus in church planting help to avoid legalism? (2 pts)

4. Based on what you have learned in this course, explain why ongoing church planting is essential for the kingdom of God to bring lasting transformation to society? (2 pts)

5. Choose a letter to fill in each blank in the best way. In church planting movements, instead of missionaries, _________ (a, b, c, d) leaders are relied upon to _________ (e, f, g, h) _________ (i, j, k, l) churches. (3pts)

a. spontaneous	e. transform	i. hub
b. trained	f. multiply	j. holistic
c. optimistic	g. preserve	k. daughter
d. cross-cultural	h. indigenize	l. existing

QUESTIONS	IN-CLASS REVIEW

6. ___ One reason church planting movements multiply so rapidly (choose the best one): (1 pt)

   a. The gospel flows along family connections.
   b. One mother church tries to plant as many daughter churches as possible.
   c. Natural leaders are selected, who are not bogged down by training, so growth is spontaneous.
   d. Carefully allocated foreign funding is contextualized.
   e. Talk about obedience is avoided so as to attract a steady stream of newcomers.
   f. None of the above, since they are God's work and Christians can do little to start or stop them.

7. ___ Which definition of the church is **not** mentioned in this lesson? (1 pt)

   a. The presence of Jesus among His people called out as a spiritual family to pursue His mission on this planet.
   b. A group of believers in Christ dedicated to obeying His commands.
   c. Jesus Christ being followed, loved and obeyed.
   d. The earthly form of the kingdom of God advancing kingdom projects.

8. Place these in order of priority for multiplying churches seeking to train believers to obey Christ (put numbers 1 through 4 in the blanks below with 1 being the highest priority). (2 pts)

   ___ The life examples and practices found in the Gospels, Acts and the Epistles.

   ___ Local wisdom that is contextualized in well-known proverbs.

   ___ Patterns of obedience tested and proven by the church traditions of the apostolic missionaries who start mother churches.

   ___ New Testament commands.

9. ___ True or False. Although churches are living organisms, they usually need to be "cultivated" to bear fruit since they sometimes fail to do so spontaneously. (1pt)

10. ___ True or False. If done in accordance with New Testament commands, funding from foreign sources can help church planting movements get started in some poor situations. (1pt)

11. Choose the answer below that is **least true** according to Keller. Churches serve their society like salt when they ______________. (1 pt)

    a. serve their city as a faithful cultural presence
    b. prevent society from deteriorating
    c. are invigorating and shaping society
    d. bring about the ultimate triumph of God's kingdom

Name: ______________________ Date: __________ ____ / 20pts

QUESTIONS	IN-CLASS REVIEW

1. Explain the distinction between having a public identity as a devoted follower of Christ and the socio-religious identity of being called a Christian. Why is this distinction important and debated among mission leaders in the Muslim world? (2 pts)

2. Why does McGavran insist that "brotherhood" between different peoples be a constant emphasis, even during the initial breakthrough in particular segments of society? (2 pts)

3. Why does Kraft say that syncretism is a necessary risk in bringing about culturally-appropriate, Christ-honoring churches? (2 pts)

4. Explain why insider movements often speak of implanting the gospel rather than planting churches. (1 pt)

5. Describe the two forces that, according to McGavran, cause new believers to be extracted from their society into a Christian sub-culture. (2 pts)

QUESTIONS **IN-CLASS REVIEW**

6. Complete the sentence in the best way by writing the letter that corresponds to the best word choice in the blank spaces. Insider movements encourage new believers to take on a new spiritual identity, while at the same time, the new believers ___________ (a, b, c, d, e) ___________ (f, g, h, i) ___________ (j, k, l, m). (3 pts)

a. become like	f. their family's	j. beliefs
b. extract	g. Christian	k. identity
c. contextualize	h. a foreign	l. kingdom circles
d. retain	i. an organic	m. cluster of churches
e. welcome		

7. Match the following movements with what is **generally true** of them. Sometime the correct answer will require more than one letter. (3 pts)

___ form new church structures	a. people movements
___ do not form new church structures	b. church planting movements
___ usually follow Christ with family	c. insider movements
___ C-5	d. a and b
___ new spiritual identity in Christ	e. all of the above
___ believe and use the Bible	f. none of the above or not applicable

8. Syncretism refers to situations in which ___________ (a, b, c, d, e) have been ___________ (f, g, h, i, j) but ___________ (k, l, m, n) has not changed. (3 pts)

a. foreign religious practices	f. implanted	k. the family network
b. biblically acceptable ideas	g. indigenized	l. insider language
c. household leaders	h. adopted	m. deep level worldview
d. missionaries	i. squeezed out	n. socio-religious identity
e. seekers	j. converted	

9. ___ What is a "Person of Peace"? (1 pt)

a. Secret believers who use their influence to protect ostracized converts.
b. Usually someone with a winsome personality who mediates disputes.
c. A recognized family or community leader able to welcome gospel messengers.
d. The kind of calm leader needed to settle tensions that arise in house churches.
e. People skilled in the kind of contemplative prayer that results in power encounters.

10. ___ What is the reason that conglomerate churches usually fail to multiply in unreached people groups? (1 pt)

a. The one-by-one approach adds new people instead of multiplying groups of believers.
b. The initial followers are often people of marginal social standing who influence few others.
c. Conversions are seen to shame and break up families and thus are perceived as bad news for the community.
d. Either converts are extracted or they are "squeezed out" and ostracized by the community.
e. Strong social relationships rarely form between converts of different social backgrounds.
f. all the above

Name: ______________________ Date: __________ ____ / 20pts

QUESTIONS	IN-CLASS REVIEW

1. Bryant puts a twist on the well-known words, "God loves you and has a wonderful plan for your life." How does he change these words? Why is this important? (2 pts)

2. What is a "wartime lifestyle" and why is it important in the life of a World Christian? (3 pts)

3. According to Livingstone, what usually happens when people ask themselves the question: "What qualifications do I lack?" Why does he instead recommend asking, "What contribution might I make?" (2 pts)

4. Some churches have ambitions to plant churches among unreached peoples. According to Miley, why have the most effective among them either started a new mission structure or formed a partnership with an existing mission structure? (3 pts)

5. ___ True or False. Reaching internationals is less challenging than being a cross-cultural missionary in another country. (1 pt)

QUESTIONS **IN-CLASS REVIEW**

6. In your opinion, which topic mentioned in this lesson offers the most hope that many more gifted and creative people will be directly engaged in cross-cultural mission? Select one and discuss why it is significant:

   Choose from: tentmaking opportunities, short-term mission, international visitors, business as mission, marketplace ministry. (2 pts)

7. There are four ways that business is being integrated with mission. Identify which of the four ways best fits the descriptions below. (3 pts, ½ point each)

   a. Tentmaking
   b. Business as Mission (BAM)
   c. Marketplace Ministry
   d. Microenterprise Development

   ___ Values well-run businesses as redemptive in society.

   ___ More about employment than beginning businesses.

   ___ Local businesses are started with the help of small loans.

   ___ Focuses on near neighbor ministry.

   ___ Like BAM, the primary interest is the unreached.

   ___ Ventures created to advance Christ's cause.

8. Hickman, Hawthorne and Ahrend write about two ways that people expect God to guide them in a life of significance using the imagery of a map and a compass. Write "M" or "C" in front of the statements below. (2 pts, ½ point each)

   ___ gives us directions, rather than direction

   ___ required for pioneering or exploring

   ___ step by step instructions

   ___ focus on purpose more than plan

9. According to Hickman, Hawthorne and Ahrend, every World Christian should expect to pursue God's purpose _____, even if it is for a season of their life. (1 pt)

   a. as one who encourages, recruits or trains others in God's mission
   b. as one who befriends and serves international visitors
   c. as one who immerses him/herself in cross-cultural relationships
   d. as one who gives sacrificially and prays for missionaries
   e. all of the above
   f. a or d

10. ___ Which one of the following is **not** one of the ways mentioned by Peterson to do short-term missions (STMs) poorly? (1 pt)

    a. Being over-impressed with how compassionate or competent STMers may be able to solve long standing problems.
    b. Acting independently of time-tested mission agencies and churches.
    c. Squandering money that could be spent on something that lasts.
    d. Using STMs as experiences to further personal discipleship.

Name: ______________________________ Date: ______________

On this page, describe some of the things you have sensed to be most important to you after the first five lessons of Perspectives. You can organize your response in any number of ways. You may describe content items that have been particularly surprising or challenging. You may want to describe how you sense God has been speaking to you. Or you may choose to present something like a personal journal entry describing changes you are experiencing because of this course. There are no right or wrong answers.

Name: ______________________ Date: ______________

Respond to what you have learned in the History section of this course (Lessons 6 through 8). There is no correct answer. You will be graded on the thoughtfulness and depth of your interaction with material learned in this class. Below are three possible ways of organizing your response. You may choose one of the ways or come up with your own way to express your response. Limit your response to the front of this page.

1. Impact from the past. Select one idea, movement, personality or statement that has made an impact on your views, hopes or life decisions. For example, describe how an idea or movement has encouraged, dismayed or informed you.
2. Meet history. You might choose to do some time travel in your response. What era or place in mission history would you want to visit with the idea of bringing back valuable insights for missions today? Where would you go? Who would you seek out?
3. Back to the Future. Identify one point of history that you would like to have turned out differently. How would you like to have altered history? What would be the outcome of these alterations?

Name:______________________________ Date: ________________

Respond to what you have learned in Lesson 9. There are many possible ways to frame your response. How did the lesson build hope or bring discouragement? Which ideas do you most want to retain and why? What did you find most surprising? Which part do you think you are most likely to recount to someone else? Your comments will be evaluated on the basis of the personal application and thoughtful dialogue with the material.

Name: ____________________ Date: ____________________

Respond to what you have learned in Lessons 10 and 11. Choose one idea or concept that was startling, pertinent, significant or outrageous to you. Describe the idea and your response. Limit your response to the front of this page.

Name: ______________________________ Date: ______________

Respond to what you have learned in the Strategic section. Select an idea that was significant to you and describe its impact on your thinking, lifestyle, obedience or mission involvement. Here's another option: Frame your answer in the form of a journal, chronicling how the class material impacted you as you processed Lessons 12 through 14. Your response won't be evaluated on the basis of your opinions or values but on how well you demonstrate thoughtfulness and personal sensitivity to the material. Limit your response to the front of this page.